CHILDCARE PROVISION IN NEOLIBERAL TIMES

Sociology of Children and Families series

Series editors: **Esther Dermott** and **Debbie Watson,**
University of Bristol, UK

The *Sociology of Children and Families* series brings together the latest
international research on children, childhood and families and pushes
forward theory in the sociology of childhood and family life. Books in the
series cover major global issues affecting children and families.

Forthcoming in the series:

Race, Class, Parenting and Children's Leisure
Children's Leisurescapes and Parenting Cultures
in Middle-class British Indian Families
Utsa Mukherjee

Out now in the series:

Black Mothers and Attachment Parenting
A Black Feminist Analysis of Intensive Mothering in Britain and Canada
Patricia Hamilton

Sharing Care
Equal and Primary Carer Fathers and Early Years Parenting
Rachel Brooks and **Paul Hodkinson**

A Child's Day
A Comprehensive Analysis of Change in Children's Time Use in the UK
Killian Mullan

Find out more at
bristoluniversitypress.co.uk/sociology-of-children-and-families

Sociology of Children and Families series

Series editors: **Esther Dermott** and **Debbie Watson**,
University of Bristol, UK

The *Sociology of Children and Families* series brings together the latest international research on children, childhood and families and pushes forward theory in the sociology of childhood and family life. Books in the series cover major global issues affecting children and families.

International advisory board:

Find out more at
bristoluniversitypress.co.uk/sociology-of-children-and-families

CHILDCARE PROVISION IN NEOLIBERAL TIMES

The Marketization of Care

Aisling Gallagher

BRISTOL
UNIVERSITY
PRESS

First published in Great Britain in 2023 by

Bristol University Press
University of Bristol
1-9 Old Park Hill
Bristol
BS2 8BB
UK
t: +44 (0)117 374 6645
e: bup-info@bristol.ac.uk

Details of international sales and distribution partners are available at bristoluniversitypress.co.uk

British Library Cataloguing in Publication Data
A catalogue record for this book is available from the British Library

ISBN 978-1-5292-0649-4 hardcover
ISBN 978-1-5292-0651-7 paperback
ISBN 978-1-5292-0652-4 ePub
ISBN 978-1-5292-0654-8 ePdf

Cover design: blu inc, Bristol
Front cover image: MIA Studio - shutterstock.com

Bristol University Press uses environmentally responsible print partners.

For my parents

Contents

List of Tables and Boxes

Tables

Boxes

List of Abbreviations

CPI	Consumer Price Index
DipTch	Diploma in Teaching
ECC	Early Childhood Council, NZ
ECE	early childhood education
ELI	Early Learning Information, NZ
ERO	Education Review Office
MoE	Ministry of Education
NZCA	New Zealand Childcare Association
NZEI Te Rui Roa	New Zealand Education Union
REITS	Real Estate Investment Trusts
SSM	Social Studies of Marketization

Acknowledgements

For many years I have wanted to write a book about my encounters with the childcare sector, having worked on this subject matter since my doctoral studies in the late 2000s. However, I never appreciated just how much input and support from colleagues, friends and family I would need to achieve this ambition.

Firstly, I am very grateful to the research participants from across Aotearoa New Zealand, who generously contributed their time and knowledge to this project. Without their willingness to engage with the research, this book would not have come to fruition.

The research informing this book received generous funding from the Royal Society of New Zealand, Marsden Fund in 2015, without which the work would not have been possible. Through this financial support I was able to build research connections with the project mentor, Professor Deborah Brennan, and the Social Policy Research Centre at the University of New South Wales. I am very grateful to Deb and colleagues for taking me under their wing and showing me how to scale-up individual research endeavours into internationally successful and impactful projects.

Over the course of the research I relied on the critical insights of colleagues within both my own university and academic communities internationally to challenge my thinking. To Carolyn Morris and Russell Prince, I am indebted to you for your attentive reading of earlier versions of the manuscript, and ultimately helping me to see the wood for the trees with your feedback. I am also grateful to Mike Roche, Juliana Mansvelt, Robyn Andrews, Regina Scheyvens, Jeff McNeill, April Bennett, Matt Henry, Stephen FitzHerbert, Glenn Banks and Trisia Farrelly for their ongoing interest and advice on the writing process. Colleagues in the Geography Programme facilitated my research leave in 2019 to begin writing the manuscript, and on return provided me crucial periods of unburdened time to meet deadlines, for which I am hugely appreciative.

Over the course of the past five years I have had the opportunity to speak about my work on a number of occasions to different audiences. I am grateful to staff in the Geography Department, National University of Galway, Ireland; The Institute of Social Science in the 21st Century, University

College Cork; The Heseltine Institute, University of Liverpool; and The Economic Geography Research Cluster, University of Zurich, who hosted me and facilitated seminars. I have also presented various aspects of this work to audiences at the New Zealand Geographical Society Conference, the Institute of Australian Geographers Conference, the Association of American Geographers Conference and the Royal Geographical Society-Institute of British Geographers Conference. Critical comments and feedback on my work during these presentations and academic visits provoked my thinking in innumerable ways.

To the series editors, Esther Dermott and Debbie Watson, and to Shannon Kneis at Bristol University Press, thank you for your patience and support in bringing the book to completion.

Lastly, I would like to thank my family and friends. To Áine, Sinéad, Louise, Frances and Henrike, thank you for always checking in on me and making me laugh, even though we live very far apart these days. My parents, Nancy and John, have always supported and trusted my decisions in life unconditionally, even though these decisions must have seemed odd at the time. Moving from the UK to Aotearoa New Zealand over a decade ago was one such decision which marked a significant change in my life circumstances. Leaving family and friends to remake my home on the other side of the world has not been easy, but I have found solace in the welcome I received into my partner's family. Thanks to Jenny and Gary for taking the time to enquire how things were going, and for the crucial childcare support. To Mary, I really appreciated the quiet writing space you provided, along with the scrumptious home-baked morning tea. What a treat! Finally, to my partner Russell and my two children, Ailbhe and Cillian. Russell, your love, patience and support has kept me going through the writing process, when my confidence wavered and life generally got in the way. I hope that one day I can provide the same in return, so that you can achieve some of your own life goals. Kids, I love you – please stop jumping on the sofa.

1

Childcare as a Market
of Collective Concern

> The childcare market is a way of describing a situation where
> the state has relatively little influence on – or interest in – how
> services for young children are set, maintained or delivered.
> (Penn, 2013: 19)

I had been in Ireland on research leave for just under a month when a
news story caught my attention. A prime-time television investigation of
a Dublin-based childcare chain was due to air, ominously titled 'Creches,
Behind Closed Doors'. The story cast a critical lens not only on the service
in question, but on all aspects of the regulation, funding and development of
the sector. In the week leading up to the documentary, my family members
and neighbours debated whether or not they would watch it at all. For
many the prospect was too emotionally confronting, confirming their
worst suspicions about care conditions in a fast-developing sector. At the
same time social media feeds were humming with the voices of childcare
workers pleading with parents to not assume this case was reflective of the
entire sector. "Don't tar us all with the same brush – We love the children
as our own", was the message. Emotions were running high. In the midst
of writing the book, it was a sharp reminder that commodified childcare is
a high stakes endeavour.
   Childcare is an emotionally charged domain, as are all spheres which
concern the care of the most vulnerable in society. However, childcare is
also now big business, bringing into sharp relief the long-standing tensions
between profit making and care giving (Folbre and Nelson, 2000; Tronto,
2013). The significant growth in demand for childcare across the OECD over
the past 20 years (OECD, 2016b) has given rise to more providers operating at
larger economies of scale than ever before. In the UK for example, a market
report by LaingBuisson (2019) estimated that 81 per cent of the childcare

sector is currently owned and operated by private for-profit interests, with two 'supergroups' alone accounting for 8 per cent of the market.[1] At the same time, the report noted the number of individual owner-operators in the UK market had dropped by 20 per cent between 2016 and 2018. Similar trends towards consolidation are apparent across most neoliberal childcare markets, like that of Australia (Sumsion, 2006). In Aotearoa New Zealand the for-profit sector now occupies about 60 per cent of the market, the inverse of 15 years ago, with full day childcare centres accounting for the majority of this growth (Mitchell, 2013).

For many, the link between the rise of for-profit provision and lower quality care is self-evident (Morris and Helburn, 2000; Sosinsky et al, 2007; Cleveland and Krashinsky, 2009; Akgunduz and Plantenga, 2014). It is argued that what we are witnessing in neoliberal, anglophone contexts like the UK, Australia and Aotearoa New Zealand is the profound reshaping of the political economy of childcare provisioning in response to growing parental demand, incentivized by government investment such that childcare becomes more about making money than the care of children (Sumsion, 2006; Penn, 2011; Lloyd, 2013). The 'scaling up' of delivery, resulting in childcare chains, corporations and more recently the involvement of shareholder investment vehicles like pension funds, are profoundly changing how childcare is being viewed and practised in society. The related business models which have emerged attempt to find the fine line between regulatory compliance and maximum financial return.

As the scale of provisioning changes in response to marketization, the basis on which value is extracted from the care relationship itself becomes increasingly complex. As Susan Prentice argues, the economic framing of childcare as a site of investment now 'extends the universe of stakeholders who will reap returns on childcare. It broadens the domain of beneficiaries beyond children and their parents' (2009: 669). As I document in this book, childcare markets are being shaped and mediated by an increasingly diverse range of actors, materials, discourses, rationalities and technologies (Lloyd, 2013; Moss, 2014). Processes of privatization and more recently financialization[2] open the sector to the involvement of a greater range of economic actors than ever before (Gallagher, 2018b, 2020). These new actors, like the shareholders, property investors and software designers I discuss later in the book, are profoundly reshaping how childcare is organized and practised in the market.

Within the context of rising concerns about marketized childcare, in this book I aim to open the 'black box' of childcare markets to critical scrutiny. Whereas existing studies of childcare have considered its marketization (Mahon and Michel, 2002; Brennan et al, 2012) and the impacts of commodification and privatization on those who use and work in childcare (Osgood, 2005; Press and Woodrow, 2005), this book takes a different approach to offer an in-depth examination of a childcare market in creation. This empirical approach seeks to uniquely highlight the everyday political, social *and* economic work of constructing childcare markets. In the process, I will ask three important questions: Who are the actors shaping neoliberal childcare markets? What work do they do to marketize care? And what does it mean for the sustainability of childcare as a crucial service for children and working families?

Although neoliberal childcare markets provide the broad analytic terrain for this book, within these markets I specifically focus on the growth of private, for-profit childcare centres. While I acknowledge that this only represents a small part of the diverse economy which exists to provide the social infrastructure of childcare, centre-based childcare has experienced the largest growth within these contexts[3] and today accounts for the paid care experiences of the majority of preschool aged children (Boyer et al, 2012; Sosinsky, 2013; Gallagher, 2017). It is within this part of the childcare sector that we can see most evidently the kinds of changes associated with processes of privatization, corporatization and more recently financialization having an impact.

Recent critical work on neoliberal childcare markets tends to criticize the state as something of an absent presence (Lloyd and Penn, 2013; Penn, 2013; Brennan, 2014). In keeping with the opening quote from UK early education expert Professor Helen Penn, it is argued that the state has very little control over, and is largely disinterested in, the operation of the childcare market. While there is evidence to support this view, certainly when read in light of the difficulties incurred in regulating childcare markets, this book questions the assumption that the state is stepping aside to simply allow markets to flourish. By reinforcing the perspective of a withdrawn state vis-à-vis the market, we accept one of the key myths of neoliberal governance. Instead, I seek to examine the role of the state in actively producing the conditions for neoliberal childcare markets to operate, a process I will refer to in the book as *state-led marketization*. Delving into this process I will examine the ways in which the childcare market is being shaped by the economic and financial strategies of a range of actors, in direct response to the conditions of state-led marketization. Tracing out the creation of the childcare market will account for expected protagonists, like parents and providers, but I will also show how state-led marketization has incentivized the involvement of other, less visible groups, such as childcare finance companies and property sales brokers, drawn to childcare as a government backed business opportunity. In doing so I aim to highlight the challenges of state-led marketization, as the resulting market inevitably exceeds the capacity of government to regulate and contain.

Neoliberalism and the rise of a market ethic

To understand the changing relationship between the state and market in the delivery of childcare, and social services generally, we need to first trace out the politico-economic terrain of neoliberalism, and the increasing centrality of markets to solving social problems. Debates over the prevalence of neoliberalism as a political ideology, policy framework and a form of governmentality have been well documented over the past 30 years (Larner, 2000, 2003; Peck and Tickell, 2002; Harvey, 2007; Birch, 2017). Although cautious not to deploy an overly coherent account of neoliberalism, at a rudimentary level it can be identified as the prioritization of the logic of the market across all spheres of economic and increasingly social activity. Economic geographer David Harvey (2007: 3) characterizes neoliberalism as the ascendance of a 'market ethic', in which contractual relations in the marketplace are deemed the most efficient and indeed ethical means to organize society. The perceived failures of the 'cradle to grave' approach of Keynesian welfarism by the late 1970s steeled governments internationally to reduce their involvement in the lives of their citizens. This political withdrawal manifested in diverse ways, such as large scale public sector funding cuts; privatization of state assets; deregulation of economies; privatization of welfare services; and the reliance on other non-state actors to meet crucial social needs, to name but a few. Under this new political imaginary it was assumed that markets, once established, could replace much of the work of government and garner benefits which a centrally planned public sector could not, undermining the need for a public sector at all (Clarke, 2004a, 2004b). In this context, the role of the state was to protect or even create the conditions for markets, and although most popular forms of neoliberal politics veered to the economic right, adherents of neoliberalization as a process of state reorganization were located across the political spectrum.

Central to most early forms of neoliberalism was the mantra of proliferating choice for citizens (Friedman, 1962). The rhetoric of choice became a driving discourse around which social policy itself was redesigned, with the deployment of markets where possible to achieve this aim (Bevir, 2005). Society came to be acted on less through collectivized strategies as it had been under Keynesianism, and increasingly through means which encouraged individualism and individual choice. Within this new form of 'governing the social' (Rose, 1996), families and individuals were envisioned to be less reliant on the state, and instead should aim to take control of their own destinies through their engagement with the labour market. In the domain of care, the use of markets or quasi markets (Glennerster and Le Grand, 1995) to meet social needs became commonplace. Recreating citizens as new consumer subjects was a necessary part of the marketization of the social to ultimately enable governance 'at a distance' (Rose, 1999; Holmer Nadesan, 2008), as consumers could theoretically regulate the market. It was claimed that the benefits to an emergent consumer society would be the generation of a broader range of goods and higher quality of services to choose from than ever before.

However, by the late 1980s in the neoliberal heartlands of the global north, countries like the US, UK and New Zealand, which had wholeheartedly enacted their own version of neoliberalism, the retrenchment of welfare, coupled with the deregulation of the economy had considerably exacerbated existing social problems. Social and economic inequalities increased rapidly as governments prioritized capital economic accumulation through the expansion of the free market economy, at the detriment of social stability (Harvey, 2007). In most westernized economies, the income gap between the top 10 per cent and the rest of the population widened to a gulf (Wilkinson and Pickett, 2010), as income redistribution became a politically suspect idea. The associated 'individualization' of society brought about new social risks and heightened levels of insecurity about the future (Beck, 1992). One domain in which this anxiety has become manifest is in the 'crisis of care' (Daly and Lewis, 2000; Brennan et al, 2012; Dowling, 2020). As all individuals became integrated into the labour market as an expectation of their citizenship, there has been a fundamental reduction in the ability of households to manage their care responsibilities across western societies (Hochschild and Machung, 1989; McDowell, 2004). The rise of a universal worker model in place of a more traditional female carer/male breadwinner version of household relations has produced a significant shortage in what was largely unpaid care labour, hidden within the reproductive sphere. The growing number of women, and mothers in particular, joining the workforce has manifested in a heightened demand for outsourced non-familial care, like childcare (Hochschild, 2012), creating new social problems to be addressed.

Addressing new social problems: making markets of collective concern

While neoliberalism has become an ubiquitous term encapsulating a range of reforms, from the early phase of market-led restructuring of welfare in the 1980s, today the term accounts for more complex associations of the state, market and third sector actors in providing welfare (Peck and Tickell, 2002; Harvey, 2007; Milligan and Power, 2010). Faced with mounting concerns over the impact of growing societal inequality, anglophone governments of the global north have attempted to offset the worst effects of neoliberal restructuring through interventions intended to 'soften' market expansion over the past 20 years. Political scientist Janine Brodie (2003) suggests that these interventions were borne out of a 'paradox of necessity': such that neoliberalism stripped away the mechanisms and institutional supports, and the capabilities of states, while simultaneously maximizing the need for social intervention because of the socially destabilizing effects of unfettered markets. In many OECD countries this political focus has led to an approach to social policy known as 'social investment', characterized by a renewed interest among policy communities in mitigating the collective problems produced under earlier 'roll back' neoliberal reforms (Jenson and Saint-Martin, 2003). Endorsed by UK sociologist Anthony Giddens (1998), the social investment approach represents a reformulation of the role of the neoliberal state to incorporate a greater emphasis on social programmes and provisioning, recognizing the importance of rebuilding social collectives through developing 'social and human capital' (Morel et al, 2012). However, while this may sound like a more interventionist role for the state, in practice a social investment approach does not signal a move away from the belief in the benefits of markets as a means of organizing access to resources. Rather, it has led to a more proactive role for the state in mediating the 'invisible hand' of the market in social provisioning (England and Ward, 2007).

Unlike earlier forms of neoliberalism, under a social investment approach government spends on welfare, but in a highly strategic manner such that social spending is expected to make tangible economic returns (Midgley and Tang, 2001). There has not been a complete break with previous neoliberal rationales, as any political commitment to social expenditure is made not as a redistributive intervention, but is recast as an investment whereby the state seeks to achieve measurable returns (Dobrowolsky, 2002). In order to reap the greatest benefits, government spending becomes highly targeted, directed to where the highest returns are to be gained in the present and importantly, the future. In an attempt to capture the benefits of this new investment paradigm, there has been a related proliferation of governmental accountability and ways of measuring the effectiveness of social investment spending, made more pervasive through the datafication of the social sphere (Power, 1997; Baker and Cooper, 2018). As I will discuss in the next section it is in this light that spending on childcare, and early childhood education (ECE) in particular as a form of human capital investment, has come to the fore of attention for neoliberal governments and their policy communities.

The breadth of work on neoliberalism over time has clearly shown that the idea of the invisible hand of the market, operating unimpeded by the state, is largely a political fiction. Critical social scientists who study processes of neoliberalization argue that today it is more analytically useful to move beyond depictions of a withdrawn 'hollowed out' state (Jessop, 2000; Rhodes, 2005), and instead trace how the state has changed in response to the political desire to extend markets into all spheres of life (Mirowski, 2013). To that end, government intervention is increasingly focused on smoothing over the worst effects of markets, rather than questioning the appropriateness of their use in meeting complex social needs. Researchers of more recent variants of 'post' neoliberal governance have documented the deepening of relations between the state and market over the past 20 years, a variable process Birch and Siemiatycki (2015) refer to simply as 'marketization'. Rather than a reduced role for the state as evident in roll back forms of neoliberalism, we are witnessing the market-based restructuring of the state itself whereby governments actively create the conditions in which a market logic dominates. Foucault in his work on biopolitics referred to this shift as the work of the state to produce 'infinitely active policy' (Foucault, 2008; Hoppania and Vaittinen, 2015), constantly revisiting policy in an attempt to sustain conditions for the market. This he suggested has engendered in many cases a political transformation 'from a market supervised by the state to a state under the supervision of the market'[4] (Lemke, 2001).

Recent literature in economic sociology on 'markets for collective concerns' (Frankel et al, 2019) builds on Foucault's observations to offer fruitful analytical insights into the ongoing political rationale informing state engagement with markets in order to solve social problems. In this work markets of collective concern are understood as markets that have been constructed as policy instruments, because policymakers expect them to offer the best possible solution to a particular collective problem. However, once these markets have been found problematic, policymaking becomes *an exercise in market organization* where attention is re-orientated towards the repair of the market so it can work 'better'. Over time, because of the crucial role these markets come to play in sustaining economic and social life, they become seen as too important to fail, and continued market organization through policymaking is normalized politically as the *only* way to achieve desired social outcomes. Drawing on this recent work, this book seeks to examine childcare markets *as* markets of collective concern. Despite considerable criticisms raised as to the suitability of marketization as a means of organizing access to childcare in countries like the UK, Australia and as I will detail Aotearoa New Zealand, these countries have remained politically committed to sustaining childcare markets in some form over the past 30 years.

As a market of collective concern, governmental and policy interventions have been directed towards repairing and solving market problems in order for the market to work 'better'. To account for the complex and varied political work of market organization and repair, especially for markets which have considerable social and economic goals attached (like childcare or education), I have developed the concept of state-led marketization. I use this term in the book to capture the highly evolving and *experimental frontier* of policy making in an attempt to mobilize markets to achieve important social goals. Moving beyond renditions of a disinterested state giving way to the invisible hand of the market, in this book I focus on the deepening involvement by the state not only in regulating markets, but in actively setting the conditions for markets to operate through the design of funding and policy mechanisms.

Inherent to state-led marketization is a desire to guide and use the market to achieve important social goals and to address collective concerns. Yet, despite attempts to govern the markets being created to do this work, these markets inevitably generate unanticipated outcomes. In the case of childcare, the use of increasing amounts of government funding as a driver to both stimulate and direct neoliberal childcare markets has incited speculative interest from a diverse range of actors, many of whom have expertise largely outside the domain in question. Consequently, state-led marketization *intersects in unexpected ways with other markets* through the attempts of diverse economic actors to access government revenue. In making this point I will suggest that there is more happening here than merely the private sector syphoning off public money. In the empirical chapters of this book, I delve deeper into some of these sites of intermarket engagement, to show how the economic logics and rationales of other markets over time *can become infrastructural*, shaping practices and processes in relation to the social problem being solved.

In sum, mobilizing markets to achieve social goals and remedy collective problems has become an experimental frontier of neoliberal governance (Gingrich, 2011). Birch and Siemiatycki (2015) highlight the importance of recognizing the diversity of this experimental frontier and the diverse forms that state-market relations can take; from privatization, to public–private partnerships, to the contractualization of service provision and more. The considerable increase in social spending as part of an investment approach within many neoliberalized welfare economies has proliferated the amount and diversity of non-state actors tasked with providing the bulk of the social infrastructure. One outcome of this trend has been the transferral of considerable amounts of public funding towards private sector actors (Raco, 2016). Rationalized through a discourse of social investment, the politics of this government spending becomes hidden under a renewed political pragmatism. It is within this context that childcare has become viewed as a lucrative and risk averse business due to its changed status as a government funded sector. Now that I have opened out the broad terrain as to why markets are being used to meet complex social problems, like that of childcare, the next section will specifically consider the childcare problem in neoliberal welfare economies, and how markets are anticipated to be the solution.

Childcare as a site of interest for neoliberal policy communities

The expansion of commodified childcare since the late 1970s across much of the OECD is now a well told story (Jenson and Sineau, 2001; Bonoli and Reber, 2010; White and Friendly, 2012). The dramatic rise in women's employment, most notably of mothers into the workforce, coupled with the increasing financial expectation in society of the dual earner household, has been a key driver behind the rising demand for childcare (OECD, 2001,

2020). The resulting dearth of reproductive labour, previously available for 'free' and associated with the private sphere of the home, has resulted in considerable pressure to find new care solutions, creating a care crisis in many contexts. As a social and economic intervention, intended to support the proliferation of childcare for working mothers (as opposed to the later redefined ECE),[5] many neoliberal welfare economies increased expenditure for the first time on childcare supports during the 1970s and 1980s, when financial retrenchment was more politically acceptable. In this sense the story of childcare markets in anglophone countries, like the UK, Australia and New Zealand, is one which sits uncomfortably within the broader neoliberal narratives of government cutbacks during this time (Peck and Tickell, 2002; Harvey, 2007).

As a governmental problem, childcare gained much greater traction within policy making communities under a social investment paradigm[6] during the 1990s. As Ruth Lister highlighted at a peak in government spending on childcare in the UK, children (rather than women) moved to the heart of social policy under a future orientated model of citizenship (2003). While childcare had been a biopolitical concern for governments for the duration of the 20th century (Rose, 1990), a new expertise of childhood[7] came to shape how children were viewed and acted upon by government from the 1990s (Millei and Joronen, 2016). Within this context, childcare took on new significance as an 'opportunity' within the lifecourse to 'maximise the mind' of the child (Millei and Joronen, 2016: 182). The findings of a number of influential longitudinal studies gave the weight of evidence to policymakers to invest in childcare as early education services (Schweinhart et al, 2005). One of the often-quoted measures found in policy briefs of the return on this investment came from the findings of the US Perry Preschool Project, which stated that every US$1 invested by the state into a HighScope Programme,[8] would save society US$7 in terms of a reduction in future welfare spending on that child (see Clarke, 2006, for a critical review of these purported outcomes). As Susan Prentice argues, spending on childcare as ECE also aligned well within an economic framing of the 'investable child' (Prentice, 2007, 2009) forming a unifying regime of truth which seemingly spoke to the diverse interests of governments, childcare providers, feminist advocacy groups, and parents at the same time. Consolidating this view of childhood, major think tanks like the OECD purported the long-term benefits of childcare as ECE, and an educational resource in its own right (OECD, 2001, 2006). Rather than simply viewed as a means of caring for children during the working day, under a social investment approach we can trace governmental encouragement of children into preschool environments in particular, as it became seen as a means to mitigate the effects of educational disadvantage for children in later life (Gambaro et al, 2014).

A final, but often less acknowledged, reason for governmental interest in childcare provisioning since the 1980s has been the stagnating, and in some cases falling, birth rates across the global north (Bauernschuster et al, 2016). For the first time since records began, New Zealand failed to meet its population replacement level in 2018. The demand for childcare is predicated on the continued replacement of the population. We would not need childcare if there were no children to care for. Aside from neo-Malthusians, many foresee significant problems for the economies and societies of advanced capitalist nations as a result. Within this context, there has been an increase in government interventions which can be both directly and indirectly considered as childcare related, to reinvigorate dwindling population numbers. These incentives include the likes of baby bonus payments in Australia (Risse, 2010). Indeed, the international shareholder prospectuses of global education corporates, like G8 Education, draw clear links between a governmental need to ensure the reproduction of the workforce in the face of an ageing population, as an indication of the continued political commitment to childcare markets. Childcare, then, has become an important point of confluence for a range of complex long and short-term governmental problems.

Markets as the answer to the childcare problem?

While childcare is increasingly emphasized as the answer to a range of complex social issues within the welfare contexts of New Zealand, the UK and Australia, marketization has been the means by which the formalized childcare sectors in these countries have been developed in response (White and Friendly, 2012; Lloyd and Penn, 2013). There are different rationales as to how and why marketization has been deployed in each country, as I will discuss in the next section, but generally speaking childcare markets have been anticipated to offer a way of effectively and efficiently meeting rising demand for childcare while minimizing costs to government. It is important to note that the use of markets in itself to meet childcare needs is not necessarily problematic, as there are examples of well-functioning markets shaped around supply side payments given directly to providers (Brennan et al, 2012). However, within the neoliberalized anglophone contexts to which this book speaks, there has been a uniform move away from supply side funding to more demand-led supports which seek to promote a competitive and consumerist approach to childcare (Warner and Gradus, 2011).

A particular imaginary of the childcare market has gained currency in neoliberal policy domains over the past two decades, whereby the state takes up the mantle of regulator rather than direct provider of services. Instead, the bulk of extra familial childcare needs are provided within a diverse and mixed economy of care, comprised of actors from across the formal/informal and for-profit/non-profit sectors. At the heart of the neoliberal imaginary of the market is the idea of an informed, rational parent consumer, who strives through their own self-interested actions to find the best solution for their care needs in a competitive market. Through demand side funding interventions, as opposed to supply side funding directly to services, parents are anticipated to be 'empowered' in the market to exercise their consumer choice, seeking out the service that best fits their needs (Plantenga, 2012). Strengthening the ability for parents to choose and move between services is thought to generate competitive pressures, which in theory will increase quality and reduce costs among providers. Those services which are capable of meeting parental demand will succeed, while those that do not will become obsolete, allowing for a more 'responsive' market environment.

Childcare markets in Australia and the UK

Before examining the development of the childcare market in Aotearoa New Zealand, in this section I will give an overview of two other anglophone childcare markets against which it is most regularly compared in the existing literature: those of Australia and the UK. Indeed, much of the critical literature which I have drawn on in the book is grounded in these contexts, as they have been key frontier sites in the debates around the privatization and more recently the corporatization of childcare. While these markets appear to have reached a common critical moment in terms of their development and sustainability (Mahon et al, 2012), their welfare histories and trajectories in reaching this point do differ in important ways. Although this book does not claim to be a comparative study, the aim of this section is to give a brief overview of these better documented and studied childcare markets, to demonstrate the different kinds of policy rationales and funding mechanisms which have been used to try to create and direct the market. Giving empirical reality to some of the conceptual claims made earlier in the chapter, this section outlines the different trajectories state-led marketization has taken in these two contexts yet highlights the eventual discursive closure around markets as the only means of meeting the demand for childcare and early education.

State-led marketization in Australia

The Australian context has offered a very active site of analysis for many working in critical social policy and education to document and critique the marketization of childcare over the past 30 years. Australia, like the other anglophone countries discussed here, has never had universal childcare, but like New Zealand it did have an existing mixed economy of care with a well-established community non-profit childcare sector before the

1990s (Brennan, 2014). Throughout the 1970s and 1980s the Australian government actively expanded non-profit services through a mixture of capital grants to providers and fee subsidies to parents to incentivize their use. Families who used for-profit services to access longer childcare hours were not eligible for fee subsidies at this time. At this point, the non-profit sector was diverse, as Brennan (2014: 155) suggests, 'delivery through community based services ensured diversity of provision, since auspice bodies were locally based and closely connected with the communities they served'.

Under the Hawke and Keating Labor governments (1983–96), childcare moved to a central position on the political agenda in Australia, gaining voice through the alignment of shared interests of the Trade Union movement and those of women's groups on work related issues (Brennan, 2002). The rising demand for childcare due to mothers (re)entering the workforce placed renewed emphasis on national and territorial governments to meet changing household care needs. Faced with the financial pressure of meeting rising demand, in 1991 the Hawke government took the key decision to make childcare funding available to private for-profit providers. At the same time, capital expenditure to non-profit community-based services was reduced. This change in the funding system initiated a key phase of marketization.

However, unlike the UK and New Zealand, the debate in favour of marketization in Australia at this time was not one of proliferating choice for parents, as there was already considerable choice available in the non-profit sector due to their obligation to the communities they served (Brennan, 2014). The primary reason used to justify marketization was instead to reduce the cost to government of a burgeoning demand for childcare, whereby the necessary capital expenditure for new facilities could be sought from within the private for-profit sector. A second rationale for opening funding to the for-profit sector was a desire to suppress what was perceived as wage inflation of childcare workers within the existing non-profit sector, such that the influence of the private sector would help to curtail wage increases and 'creeping credentialism' within the workforce (Press, 2015).

Marketization of childcare accelerated in Australia with the election of a centre right government under Prime Minister John Howard (1996–2007). The most notable change under this government was the introduction of two commonwealth level funding schemes, with the aim to subsidize parental fees as a key barrier to access for many households. The first scheme was the Childcare Benefit introduced in 2001, which offered a means-tested benefit to low-income working families of up to 50 hours of childcare per week within approved childcare and early education settings. Parents could use this subsidy at any registered provider, but despite the intention to reduce childcare costs, parental fees remained high as there was no cap on the rate of fees which providers could charge. To address the issue of cost, a second childcare rebate scheme in 2004 offered up to A$4000 off the remainder of the cost of care for parents after the childcare benefit was deducted. This was not means-tested and was most explicitly directed to those families paying higher fees. An unfortunate outcome of this subsidy was that in effect the continued fee increases by childcare services could be largely absorbed by increased government funding. Reflective of this issue, between 2002 and 2007 the cost of childcare increased by 88 per cent (Brennan, 2014). As Brennan et al have suggested, ultimately the subsidy schemes were seen 'as a bonanza for business' (2012: 384), which led to a considerable proliferation of for-profit providers attracted by the security of government funding to services.

In 2008, the incoming Rudd Labor government made a decision to refocus childcare spending towards early education in keeping with a social investment approach (Logan et al, 2012). Influenced by OECD reports and the emphasis on early education as a social and economic policy objective, government expenditure in Australia on ECE increased by over 60 per cent in real terms between 2008 and 2012. However, as Adamson and Brennan suggest, this investment occurred at a point when marketization was already well underway, and a strong private for-profit sector had developed. Ultimately the for-profit sector saw the biggest financial gains from this wave of government spending. Like the UK at this time, economies of scale in the delivery of childcare also began to change, with service consolidation becoming apparent. One of the most notable examples of corporatization was ABC Childcare Australia, which gained significant dominance in the market throughout the 1990s and early 2000s. In 2001 it took the relatively novel step at the time of listing on the stock exchange, gaining access to increased amounts of financial capital through shareholder investment to allow further service expansion. Engaging in an aggressive acquisition strategy of non-profit and other corporate providers, by the mid-2000s it had amassed a considerable share of the Australian childcare market (Brennan, 2007), providing up to 50 per cent of childcare places in some locations.[9]

An emphasis on early education in policy led to an attempt to raise and align staffing and regulatory standards across the sector through the introduction of the National Quality Framework in 2009. While professionalization of the sector was acknowledged as an important part in achieving the educational goals for children in ECE, critics argued that these ambitions were undermined by the profit-making objectives and business models of a burgeoning for-profit care sector which had been growing over the previous 15 years. Raising quality in early education through increasing skills levels was mitigated by the lower levels of remuneration in the for-profit part of the sector, where a significant proportion of the workforce was also comprised of migrant workers (Hamilton et al, 2021). Despite the policy desire for professionalization, subsequent research showed a consistently high staff turnover in the sector, up to as much as 50 per cent in more remote areas (Jovanovic, 2013). Indeed, current predictions suggest that there will be a need for an additional 5800 qualified early education teachers each year until 2023 to meet a burgeoning teacher shortage (Early Learning: Everyone Benefits, 2019).

Currently in the Australian childcare market there remains a distinction in the kinds of services available to parents; with long day childcare centres and in-home childcare tailoring primarily to the needs of working households, and preschool services offering sessional or short hours for children in the year or two before school (Adamson, 2017). The costs to parents between the two types of services remain considerable, with a nominal fee paid for non-profit preschool services, compared to an average weekly cost of A$460 to parents for full day care, before the childcare rebate is deducted. In 2018 there were 1.8 million children accessing the childcare benefit for registered childcare services, with the majority of this funding being used in long day, centre-based childcare which remains largely provided in the for-profit sector (Early Learning: Everyone Benefits, 2019). In the same year a Productivity Commission report noted that low-income families were spending twice the proportion of their weekly income on ECE as high-income earners (Productivity Commission, 2019). The report acknowledged that the various forms of childcare subsidies which had been introduced had failed to significantly improve the cost of care for many families, in large part because of the uninhibited ability of the for-profit sector to raise fees.

State-led marketization in the UK

By comparison with Australia, in the UK there was very little interest in a formalized childcare sector from a government perspective until the late 1990s, and the system evolved as a mixed economy of care without large scale intervention from government (Lewis and West, 2017). Some specific funding had been available to non-profit services from local authorities for communities in socially and economically deprived neighbourhoods, and there was also a minor funding commitment for early education through state-maintained nursery schools[10] for children just before starting school. However, provision across the country was largely ad hoc, and did not explicitly cater to the needs of working families. To that end, by the early 1990s only 1 per cent of children had access to centre-based childcare, almost all of which was in the private and voluntary sector (Penn, 2007).

Under the New Labour government (1997–2010), expansion of the formalized childcare and ECE sector accelerated with the introduction of the first National Childcare Strategy (DFES, 1998), and a political desire to expand the amount of services available for working households. From a policy perspective, childcare and early education became viewed as a linchpin aligning many of the social and economic ambitions of the New Labour government, such as improving social inclusion and mobilizing women into the workforce (Ball and Vincent, 2005). Like Australia, the advocacy work of the National Childcare Campaign coupled with the political activism of feminist politicians, furthered childcare as a pressing policy issue (David, 1999). Under a more targeted social investment approach, a key policy initiative was the introduction of 'Sure Start' childcare services for children and families in 1998. This initiative explicitly acknowledged the necessity of childcare services in order to facilitate parents into education or the workforce, and co-located childcare centres alongside other wraparound counselling and parenting resources for families in economically and socially deprived neighbourhoods.

From 1997 until 2010 there was a rapid expansion of the childcare market through a significant introduction of funding into the sector. Unlike previous forms of support, which were supply side and given directly to non-profit services for their work, the new funding was largely demand-led spending on the sector. In 1998, alongside the Sure Start initiative, the Labour government introduced 12 hours of free early education in nursery schools to all four-year-olds, for 33 weeks of the year. This was increased in 2010 to 15 hours free to three- and four-year-olds. However, the existing nursery sector did not have enough capacity to meet the rise in demand for ECE that the new spending was set to incite. In response, the government envisioned a new role for the for-profit sector to fill the gap through expanding day care nursery provision. Participation by children in the free hours scheme was high, with around 95 per cent of three- and four-year-olds participating by 2015. In addition to the free hours scheme, a means-tested tax credit system was introduced for parents to meet wider childcare needs, especially for children under three whose care received less subsidization. By 2006 the tax credit system covered up to 80 per cent of the cost of childcare, to a ceiling amount, for low-income families where both parents were working up to 16 hours a week. For families not eligible for the tax credit, a childcare voucher system was extended in 2005 which offered income relief for parents whose employers were participating in the scheme. Yet, like the Australian context, there was no cap on the fees providers could charge parents, and much of the cost of care remained on the shoulders of families as fees outside of the paid hours increased alongside government subsidization.

The introduction of the Children Act (2004) required local authorities to 'close the gap' between families by providing access to ECE. As Lloyd (2007) suggests, how this was enacted was firmly shaped by a market logic, with priority to be given to for-profit providers whereby local authority provision a last resort. Instead, local authorities had an obligation to conduct 'childcare market management' to proliferate the supply of services through a range of interventions like business and enterprise grants and mentoring programmes for owner-operators (Osgood, 2005; Robert-Holmes and Moss, 2021). The private for-profit sector accelerated its market share between 2002 and 2008 in response to demand-led funding, with a 70 per cent increase during this time (Lloyd and Penn, 2010: 153). By the end of the 2010s service consolidation was apparent, with 19 of the top 20 childcare companies corporately owned (Penn, 2011). Despite the rhetoric of increasing access to quality early education, these aims were ultimately undermined by a lack of political interest in the rise of the for-profit sector in response to government spending. The failure to differentiate in funding terms as to the auspice of the service providing childcare and ECE has been seen as a major fault in the initial conception of the UK childcare market.

To oversee the changing emphasis on ECE in policy, the governance and regulation of services was centralized under the Department of Education and Skills, and a separate Minister for Children was created in 2003. The Children Act (2004) set out a basic agenda for all children's services, and within childcare and ECE it sought to standardize quality and care practices across the sector. As Penn (2007) suggests it was also an attempt to level the playing field across the range of diverse providers in the for-profit and non-profit sectors of the market. Some of the key changes included trying to raise the qualifications of the workforce through funding initiatives like the Transformation Fund for staff training, by regulating structural elements such as staff/child ratios, and by introducing the Early Years Foundation Stage Framework (EYFSF) curriculum in 2008.[11] Adherence to these regulatory tenets were monitored at a national level by the newly established Office for Standards in Education (Ofsted) (Penn, 2013).

While from 1997–2010 the focus of the Labour government was on proliferating choice and improving quality in the childcare market, Lewis and West (2017) suggest that since 2010 the emphasis of subsequent government policy has been on forging the childcare market first and foremost. Following the election of a Conservative/Liberal Democrat coalition government in 2010, policy goals reverted to an emphasis on facilitating mothers' employment and the role of the private sector in meeting ongoing demand as childcare rather than ECE. In the process the social investment emphasis on children's educational development dropped from political view. These changes also took place in the context of considerable economic austerity in the wake of the global financial crisis. During this period, important regulatory levers for the market, such as provider registration and service inspection, all underwent some form of deregulation (Lewis and West, 2017), conducted in the desire to reduce 'red tape' for owner-operators to allow them to provide childcare in a more cost effective and flexible manner.[12]

Faced with the need to rethink the cost of government spending on ECE under a renewed era of fiscal austerity, the reliance of the state on the market to meet childcare needs changed during the 2010s. This can be evidenced by the discontinuation of existing supply side funding for Sure Start services which catered explicitly to families in lower socioeconomic communities. While the wraparound support services were still available at Sure Start centres, the cost of childcare was now placed back on the parents, unlike the original government funded Sure Start initiative. Eventually in 2011 the policy commitment for Children's Centres to provide services in 30 per cent of the most disadvantaged areas was abandoned, creating deepening inequalities of childcare provision in the market (Smith et al, 2018).

Attempts to address concerns over rising cost and limited availability of childcare in the market during the early 2010s were addressed by the coalition government through a reformulation of the funding system. In 2013 a tax-free childcare system replaced the childcare voucher scheme, which studies showed was only reaching a third of families and was dependent on whether employers chose to take part. The tax-free system covered 20 per cent of the cost of childcare up to £2000 per year per child. To address the spiralling costs for lower income families, a second means-tested Universal Credit system was also introduced, which covered up to 85 per cent of childcare costs to a limit of £175 per week for one child and £300 for two children. The free childcare hours payment for three- and four-year-olds, introduced under the previous Labour government, was increased in 2017 to 30 paid hours per week for up to 38 weeks of the year for families in receipt of the Universal Credit payment. While these subsidies and payments have gone some way towards improving the cost of care for families at the lower end of the income ladder, as attempts to 'fix' the problems of affordability and availability they have, however, produced a highly complex funding system for even the most informed parents to navigate (Rutter, 2016).

The childcare workforce in the UK (excluding funded nursery schools) remains among the lowest paid within the education sector, with those in for-profit services reporting the lowest skills and pay (Gambaro, 2017). While state-funded nursery services have fully qualified teachers, only 13 per cent of paid staff in for-profit full day care services were equally qualified by 2015. Given this is the fastest growing part of the UK childcare market, it poses questions as to the quality of care and education in these settings. Since 2010 for-profit childcare provision has grown exponentially in the market to meet the increase in government funding. By 2019 almost half of the 1.7 million childcare places available in the UK were delivered by the for-profit sector. Moreover, corporate ownership of centre-based childcare has made a notable increase since the mid-2000s, with two supergroups alone accounting for 8 per cent of the market in 2019. By contrast, the number of maintained nursery schools has dropped significantly, with only 389 remaining in England at the time of writing, many of whom were citing significant financial problems (Adams, 2021).

A second ongoing problem with the market has been the cost of care to parents, which despite the UK government spending £6 billion on childcare each year remains one of the highest in the OECD (OECD, 2021). In 2018 childcare services received just over a quarter of its funding for two- to four-year-olds from government (Blanden et al, 2020), leaving a considerable shortfall for parents to meet.[13] According to Blanden et al (2020), the average price for full time care (50 hours per week) in a daycare nursery for an under two is nearly four times as much as the average household spends on food. Findings from a recent childcare survey suggest that only half of local authorities report they have enough childcare for full time working families, with a particular shortage for children under two (Coleman and Cottell, 2019). The recent extension of the childcare free hours payment to 30 hours for some three- and four-year-olds before school has produced considerable tensions in the sector, and made evident the reliance of for-profit business models on the need to raise parental fees, something which was envisioned to be mitigated by the paid hours scheme. To that extent, setting the hourly rate for the 30 hours of care has been argued to have overly intervened in the business of care, such that providers with higher-than-average operating costs can no longer remain financially viable on the amount provided by government. Some evidence suggests that service closure is occurring in response (Spanswick, 2016).

In sum, there are notable differences in the childcare markets of both the UK and Australia in terms of how childcare has been funded, viewed and organized. Yet, as Mahon et al (2012) have suggested, what we may be seeing in more advanced neoliberal childcare markets is ultimately policy convergence around systems of organization, in large part because of the impact of ECE policy transfer through international think tanks like the OECD. There are two key points which I will highlight from the earlier accounts which speak to the broader theoretical argument of state-led marketization as outlined in this book. Firstly, despite different means of organizing and funding childcare, there has been considerable political commitment to the market ideal, irrespective of political leaning of the parties in power over the last 30 years. In both Australia and the UK, despite some existing government support of an established community, non-profit childcare sector, the idea of the childcare market gained political traction under periods of public sector reform and a revised relationship of the state to public service provisioning. As Lewis and West (2017) have suggested, over time the main difference in childcare policymaking in the UK became how the role of the state was conceptualized in managing the market, rather than whether or not the market system was meeting the policy objectives for families and children. To that extent, what is apparent in tracing the evolving policy, regulatory and funding trajectories of the UK and Australia is that the work of policy over time became one of 'fixing' the market through the levers of funding in order to make it function more efficiently and effectively.

As Hoppania and Vaittinen (2015) suggest with regards to care provisioning, the nature of the market intervention significantly shapes the kind of care market which emerges. Indeed, within neoliberal childcare markets there have been a number of common policy and funding trends which have been noted, in particular the change from supply side payments directly to services, in markets where they already existed, to demand-led funding to parents as consumers. One of the primary differences here is that income is no longer predictable to services under a demand-led system, as it is linked to parental choice. Moreover, within the different demand-led approaches to funding visible in neoliberal childcare markets, voucher and tax deduction systems have tended to foster 'commodification without regulation' (Adamson, 2017), reproducing low waged and low skilled care economies, many of which rely on the steady flow of migrant labour. In comparison, subsidized or payment-based interventions, like the 15 free hours in the UK and the 20 free hours in New Zealand, have tended to be linked to higher expectations in the market around workforce professionalization and standards of practice in order to be eligible for funding, thus leading to generally higher levels of structural quality. Yet, as I will discuss further in the book, opening these schemes out to for-profit providers on the same terms as the non-profit sector has led to highly risky financial practices in the delivery of childcare, as these models rely on competition for the parent consumer.

Overall, research in the aforementioned contexts suggest that the different approaches to demand-led funding have largely stimulated a significant increase in market presence of the for-profit sector, and a related stagnation or even shrinkage of the non-profit sector where it existed (Penn, 2013). As already discussed, relying on the for-profit sector has been viewed as a necessary part of meeting childcare demand by government, as it expeditiously creates childcare capacity in the market and is thought to stimulate competition which will benefit parent consumers. These benefits are anticipated to be manifold, such as lower costs for parents and purportedly higher quality of care for children. Yet as Gillian Paull (2013) cautions, there has been no convincing evidence to suggest that competition in childcare markets leads to better quality. More often the inverse has been shown to occur. As Cleveland et al (2007) detail in their comparison of quality between the non-profit and for-profit sectors in the Canadian context, in competitive markets for-profit providers are generally not aiming to produce high quality care, but rather to offer childcare of moderate quality and cheaper price. In such 'thick', competitive markets, for-profit providers often invest more into the appearance of their premises, have more developed marketing strategies (around fees for example) and are better placed to capture the attention of parents through their advertising capacities, than non-profit services (Paull, 2013).

Although for-profit care services have been present in the aforementioned childcare markets for a long time, the injection of demand side funding has also provided impetus for a reconsideration of scale economies around childcare, a topic I will revisit in Chapter 4. One clear example of this has been in the proliferation of childcare chains and corporatized entities,[14] in lieu of what were more traditionally a single owner-operator model within the market. Indeed, a tandem drop in individual owner-operators has been noted in the UK, Australia and New Zealand markets, with evident attempts to rationalize service ownership over the past 20 years. A change in ownership models has significant implications for how childcare is organized and practised at every level. For example, as Kamenarac (2021) has illustrated in the New Zealand context, childcare workers in corporate childcare settings have a very different understanding of their job, through heightened potential for promotion within a larger management structure for example, than workers in non-profit service. At another level the tendency towards corporatization has implications for parents and children, as the rationalization of service ownership also undermines the extent of the 'choice' they may have in the market, both in terms of type of service but also in terms of cost. While it is clear that not all for-profit provision in the market is problematic, many have argued that it is especially in the domain of childcare chains and listed childcare entities where the tensions between care giving and profit making are especially pronounced. Ultimately it becomes challenging to meet the expectations around quality of care when services are also trying to meet the expectations of investors (Brennan, 2014; Mitchell, 2019b).

Approach of the book

As the book unfolds, I aim to make an empirical and theoretical intervention into our understanding of the interrelationship between states and markets in the delivery of childcare in the current post-neoliberal moment. In the process I will examine neoliberal childcare markets as highly contingent, actively created endeavours. The analysis presented will prioritize *market making as a process*, developing an approach which shifts our analytical gaze from primarily studying the negative impacts of the market on the delivery of childcare, to considering the political and economic work which, seemingly against a weight of criticism, sustains a particular form of market-based organization over time. One of the absences within existing work on childcare is a considered exploration of the daily, often benign, work of marketizing care. Existing studies tend to start from the position of an already existing market, and then offer a critique of commodified care for those who work in and use childcare services. While cognizant of these critiques, this book proposes to take a step back from the delivery interface to consider the broader political, social and economic drivers which are shaping the very possibilities for how childcare is practised under neoliberalism.

Focusing on a market in creation also draws our attention to the diverse actors involved in this work, their claims to expertise (which as I will document in later chapters is often far removed from the care and education of children) and the kinds of techniques, discourses and materialities involved in maintaining or repairing the market itself. The second key contribution of this book is to bring into conversation existing work on childcare markets with recent developments in the Social Studies of Marketization (SSM) literature, to provide a conceptual language that allows for more insight into the diverse logics, values and actors (human and non-human) at work in the construction of childcare, and potentially other care markets as well.

Analyses of childcare markets, like other morally contentious domains, have been shaped by a host of dichotomies; private versus public, business versus care, individualized versus collective to name but a few, all of which make studying and writing about childcare, and indeed other care sectors, a highly politicized field. Bearing this in mind, there are two important provisos to reading this book. The first pertains to how I understand the private for-profit sector. It is becoming unquestionable that highly competitive childcare markets are fraught with problems that many attribute to the growing prevalence of for-profit actors in childcare. However, many critics of the trend towards privatization tend to focus on the fact that there are profit-making interests involved, as an a priori problem for how childcare is delivered, rather than the volatility of the sector as a result of privatization (Bushouse, 2008). As a point of clarification, I do not want to make the claim that all for-profit childcare centres are bad or lead to uncaring environments simply because they operate as a business. Many for-profit childcare owners work with their staff, parents and children in respectful and mutually beneficial ways. Mindful of Viviana Zelizer's caution to not hastily assign moral judgements based on the assumption 'that social relations divide sharply into spheres of sentiment and solidarity on one side and rational self-interested calculation on the other and that contact between these hostile worlds tends to produce mutual contamination' (2010: 289), there is much evidence that commodified childcare can also be deeply caring (see for example Boyer et al, 2012). Payment itself is not necessarily the problem, but the context and organization of commodified care can be highly problematic. Ultimately, as I will argue in this book, for-profit centre-based providers are responding to the conditions of the market as set by the state, and their economic subjectivities and behaviours need to be contextualized within changing state-market relations, rather than be viewed as an inevitable outcome of for-profit incentives.

The second proviso pertains to the private versus public debate, most readily seen in calls for the state to step into childcare markets and take greater responsibility for the daily delivery of childcare, as a foundational aspect of our economy and society (Foundational Economy Collective, 2018). I suggest that the failure of policy advocacy groups to encourage the state in neoliberal contexts to remedy the problems of childcare privatization over the last decade in particular, fundamentally overlooks the nature of the relationship between the state and processes of marketization. As I will demonstrate, state-led marketization involves the deepening of state involvement in the childcare market over time but done in an attempt to sustain and repair it, rather than significantly change it. The analysis which follows steps back from the public versus private debate around neoliberal childcare markets, to instead focus on the complex interrelationship between state and market which blurs the boundaries of these political distinctions. I do this with the intention to better understand the contours of neoliberal childcare markets, and the work and actors involved in their creation, as an important first step in rethinking our political engagement with them.

Chapter overview

In order to open up a consideration of neoliberal childcare markets as markets of collective concern, Chapter 2 outlines the theoretical and conceptual terrain of a Social Studies of Marketization approach. When we document the centrality of markets to neoliberalism, we reinforce the all-encompassing narrative of the reach and spread of processes of neoliberalization into all aspects of life. This project aims to move away from this grand narrative to consider what childcare markets actually look like in place, recognizing that markets do not impose themselves naturally: they have to be constructed. Within this context Chapter 2 outlines a project for the consideration of markets and how they are stabilized within their particular socio-historical context. It encourages us to step back from the immediate impacts of markets to consider what the problem was to which marketization became the answer, and who the actors (human and non-human) are involved in realizing the market as a solution. Bringing together insights from SSM and other contingent literature from geography and economic sociology, this chapter lays out the broad political project as to why markets themselves require scrutiny; to open the black box around marketization, more than simply critique its effects.

Chapter 3 gives a situated account of the creation of the New Zealand childcare market since the late 1980s, reflective of its emergence at the frontier of neoliberal politics during that time. As I will document the marketization of childcare in Aotearoa New Zealand began even earlier than that of the UK and Australia. New Zealand offers an important empirical setting for thinking about childcare markets as it is considered internationally to have a high level of structural quality regulations in place

(White and Friendly, 2012), and as such is often referred to as a successful comparison to other neoliberal childcare contexts. It was also an early adopter of market governance within social provisioning as part of the (in)famous 'neoliberal experiment' of the 1980s (Kelsey, 1997). As such, childcare has occupied an important position on the frontier of neoliberal politics over the past 30 years in Aotearoa New Zealand, with considerable oscillations in political thinking about how best to organize the market. Within the other neoliberal policy contexts which have relied on market-based systems as a means of addressing their childcare demands, the New Zealand context stands out. As White and Friendly have suggested, its uniqueness within studies of childcare markets is borne from the fact that it shows 'even when a government attempts to develop standards regarding planning, delivery of services, staffing and training, the choice of delivery agents can undermine those efforts' (2012: 306). Drawing on the insights of SSM, Chapter 3 considers the political and economic work of state-led marketization involved in the initial framing of the childcare market, showing also the points at which these efforts were contested and prone to failure.

State-led marketization has fuelled the privatization of childcare services, with a range of for-profit providers now evident in neoliberal childcare markets. As a means of exploring the diversity of the growing for-profit sector, Chapter 4 traces out the business strategies of two key types of providers in the New Zealand market: a publicly listed childcare chain and small scale owner-operator. In the context of an ECE skills shortage, accessing and maintaining qualified staff has become a central financial calculation within the business models of for-profit providers. Emphasizing the complex financial landscape within which for-profit providers at all scales now operate, I document the proliferation of new financial actors and business practices in response to the problem of paying labour. I also query the role of certain forms of economic knowledge deployed by international economic consultancies, that neoliberal childcare markets are ripe for consolidation and that 'bigger is better' in the business of care.

One of the primary ambitions of this book is to highlight the diverse, and often unanticipated outcomes of marketization which disrupt the best laid market 'blueprints'. Chapter 5 documents the growth of an urban childcare property market off the back of the marketization of childcare. The relatively secure nature of childcare as a government backed business has stoked investor interest in the sector, both from the perspective of institutional investors like pension funds, but also from small scale 'mum and dad' investors keen to consolidate their retirement provisions. I document how urban childcare property since 2012 has become a highly sought-after passive investment for 'mum and dad' investors in New Zealand, considerably reshaping the conditions in which private providers deliver childcare and exposing the sector to new axes of financial vulnerability through rentiership.

The penultimate chapter traces the formative work of another hidden, yet now crucial aspect of childcare markets: childcare management software. The significant uptake of childcare management software in New Zealand, and across other neoliberal childcare markets, has in large part been precipitated by the demands of state-led marketization. With increased funding under a social investment rationale comes increased expectations around compliance and an interest in the *value* of childcare expenditure. Set within the context of the increased datafication of welfare, this chapter details the role of the software platforms as a key non-human part of the market. The mass integration of management software into the operation of childcare services has created new relationships, ways of governing the sector and ways of organizing commodified childcare. More than that I suggest that the data produced through these digital platforms has taken on a somewhat unintended life, forming a central part of the digital infrastructure which now underpins and stabilizes the market.

The book's conclusion reflects on childcare as a market of collective concern in the context of the current post-neoliberal moment. I will discuss the benefits of taking childcare markets, and indeed care markets more generally, as an object of study through the lens of SSM, and point to some of the challenges in establishing new accountability structures for childcare markets, as they become increasingly interwoven with the economic logics and practices of other kinds of market actors, far removed from the care of children.

2

Childcare Markets as an Object of Study

In the introductory chapter I outlined my working definition of state-led marketization, as one way to apprehend how states are involved in the active construction of markets to solve social problems. Moving forward, this chapter will develop a framework through which to explore state-led marketization in action, drawing on the conceptual language of a broader social science literature called the Social Studies of Marketization (SSM) (Callon, 2007a; Muniesa et al, 2007; Berndt and Boeckler, 2012). This work, largely housed in the domains of cultural economy, economic sociology and economic geography, seeks to take markets as an object of study, paying analytical attention to the everyday, mundane practices and objects which are involved in their construction. While care markets have not tended to be a focus of research in this field, with commodity and financial markets dominating analyses, I suggest that SSM offers a conceptually sophisticated language to open the black box of childcare, and other care markets, to more engaged scrutiny. Bringing the literature on childcare markets into conversation with the insights of SSM, this chapter will lay out an alternative approach which seeks to better account for the dynamic and often unseen work involved in their creation. In doing so I will move from a critique of markets as an ideology or 'handmaiden' of neoliberalism as outlined in Chapter 1, to markets as an object of study in their own right.

A central aim of this book is to explore the changing relationship of the state vis-à-vis the organization, regulation and delivery of childcare in neoliberal contexts. This chapter will provide further background for this aim, by outlining the fundamental critiques of marketized childcare and the role of the state within these conversations. In the process I will consider why many argue that childcare should be organized and provided as a public good. Common to much of this literature has been a desire to explicitly address the ongoing devaluation of childcare under neoliberal forms of governance, whereby care has become viewed as an individualistic, commodified and privatized experience purchased through the market (Pratt, 2003; Press and Woodrow, 2005; Gallagher, 2018b). Highlighting the damaging effects this approach has on the distribution of and access to childcare, there has been strong feminist advocacy directed towards the (re)socialization of care, through calling for a more central role for the state in its provisioning as a foundational aspect of society (Lloyd and Penn, 2010; Mitchell, 2019a).

With these aims in mind, the chapter proceeds as follows. I will first give a selected summary of the current critical literature on marketized childcare, an extensive body of work which draws on broader debates around the neoliberalization of care. A SSM approach will be outlined and put into conversation with the existing childcare markets literature, to highlight what this approach may offer our existing studies. The chapter finishes with a reflection on the research methodology which informs the book, and the challenges of taking SSM into the field.

Who cares? Critiques of marketized childcare and the role of the state

In the previous chapter I discussed the political rationale for the continued use of markets to meet childcare needs, as an example of a market of collective concern. However, as discussed thus far, it has been increasingly apparent that marketized childcare has become highly problematic for those who provide, govern and use these services. In this section I will engage directly with critical literature pertaining to the marketization of childcare, to outline in more detail the problems which have been identified with this means of provisioning. Considerable attention has been paid by academics across the fields of social politics, education, social geography and social policy in particular over the past 30 years, to the failures of the market to deliver equitable and high quality childcare (Brennan, 2007; May and Mitchell, 2009; Lloyd and Penn, 2013; Mitchell, 2013). Influenced by broader critiques of the neoliberalization of care from feminist political economy (Bezanson and Luxon, 2006; Bakker, 2007) and an ethics of care literature (Tronto, 1994), much of this work is also shaped by a strong feminist praxis which seeks to find better care solutions for carers, working families, and their children.

From the outset, a wealth of research to date strongly suggests that childcare markets in practice deviate in profound ways from the theory of supply and demand inherent in neoclassical economic renditions of market behaviour (Plantenga, 2012; Lloyd and Penn, 2013). Illustrating this discrepancy, considerable attention has been directed at the notion of the parent consumer, a figure central to neoliberal framings of childcare markets and the commodification of childcare more generally. As many have documented, the expectation of how parents source childcare in a market-based system sits in tension with the lived emotional and affective experience of obtaining suitable childcare (Roberts, 2011). Parents are rarely as well informed as they might need to be in order to make 'good' decisions in the market, due to time constraints or educational limitations for example (Plantenga, 2012; Kuger et al, 2019). This situation is made even more challenging by the competitive nature of childcare markets, whereby services are often reluctant to make their fees easily available for potential parents (and competitors) to see.

Indeed, the notion of the individualized parent consumer, making rational decisions based on their assessment of their own familial needs, bears little resemblance in practice to parenting as a relational and situated experience (McDowell et al, 2005; Meyers and Jordan, 2006). As has been shown, parental decision making around care does not take place within a social vacuum; it occurs within particular childcare cultures, where parents rely on existing social networks and friends as the basis for finding suitable care (Holloway, 1998). Carol Vincent and Stephen Balls' in-depth study of middle class mothers in the UK found that parents attempt where possible to personalize the transaction of care within the market, through sourcing recommendations via friendship networks for example (Vincent and Ball, 2001; Vincent et al, 2004; Vincent et al, 2008). In these instances, parental choice was driven as much by emotion as it was by more objective measures like distance and cost (Viitanen, 2005). Consequently, what qualifies as 'good' care is often reproduced within place-based (and class-based) networks,[1] and may not be of an ostensibly high quality at all.

The idea that parents as consumers can move between care services to find one which best fits their diverse needs is counter to how parents understand their role in the market. As any parent will attest, removing a child from a care environment they are accustomed to often results in a significant disruption to family life, and cannot be viewed as an active strategy for parents to use. In that sense, childcare has an emotional 'stickiness' (Bondi, 1997), such that parents are loathe to leave a service unless necessary. Moreover, as childcare as an educational resource occupies an increasingly central position in policy domains to achieve complex social outcomes, parental choice for many families becomes narrowed around which paid care setting to use through the structure of the funding schemes themselves (MacLeavy, 2007, 2011). The idea of caring for your young child at home becomes reframed through a primarily econometric lens, as only families who can afford to do so have the option. Under more punitive social policy contexts, where participation in work has become prioritized as a means of reducing welfare dependency, choice is something which is exercised by some, but constrained and contingent for many[2] (MacLeavy, 2011; Gallagher, 2013). The overwhelming conclusion reached within this critical literature is that the notion of parental 'choice', and the idealized version of the rational parent consumer within childcare markets, is ultimately a neoliberal fiction.

Making childcare into a commodity for sale in a market environment has exacerbated many of the existing inequalities which have structured childcare as 'women's work' under capitalism (Federici, 2012; Fraser, 2013). As a highly gendered form of labour, it has opened up new axes of inequality between women. A key site of concern for many feminists has been the growing inequities in terms of who now does the majority of the reproductive labour in childcare markets (Lawson, 2007; McDowell, 2008). Placing it into a cash–care nexus has resulted in the ability of some households to outsource much more of their childcare responsibilities than others, by virtue of the fact that they can afford to do so. This has implications for families who cannot afford the cost of outsourced care on one hand, but it also impacts who now provides much of this commodified care work in childcare markets. This resulting differentiation between women has an evident class dimension, as the childcare workforce in many less regulated contexts is sustained by women of lower socioeconomic status and women of colour (Pratt, 2003; Ehrenreich and Hochschild, 2004).

A more foundational critique of childcare markets within the broader social science literature has been focused on exploitative labour relations under capitalism. The devalued status of childcare work is understood to have become more extreme with the privatization of childcare as it becomes a service for sale. Indeed, many have shown how the increasing privatization of childcare in neoliberal contexts has occurred at the detriment of childcare labour conditions (Kamenarac, 2019; Neuwelt-Kearns and Richie, 2020). Generally speaking, despite the significant demand for childcare, the care workforce remains among the lowest paid and least unionized within most neoliberal policy contexts (Brown, 2009). The proliferation of the for–profit sector to meet the demand for childcare has been shown to result in the related suppression of workforce professionalization and remuneration in direct response to maintaining profit margins. Although it is conceivable that corporatization may lead to improved career progression for some due to higher managerial structures, most have found that the dominance of larger childcare chains and corporatized entities overall suppress workforce advancement (May and Mitchell, 2009; Weaven and Grace, 2010). At the heart of these narratives about privatization is that a profit-making incentive will take precedence over the quality of care for children in their charge. Providing childcare through a competitive consumer driven market is argued to undermine the relational nature of the work, which often leads to highly perverse outcomes. This has been most clearly articulated through recent analyses of large scale privatization in the UK and Australian childcare markets, with the conclusion that more often than not this situation produces what Viviana Zelizer would term 'dangerous mixes' (2013). In competitive childcare markets, where demand side funding incites the interest of the private sector, the concern is that many childcare providers are involved for the wrong reasons, that is to say to run a profitable business potentially at the detriment of the care given.

As a discursive counterpoint, studies of non-profit and community-based services from contexts like New Zealand and Australia signal a different set of business rationales and childcare practices than those outlined earlier. In these debates, non-profit childcare, which is often locally based and driven by the needs of their parent community, has offered a pertinent alternative against which to measure the development of the privatized sector. Unlike the for-profit sector, the structure of these services mean that they are legally unable to make a financial gain for their members, which many suggest is a crucial difference in their operation. Research suggests that overall, non-profit services tend to have better working conditions, as they are more likely to adhere to collective bargaining agreements for their workforce than for-profit services. More often identifying as ECE, rather than childcare services, they also tend to place higher emphasis on the qualification level of staff and have been shown to work to higher structural quality indicators, such as child/staff ratios (Cleveland and Krashinsky, 2009).

Within highly competitive childcare markets, key democratic principles of equity of access and quality of care for all children are undermined (Moss, 2014; Mitchell, 2019b). Research has demonstrated the tendency of for-profit providers to be concentrated in higher fee paying areas, producing childcare deserts for many (Prentice and White, 2019). To that extent the social and educational goals for children, as derived from the International Convention on the Rights of the Child, are unobtainable through a competitive ECE market (Davis, 2005). In this vein, Fielding and Moss (2012) argue for the promotion of ECE systems which view young children as citizens, who are therefore entitled to publicly provided care and education which ensures their wellbeing. This sits in contrast to a reliance on consumer-based forms of provision, which fuel the negative impacts of competition outlined earlier, and produces a system which is largely outside of public control.

In the face of these concerted problems, many argue that the central role of childcare services for working families and a site of educational intervention into the lives of young children would suggest the need for neoliberal governments to take a greater role in directly meeting childcare demand (Lloyd and Penn, 2013). While funding for childcare in neoliberal policy contexts has dramatically increased over the past 30 years (OECD, 2021), relying on a market to achieve the key social and economic ambitions associated with this spending has produced highly perverse effects. Suggestions for how the state could step in to remedy the problems of marketized childcare have been varied, including: greater regulatory oversight, especially of the for-profit sector; changes to the funding systems to directly pay services thus reducing the competitive nature of the market; or even to decommodify childcare entirely by making it a publicly provided service (Jenson and Sineau, 2001; Moss, 2014). Acknowledging the political apathy for the latter option on the grounds of increased cost to government, feminist economists have sought to couch the debate in favour of publicly provided childcare in economic terms. In *Valuing Children: Rethinking the Economics of the Family* (2008) Nancy Folbre speaks directly to a more economic understanding of care by clearly outlining the significant financial benefits of investing in children as future taxpayers and workers, pushing back against the neoliberal discourse of care labour as a burden to society. She offers a credible dollar amount for the time spent by parents with their children, and asks what we would need to spend as a society to get a viable substitute for this labour, in turn provoking us to reflect on the real hidden costs of care in order for it to be meaningfully recompensed. A similar argument is put forward by an academic collective at the University of Manchester, UK, in their development of the notion of a *foundational economy*, in which they suggest childcare should take its place as one of a range of what they term 'providential services' central to the reproduction of society, rather than be treated as an individualized endeavour bought and sold through a market (Foundational Economy Collective, 2018).

While the research summarized this far has given important insights into the fundamental problems of marketized childcare, in this book I want to contribute to this body of work in another way, by opening out lines of engagement with recent critical studies of marketization. More specifically, I want to move beyond critiques of the problems of marketized childcare to a consideration of how childcare markets themselves are created, sustained and remade in the face of their considerable shortcomings. In taking this approach the ambition for the research is to gain a better understanding of how childcare markets operate, accounting at the same time for more than the human agents involved in their creation. As Deville (2015) suggests, exploring the relationships which give rise to markets requires us to consider how much of what happens is shaped by their social *and* material infrastructures. Tracing the material and social aspects of childcare markets requires a much closer reading of the everyday, mundane work which goes into organizing and delivering commodified childcare and pushes us to look beyond the state–parent–provider research nexus. To develop these aims further into a methodological framework, in the next section I will outline the key tenets of a post-structuralist body of work, situated within economic sociology, cultural economics and economic geography, collectively known as the Social Studies of Marketization (SSM).

Social studies of markets

Stepping out of my car I was met with the sound of children running around the childcare centre playground, located at the back of the bright single-storey building. The sound was a mixture of laughter and tears, as childcare environments can be. Walking up to the front door I passed through two security gates, a reflection of the relative proximity of the centre to a busy main road. Trying to catch someone's attention, I waited for some time watching play in action and cuddles being given to a child for a fall. I reflected on how the immediacy of the interaction between carers and children sits in sharp relief to the detailed documentation and compliance work which goes on behind the scenes. The interactions in the room also belied how organized the scene actually was: the ratios of adults to children, the differentiated funding levels accorded to each child depending on their age, the level of qualified teachers, all of which directly shapes how childcare is being commodified. Finally, I am seen by a carer. She allows me to enter, but not before I add my details to the electronic record keeping system via the tablet on the wall by the entrance. I am shown through the hub bub to my interviewee, the owner-operator, deeply ensconced in her office beyond the playground.

Childcare centres are made up of a diverse amalgamation of people, practices, rules regulations and objects. Childcare centres appear lively and somewhat chaotic, but they are highly ordered and structured, mediating the interaction between carer and child in largely unseen ways. Moreover, childcare markets are not discrete closed entities, but rather intersect with a host of other markets and economic actors. To that end the construction of childcare markets increasingly involves a range of unanticipated actors and knowledges; like accountants, business training groups, childcare finance services, property brokers and software companies, some of whom I discuss in subsequent chapters but all of whom now play a role in the marketization of the sector. As my opening narrative suggests, childcare also involves a range of other material, non-human components, like the built care setting, computer technologies, and regulatory documents to name but a few. The empirical project informing this book aims to examine how ways of practising marketized childcare have been normalized over time in the New Zealand context, to lay bare the often tentative and precarious conditions which sustain market relations.

The performative turn in the social sciences, coupled with the ontological insights of Actor Network Theory (ANT) has generated a new research field in the study of markets, encapsulated in the SSM approach (Callon, 2007b; Çalişkan and Callon, 2009; Berndt and Boeckler, 2012). Bringing together the work of geographers, anthropologists, and sociologists, there is now a well-established interdisciplinary literature which offers an empirically detailed understanding of how markets are made (Mackenzie et al, 2007; Berndt and Boeckler, 2009). Born from a 'pragmatic turn' in the social sciences (Muniesa et al, 2007), this approach has sought to produce an anti-essentialist account of markets and the actors involved in their creation, one which privileges neither the actor nor the system (Deville, 2015). Taking a highly social understanding of markets (Polanyi, 1944; Zelizer, 2013), nothing is assumed as having an a priori existence outside networked, market relations. To outline fully the contributions of a SSM approach to the study of markets is beyond the scope of this book (see Ouma, 2015); however, in the remainder of this section I will summarize five key provocations of the approach which are important for the analysis to come. Within this discussion, I have italicized the key concepts which I will draw on in subsequent chapters.

1. Markets are not naturally occurring, they are 'practical accomplishments'

One of the criticisms raised about more prevalent political economy analyses of neoliberalism and the reliance on markets has been that markets themselves are ceded an unquestioned existence (Christophers, 2014; Cohen, 2017). Research tends to focus on the implications of marketization under capitalism, but the markets themselves remain largely black boxed in the analysis as a means of reproducing unequal social and economic relations. We can trace the impact of this perspective in how childcare markets have been studied, with a strong feminist political economy focus on the unequal labour relations which have been sustained through the marketization of care for example (Pratt, 2003; Ehrenreich and Hochschild, 2004; McDowell, 2008). In comparison, the SSM approach makes an analytical shift away from 'the market' and a related critique of the impacts of marketization, to studying markets themselves as particular arrangements of practices and material elements always in formation (Berndt and Boeckler, 2009). As such, studies in this vein seek to avoid reducing markets to a singular object ('the market'), acknowledging that there are multiple ways of structuring and ordering markets (depending on whether it is a care market or a market for financial derivatives, for example). The emphasis then is to focus analytical attention on market making as a 'practical accomplishment' rather than a pre-given outcome (Berndt and Boeckler, 2009).

2. Market failures are the norm, not the exception

Market creation is essentially a process of boundary making, of selectively closing off some things over others (Ouma, 2015). The stabilization of a particular form of the market involves a highly selective process of linking up specific economic agents into a relatively bounded and ordered network, a process Michel Callon calls *framing*.[3] As he suggests, 'to frame means to select, to sever links and finally to make trajectories (at least temporarily) irreversible' (Callon, 2007a), giving rise to stability in the market. For a market to become stable these links need to be constantly re-performed into being, highlighting the deeply social and relational nature of market encounters. Denaturalising the idea of markets as rational or pre-social entities makes visible the fragility of market making as a process. In reality, attempts to stabilize or frame the market are regularly tested (Callon, 1998). The economic actors enrolled are connected to different networks and lifeworlds, through which other economic and non-economic logics emerge to destabilize market relations. The result of such destabilization leads to an unintended *overflow* in the market. Indeed, rather than view market framing as the norm, and processes of overflow an example of 'market failure' in neoclassical terms, proponents of SSM trace how overflows are instead the norm and that the successful framing of markets is actually a highly unlikely outcome.

3. Markets are a socio-technical assemblage of human and non-human elements

Drawing on insights from Science and Technology Studies (STS) and ANT, markets are viewed as diverse heterogenous assemblages: that is to say arrangements of things, people, discourses, rationales and socio-technical devices which are organized in such a way as to create the conditions for the commodification and exchange of an object, good or service to occur. Stepping away from the analytical dichotomy of humans doing the organizing versus the things which are being organized, agency to shape the market is understood as occurring within a 'human non-human working group' (Bennett, 2010). Market actors are made up of human bodies, but importantly their agency is aided by a range of 'prostheses': such as tools, equipment, technical devices, or formulae for example. These non-human elements allow actors to successfully engage in the market, by allowing them to make calculated market decisions. As Ouma (2015: 86) astutely describes,

> the practically grounded knowledge involved in building a market must neither be understood as a mental substance inscribed in individuals, nor can it be imagined as a self-standing body of knowledge (an object) or an all-embracing discourse; it is instead a process inscribed in collective practices and material devices (for example management handbooks, contracts etc).

This opens the analysis to include what may be perceived as a range of benign, material aspects of market making.

To function, markets require the actors involved to have *calculative agency*. Calculation in this case should not be read as an innate cognitive disposition, like that captured in the idea of homo economicus (Kirchgässner, 2008). Rather it is a socially externalized process, referring instead to the acquired ability of actors to make decisions on how to proceed in the market. In practice, for an actor to have calculative agency, they need to be able to consider the range of options available to them, to rank these options, and be able to proceed to achieve their desired outcome through the market. The extent to which an actor can acquire calculative agency is shaped by their location in the broader market assemblage. Moreover, the capacity to act in calculable ways is made possible by the various tools, rules and routines that aid in the task of differentiation between goods and services. Calculative agency, then, is *distributed* among humans and non-humans in the market, 'the outcome of the organizing work conducted by the actors and devices involved' (Frankel et al, 2019).

While this understanding of market relations opens the analysis to account for a potentially endless amount of 'things' which could shape the ability to exercise calculative agency, not all things carry the same weighting in terms of their market effect. Which non-human elements of the market assemblage are crucial is itself an empirical question to answer within the particular market under study. However, it is clear that some have more agency to invoke change, shape or lock-in practices than others. These are ultimately called *market devices* (McKenzie et al, 2007). Applying this analytical focus to the context of childcare, we can examine which objects become market devices and how those shape who has calculable agency in the market and how they can use it. A well recounted example of a market device within studies of consumer markets is that of the shopping cart and its impact on everyday consumption practices. As Frank Cochoy (2009) describes, the shopping cart became more than a material object in the practice of shopping: its introduction profoundly shaped *how* we shop. Studying the work of market devices draws attention to their ability to shape the decision-making capacities of individuals.[4] Market devices are crucial to processes of marketization, through setting the rules of markets in terms of the kinds of products and/or services deemed as having value (as nothing has value a priori in the market) and through setting the basis for their commodification and exchange (Müller, 2015).

If the market is an assemblage of diverse elements and actors, each playing a role in the creation of the market, how then can we understand power or the ability to shape the assemblage within this flattened ontological framework? Drawing broadly on post-structuralist understanding of power (Foucault, 2001), capacity to change or to shape market relations stems from a distributed agency, which ultimately exceeds the capacity of any one actor (even the 'state'). It is relationally constituted, the outcome of an actor's location in relation to other material elements, devices, discourses and even embodied skills, which come to situate them favourably within the market. To that extent, there is no naturalized sense of agency as something innate to the individual, but rather the ability to invoke change is either enabled or limited within the conditions of the assemblage. Making this analytical step removes the desire to implicitly attribute moral or normative judgements to actions as merely the result of self-interest or selfishness on the part of the individual actor (that all for-profit providers seek to extract profit at the detriment of children's care for example), but rather to see how their actions and behaviours are produced as a result of the conditions of the market assemblage.

For proponents of SSM the commodification of goods and services only occurs through the market assemblage, meaning that nothing has any a priori value before entering the market. The qualities of a good or service are not stable: they need to be worked on to render them into something which can be easily exchanged. In that sense they too need to be framed. Central to the process of framing a commodity is its *pacification*. This refers to 'how things and services are represented as describable and predictable "packages" within fixed qualities to which value and price can be attached' (Williamson, 2020: 5). There are two key aspects to this process irrespective of whether it is a good or a service; the devices and forms of knowledge used to assess the good (such as forms of accounting, valuation, and metrology) and how the resulting evaluations are used to distinguish one good or service over another similar one in the market. As Callon suggests, all qualities of goods 'are obtained at the end of a process of qualification, and all qualification aims to establish a constellation of characteristics, stabilized at least for a while, which are attached to the product and transform it temporarily into a tradable good in the market' (2002: 199). When we consider the diverse forms of childcare which exist, across both the formal and informal economies, it is worth considering what *kind* of childcare is framed within the market and the means by which this occurs. The emphasis on formalized, regulated and licensed childcare within the childcare markets in question speaks to attempts to pacify and ultimately singularize childcare as a service. That is to say to ensure parents as consumers are attached to a particular form of care over others. Of course, this is exceptionally hard to achieve. The burgeoning conversation around the need for childcare outside the traditional working hours, in the face of a 24/7 service economy, is one terrain in which we can see the divergence between the expectations of parent consumers and what is currently pacified under state-led marketization (Rutter and Evans, 2012).

4. Markets need to mobilize adherents

Recognizing the extent of the heterogenous elements involved in the construction of a market indicates the challenge in wrangling these elements together and holding them in a relatively stable relationship over time. How then are diverse actors drawn into market assemblages as actor networks? According to Latour (2005), this process involves multiple distinct steps, some of which I will deploy in later chapters to explore the creation of the New Zealand childcare market. Initially it involves *problematization*, or the identification and treatment of something as a problem at a specific point in time, in a way that generates a heightened level of involvement between a range of actors. Secondly, it entails *enrolment*, where actors are engaged into roles which have been defined for them in the process of solving the identified problem. To achieve this step, the interests of these different actors need to be aligned with those of the actor network (in this case the market), such that they can become invested in solving the problem at hand. In doing so they will have 'skin in the game', which becomes the basis of their dependency on the success of the network. However, this is not a one-way process. Enrolment involves a change not only in the subjectivity of the actor being enrolled, but also in the network itself to accommodate the interests of this new entrant. In the context of childcare markets, where there is a burgeoning presence of for-profit actors, this process of enrolment offers much to our understanding of their growing agency in the market assemblage. Over the coming chapters I will consider the process of enrolment to show how the for-profit sector has never been completely enrolled into the market in the way aspired to under state-led marketization, leading to continued divergence today between their practice in the market and what government aspired to achieve. Bringing these insights across to studies of markets of collective concern, where a particular problem is being solved through the actor network of the market, it is evident how challenging the process of enrolling market adherents to achieve social goals can be.

5. Markets are highly contested spaces

A primary concern raised in relation to the 'flat' ontological approach of SSM is that the question of power is lost (Miller, 2002; Fine, 2003; Christophers, 2014). As with criticisms of ANT more generally, concerns have been raised about the move away from systematic analyses of markets inequities under capitalism, in favour of fine grained descriptive market ethnographies which some argue lack a broader explanatory capacity (Christophers, 2014). Questions of agency and material resource distribution are certainly important, as markets are very seldom egalitarian in their outcomes. As markets extend into ever expanding parts of our lives, they have become the terrain through which hegemonic societal struggles increasingly take place (Cohen, 2017). Marketization is essentially a process of establishing and severing linkages, it is about incorporating and expelling places, people and things (Berndt and Boeckler, 2009: 566). More recent work in SSM has built on this provocation to engage with questions of power and contestation, by offering a historicized rendition of market making, highlighting that the attributes and actor networks of markets are not neutral, but historically grounded in existing struggles (Ouma, 2015). All actors are not situated in favourable positions within the market, and not everyone has the same capacity to set the 'rules of the game'. Yet, as proponents of SSM have argued, power to act in the market cannot be achieved without the help of a host of other objects, again emphasizing the tenuous claim to such agency and the need to continuously stabilize the market in order to maintain this claim. A close reading of work in SSM shows scope for a critical account of how inequality is (re)produced through markets, with the strength of its contribution in its detailed examination of power relations as expressed in and through markets making processes, taking account of the discourses and material devices involved in maintaining them (Berndt and Boeckler, 2011). However, within childcare markets, which are already overdetermined by capitalist relations that undermine the social and economic value of childcare labour, what can SSM offer existing critiques of commodified care? In the next section I will consider what this approach can bring to the study of neoliberal childcare markets.

Childcare markets from an SSM perspective

There are a number of ways which I suggest an SSM approach can advance our understanding and study of neoliberal childcare markets. Firstly, it offers a means of delving into the complex interrelationship between the state and the market which has allowed for the marketization of childcare to continue to occur. Existing studies of childcare markets underestimate the depth of material and discursive involvement of the state in creating the conditions for the market. As indicated in Chapter 1, childcare markets are relied upon to solve a range of collective social problems, and the work of the state has become one of repair and maintenance of markets, rather than an openness to envisioning new systems of organization. Deploying an assemblage approach engenders a more situated engagement with the particular logics, rationales, discourses, technologies and practices of the state in facilitating marketization. This shifts our attention away from a state imaginary of an absent or reluctant state in childcare, and instead looks to the ways in which the state is *actively complicit* in its marketization. As I will detail in Chapter 3, the state has been deeply involved in the creation of a childcare market in New Zealand since the 1980s, at the height of neoliberal policy orthodoxy. Thus, the seeming inefficacy of calls to make childcare a publicly funded service, or for the state to take a greater role in the delivery of childcare, should be read in light of the reliance of the state on the market under neoliberalism. In this context, an SSM approach offers a means to more closely examine state-led marketization at work.

The ability to purchase care through the market has become a taken for granted response to the burgeoning crisis of care across most OECD countries (Hoppania and Vaittinen, 2015). As care becomes rendered into a commodity it is increasingly made measurable and quantifiable for exchange in the market. In the context of state-led marketization, where childcare is being deployed to meet particular social goals, I suggest that the work of pacification becomes central to achieving those aims. Indeed, criticisms of an emphasis on 'quality' in early education over the past 20 years as a story of 'control and calculation, technology and measurement' (Moss, 2014: 3) captures these pacification tendencies. Using the language of SSM we can see how state-led marketization *requires* diverse childcare practices to be pacified for them to be successfully exchanged in the market. Yet the nature of childcare, which is shaped by non-economic logics like trust and reciprocity, and which already exists within other diverse economies across the informal and unpaid care sectors, continually undermines its ability to be sufficiently pacified. Focusing on attempts to pacify childcare in the market offers insights into the incomplete nature of care commodification (Radin, 1996), noting as Nancy Fraser suggests that nothing can be commodified 'all the way down' (Fraser, 2014).

While existing work has demonstrated how childcare markets deviate in reality from an idealized neoliberal market imaginary, an SSM lens offers a different way into studying this tension through the lens of calculative agency. Attempts to create childcare markets have inherent within them a 'blueprint' as to how the market should work. Central to realizing these theoretical versions of the market are attempts to bring to the fore particular kinds of calculating subjects, like the parent consumer or the competitive for-profit provider, who between them are understood to find the best price and level of quality in the market. However, as discussed earlier, calculative agency is not something innate to the individual, but a disposition to exchange which is shaped by where the actor is located in the market assemblage, and enabled by engagement with a broad suite of market devices. While markets require actors to have calculative agency, in reality it is often not achieved equally, such that some have more agency than others. Mindful of the findings of existing work which has pointed out these inequities in the market (that parent consumers do not have sufficient information to make informed decisions in the market for example) I will delve into two things in the following chapters. Firstly, how calculative agency is engendered as a crucial part of state-led marketization of childcare, and secondly how calculative agency is exercised to a greater extent by some actors over others in the resulting market assemblage. I will suggest this work can offer new insights into the inequitable dynamics of neoliberal childcare markets.

Understanding why childcare markets persist as a means of achieving an increasing range of important social and economic goals, even in the face of considerable criticism, also requires us to be more attentive to the host of diverse *things* which are involved in framing the market. More specifically I suggest it involves a more serious consideration of how techniques, formulae, devices, and other seeming ephemera of the market are implicated in organizing and practising childcare. The opening narrative to this chapter gives some insight into the extent of the socio-technical elements now involved in the daily work of childcare, from tablet computers to charter manuals, specialist play equipment to attendance sheets. Understanding how these elements shape action in the market, overflow it or become market devices in their own right is an important part of engaging with the ongoing development of these markets.

Finally, at a more political level a market assemblage approach seeks to highlight the fragility of market framing. Creating a market is not an inevitability but a hard-won practical accomplishment, one which is continually prone to failure. Childcare markets are located at a complex intersection of a host of economic and non-economic logics and values, and as such they are sites which require considerable market making work. Viewing childcare markets as fragile arrangements of human and non-human elements, we can begin to account for the myriad ways in which these markets become increasingly difficult to manage once they leave the policy 'laboratory' under state-led marketization. As I will show, through an assemblage lens we can trace how the incentives of state-led marketization has precipitated the engagement of a host of actors located in other markets, such that childcare is subject to the rationales and logics of these new actors in fundamental ways. While tendencies towards market overflow are always there, I suggest that the increased financial incentives offered by state-led marketization to other economic actors has proliferated this occurrence, such that neoliberal childcare markets have become increasingly unstable and prone to failure.

Methodology: studying childcare markets anew?

Building from the conceptual framework outlined earlier, the key research questions which guide this project are the following:

- What do neoliberal childcare markets actually look like, taking account of their diverse human and non-human elements?
- How have they gained political prevalence and relative stability over time as markets of collective concern?
- What kinds of diverse actors are now involved in framing childcare markets and what is their impact on how childcare is organized and delivered?

The methodological approach which was envisioned for this research was an 'ethnography of marketization' (Ouma, 2015). While many who work through an SSM lens use a more traditional ethnographic approach to study market making processes on the ground (Mackenzie et al, 2007), as Ouma suggests the use of the term ethnography here is intended not as a commitment to a particular method (observation), but rather reflects a research disposition. This disposition takes seriously the everyday, banal work of marketization: such as points of problematization, attempts to pacify and commodify goods and services, the enrolment of actors, and the overall stabilization of the market assemblage. This approach is also attentive to the potential for market failure, or processes of overflow and destabilization, as a key aspect of the politics of the research itself. In practice, it encourages the researcher to script the research process in such a way that field sites, and ways of engaging with them and potential participants, emerge reflexively as new market locations become apparent. Resisting a desire to overly pre-assign values or roles in advance of the research, this process encourages the researcher to enter the field with a willingness to try to 'follow the market' (Latour, 2005) within and between markets making sites.

As a result, the methods outlined in what follows and in the subsequent chapters read as somewhat of a bricolage (similarly see Ball, 2012). Identifying the kinds of actors who are influencing the childcare market, and to allow space to pursue them and their work, meant that the methods had to be adapted in relation to the research participants and the conditions of the market. In that sense the methodology was relational, one which was shaped to a large extent by the research actors. However, such a relational methodology is also one which is necessarily shaped by what was *possible* to conduct, based not only on the participants but also by the researchers other work–life commitments. Over the course of the five years it has taken to conduct this research, my own life circumstances have changed. While at times a more sustained engagement with market making sites would have been advantageous, having two children during the course of the five-year project profoundly shaped what it was possible to achieve. It also shaped my own positionality in terms of the research and views on the sector, inevitably oscillating between researcher and parent consumer of childcare as I began life as a working mother.

As a consequence the ethnographic ambition of the project to follow the market became tempered, and finding extended periods of time that I could spend in the field was limited by family commitments. In the process the research came to rely more on methods like semi-structured interviews, archival work and documentary analysis. Much of the information drawn on in the chapters that follow were derived from semi-structured interviews with 44 participants between 2016 and 2019, who I identified as significant market making actors within the New Zealand market assemblage (see

Table 2.1). Over the course of the project, I interviewed some of these participants several times. They included expected protagonists in childcare markets, like representatives for ECE in the Ministry of Education (MoE), a previous Minister of Education, representatives for the main advocacy groups in the sector, union executives, and owner-operators of for-profit childcare centres. However, over time the list of interviewees changed from the expected to the surprising, reflective of my attempt to trace market relations beyond the state–parent–provider nexus. These interviews were conducted with childcare property sales, building and evaluation specialists, software developers and finance companies. Where possible, I have tried to maintain anonymity for participants and names used in the following chapters are synonyms. The research process took me to a diverse range of field sites. In many instances I was invited 'back-stage' to research settings. For example, two childcare management software companies allowed me to stay for the afternoon to watch how they engaged with their childcare provider 'clients'. It was through these more sustained encounters that I got a better sense of the day-to-day work they did in the sector.

Political concern about the value of childcare spending under a social investment policy focus has proliferated the desire for data about the childcare sector, an issue I will consider more in Chapter 6. The generation of new forms of 'evidence' to demonstrate the benefit of government investment into the sector offered a very fruitful source of quantitative knowledge for this project. The most notable of these datasets was the MoE Education Counts data, which is publicly available online and contains a detailed repository of information about the sector from 2006 to present day. The repository contains extensive information about childcare services (type, number, and change over time), funding information, childcare workforce and children's participation. This data was invaluable in allowing me to build up a picture of change within the sector, tracking in particular the move in the market

Table 2.1: Research interviews

Participants	Number of interviewees
Property brokers, sales and evaluation specialists	8
Childcare software company owners and staff	8
Ministry of Education officials	3
Childcare centre owners	8
ECE representative organizations	10
Childcare finance companies	2
Union executives	2
ECE academics and advocates	3

from a majority of non-profit to mostly for-profit providers after 2008. However, I also recognize that the production of this data was not politically neutral. Over time the need among providers to meet new MoE reporting data expectations came to have important performative agency in reframing the market, an issue I will return to in Chapter 6.

Chapter 3 offers an analysis of the creation of a childcare market in New Zealand from the late 1980s. While some interviewees who were advocates and union representatives for childcare and ECE could speak to their experiences from this time, most of the research informing this chapter was derived from archival sources. Data drew primarily on thematic documentary analysis of Parliamentary Hansard from 1986 to 2014 which considered the political debate and discursive framing of childcare and ECE at key points in the construction of the market. The chapter was supplemented with analysis of a repository of resources about the childcare and ECE sector housed in the Turnbull Library, Wellington. This library repository held a host of documents relating to the policy, media and broader sector-wide debates which were occurring around the introduction of the major governmental interventions into the sector.[5] To a significant extent, the background work for the book benefitted from the endeavours of a number of childcare sector advocates and academics housed in the discipline of education and social policy, who have meticulously documented the ebb and flow of the sector over the past 30 years. As a non-native to the shores of Aotearoa New Zealand, and to the discipline of education, these accounts offered an invaluably rich reflection of the time.

Chapter 4 considers the different business strategies of for-profit providers, as particular kinds of calculative agencies in the market since 2008. In many ways the material for this chapter posed the largest challenge to work with, as it involved delving into the financials of major childcare corporates through their shareholder prospectus, and other publicly available financial information. I was guided in this work by colleagues in New Zealand education union, NZEI Te Rui Roa and a university colleague in financial accounting. Towards the end of the research process in 2019, as it was becoming increasingly evident that the childcare sector was in crisis on a number of fronts, I worked with the union to create, administer and analyse an online 'ECE Financial Wellbeing Survey'. This survey was sent to a discrete mailing list of 2500 licensees of childcare centres in New Zealand, compiled from the MoE Education Counts dataset. Combined with semi-structured interviews with eight for-profit childcare centre owner-managers and three specialized childcare finance companies, this survey gave crucial insights into the extent of the financial pressure on the sector at that point in time.

Chapters 5 and 6 seek to examine two significant, yet largely unseen actors in the childcare market: childcare property specialists and childcare management software companies. As these actors tend to be viewed as peripheral to the core business of childcare, data on their involvement was not straightforward to glean and took a range of forms. Much of the data for Chapter 5 on childcare property investment was compiled from online property news media and advertising ephemera. Document analysis of 47 online sale articles, property advertisements and related news articles gave a rich insight into the changing discourse around childcare property as a lucrative investment. This material also served as the basis from which to compile a list of potential interviewees who were deemed to be key protagonists in the childcare sales and investment space. Although not an exhaustive list, this approach led to nine semi-structured interviews[6] involving two property brokers, a director of a specialist childcare building company, a childcare sector planner, four property sales specialists, and a key MoE official during 2018 and early 2019.

Chapter 6 considers the emergence of childcare management software as a market device and the work of software companies as infrastructural to the childcare market itself. Research informing this chapter stemmed from interviews with four childcare management software company owners and four of their design staff, coupled with two four-hour observation sessions at two of these companies' offices. The generation of childcare data and the use of these new software packages were also focuses of the questions in interviews with aforementioned MoE officials and for-profit providers at different scales of operation, which contributed to the analysis for this chapter.

With any research methodology, there are inevitably limitations. Attempting to cast the research net wide enough to grasp the changing nature of the childcare market and the kinds of actors taking an interest in this sector meant that there are gaps and absences in the research. The voices of parents, children and childcare workers are notably absent. In aiming to trace market relations I also found myself needing to upskill in order to understand and analyse the information I was engaging with. This was especially the case in relation to the building and property interviews and in finding and interpreting the financial information of childcare companies and corporates. To that extent, I relied heavily on the expertise of colleagues in these research domains.

Childcare and ECE in Aotearoa New Zealand is a highly politicized field. In an attempt to embrace the research approach of an 'ethnography of markets', which aims to enter research field with a more agnostic understanding of market actors and their work, I found myself at odds with the research tenor of the moment. For many who are strongly in favour of the state stepping in to slow down or even reverse the growth of the for-profit sector, and in doing so promote the work of non-profit childcare services, claiming research agnosticism created confusion and sometimes suspicion as to my motivation. Indeed, questions about my motivation for the work also came from research participants themselves. Asking questions about their work in a highly competitive childcare market brought concerns about commercial sensitivity to the fore, with many needing heightened assurances that information given would not be passed between 'competitors'.

Conclusion

This chapter has sought to outline both the theoretical basis for the research informing the book, and the conceptual terrain which I have developed to explore childcare markets. Childcare markets have been shown to be problematic, from the perspective of carers, parents and increasingly the children in their care. Yet, despite these problems, neoliberal policy communities continue to rely on them as a means of meeting complex social and economic needs. Questioning this assumed dependency, this chapter has sought to open up a research agenda for studying childcare markets as constructed arrangements of human and non-human elements, which are inherently prone to failure. In the next chapter I will mobilize this approach to examine the creation of the childcare market in Aotearoa New Zealand, highlighting the contested work of state-led marketization in action.

3

State-Led Marketization: The Creation of the New Zealand Childcare Market

This chapter traces the creation of a childcare market in New Zealand between 1989 and 2019. As a highly active political front for neoliberal politics, childcare has been shaped by quite differing understandings of what it is and how it should be organized over this period. However, despite different political parties in power, the fact that childcare is provided through a market-based system has remained constant, indicating the resilience and malleability of the market ideal. The research period in question details two key moments in the formation of the market; the Before Five reforms in 1989 and the Strategic Plan in 2002. The initial phase of marketization in 1989 led to the first major funding intervention into the sector: bulk funding. The second intervention 12 years later sought to remedy the issues of the first market framing and reflected a more active involvement by government in keeping with a social investment approach. In detailing the work of market making in this chapter, I will focus on the important differences between both phases of market creation. In doing so I will emphasize how the figure of the parent consumer has been understood within state-led marketization, as one of the key calculating actors charged with both regulating and governing the market. While I recount the emergence of the childcare market in New Zealand, in telling this story I also want to consider the highly experimental work of state-led marketization, as childcare policy making becomes an exercise in market organization (Frankel et al, 2019).

Bringing forward the analytical framework of SSM, there are two key arguments about state-led marketization which I will ground empirically in this chapter. Firstly, as discussed in Chapter 2, state-led marketization involves the creation of calculative agencies, capable of making differentiated and informed decisions about childcare in the emerging market. Picking up on the discussion of the parent consumer introduced in Chapter 2, I will show

how this figure is not static in approaches to the market but is reframed in line with the two key periods of market creation in New Zealand. This analysis offers a different set of insights to the existing literature, which is typified by a discussion of how the rational parent consumer ideal deviates in reality from how parents meet their childcare needs. Instead, I argue that there are different understandings of the parent consumer being mobilized within and across childcare markets, as a result of how the market is being framed.

The second analytical contribution of this chapter pertains to how childcare is being commodified. A central problem for state-led marketization has been the establishment of common standards and quality of practice within childcare markets, a process I refer to as *pacification*. As critics of commodification have long argued, care remains uncommodifiable to some degree (Fraser, 2014), as it shaped by non-economic logics like emotion and sentiment. The challenges of pacifying childcare, or making it measurable and standardized for market exchange, produces market overflows which force a reframing of market logics, rationales and relations. It is at these contested junctures that we can see the politics of market framing, where the possibilities of other ways of doing and organizing childcare can be made visible.

This chapter takes a more historicized approach to analysis of the childcare market, facilitated by the fact that childcare and early education in New Zealand is already well recounted in existing literature (May, 2009; Mitchell, 2013, 2015). Over the past three decades, research on these sectors has burgeoned in line with its professionalization. While acknowledging that all accounts are selective and written from somewhere, my own included, the dominant narrative of the childcare sector is one of a feminist battle against the patriarchal tenets of the state, whereby the care of children remained a largely domestic responsibility under the influence of a strong social conservatism. Feminist activism from the late 1970s gained traction through the changing face of the trade union sector but also via the rise of 'femocrats' (Brennan, 1994) within the ranks of the Labour Party, which brought women and children's issues to the forefront of politics. While I will draw on these historical accounts, in this chapter I will narrate this story differently, re-reading the involvement of some key childcare advocates and femocrats as central to market framing. Ultimately, the intention of this alternative interpretation is to highlight how feminist critiques of the childcare market became folded back into moments of market (re)framing, recognizing the importance of their written and activist work not solely as a critical voice, but also as producing knowledge which in itself plays a performative part in the market making process.

This chapter is orientated around three primary empirical questions:

- Why did childcare become a site of governmental intervention at the peak of the neoliberal policy paradigm in Aotearoa New Zealand?

- What practical problems arose for government in meeting childcare needs?
- Relatedly, how was marketization used as the means to solve these problems?

Childcare as a neoliberal policy solution in New Zealand

While I begin my narrative around the formation of the childcare market in the late 1980s, it would be disingenuous to say that childcare was not available before this time. However, provisioning was piecemeal, with a wide variety of forms across both the community non-profit and for-profit sectors. New Zealand had a strong kindergarten movement[1] from the turn of the 19th century, along with other parent run and non-profit services (May, 2009). A common story across many OECD countries, full day childcare services (as opposed to more educationally endorsed preschool services like kindergarten) gained popularity from the late 1960s onwards, when women's labour participation began to increase. Evidencing this trend, although the numbers were still quite small, the percentage of children in full day childcare increased by 164 per cent between 1963 and 1972, compared to a 33 per cent increase for those in existing sessional preschool services like kindergartens, suggesting the need for care during working hours (Pollock, 2021). By the late 1970s, it was clear that there was impetus for greater access to childcare in line with the move away from the male breadwinner model, which had been largely protected under the extensive welfare system in New Zealand (Kingfisher, 2013).

The 1980s in New Zealand are renowned for a sweeping ideological shift to the economic right which deeply impacted all areas of policy making (Larner, 1996). As outlined more generally in Chapter 1, the neoliberal retracing of the boundaries of what constituted public and private sectors occurred under a social democratic Labour Party, spurred on by an economic recession and a critique of what had been a strongly centralized welfare state (Kingfisher, 2013). This era, labelled by some as the 'New Zealand neoliberal experiment' (Kelsey, 1997), was defined by widespread economic deregulation, and the privatization of domains which had traditionally been the preserve of the state. Markets were introduced where none previously existed, such as the domains of healthcare and education (Gordon and Whitty, 1997; Prince et al, 2006). The impacts of economic reforms were swift and brutal, felt especially hard for those who were already in a position of social and economic vulnerability. The legacy of colonial relations in Aotearoa New Zealand meant that indigenous Māori populations were overrepresented among the socially and economically vulnerable, producing stark intergenerational inequalities for many (Ongley, 2013).

Yet it was under this particular political optic of cost saving and financial retrenchment that childcare as early education gained governmental attention and funding. In 1984 the incoming Labour government signalled a profound change in how early childhood services were to be viewed and supported by the state. As part of an entire review of the education system in 1986, driven by neoliberal incentives to put markets to work in achieving new social and educational goals (Gordon, 1992), New Zealand was among the first countries in the world to reconceptualize the place of early childhood services within the broader education system. While this may seem like a benign shuffling of deckchairs to derive some greater public sector efficiency within education, the redrawing of governance structures marked the first step in the process of boundary making for the emergent childcare market. It also made the childcare sector subject to the same neoliberal logics of reform as the rest of the education system (Manning, 2016).

Against all odds, and counter to advice from the Treasury – which held a strong new right economic position, Prime Minister David Lange committed for the first time in 1988 to invest in childcare as a crucial service for children and working families. The commitment to spend on childcare as early education, at the pinnacle of neoliberal thinking and a broader incentive to reduce government expenditure, should be read as a reformulation of biopolitical and economic agendas in the context of early childhood (Prentice, 2009). Leading up to this announcement, there were important alignments of discourse and knowledge which brought early childhood into the political domain. The much-heralded visit of Dr David Weikart in 1987, chief investigator of the influential Highscope/Perry Preschool Longitudinal Study which profoundly shaped political perceptions internationally of the economic and social value of early education (Schweinhart et al, 2005), gave significant validation to proposed governmental spending. The evidence presented by Weikert on his trip of the long-term benefits of spending on early education, dovetailed at a domestic level with the publication of an influential review of the prison system, commonly known as the Roper Report.[2] As this report argued, the foundations of a life of crime were set in early childhood, and consequently interventions should be prioritized in early life. Links drawn in parliamentary debate between the Roper Report and the need for increased childcare spending were unequivocal. The deputy prime minister at the time captured this sentiment stating that

> The Budget will ensure that children get a head start in life. ... We were told by the Roper Report some time ago that if we wanted to deal with violent crime successfully it was necessary to tackle the problem of the way in which children are brought up and early childhood education is organized. (Palmer, 1989: 11737)

Funding childcare as ECE was seen as a means of supporting 'at risk' children and their families. The long-term welfare savings to be generated from this kind of spending were anticipated to be manifold.

While the importance of early education for achievements in later life became a cross-party mantra by the late 1980s, the means of achieving a robust childcare system was subject to the particular neoliberal optic of the time. Key members of the Treasury were unconvinced as to the benefit of increased spending, preferring to view the care of children as a private family responsibility, stating that 'education shares the main characteristics of other commodities traded in the market place ... State intervention is liable to quash or discourage the development of new or exceptional forms of education provision' (May, 2009: 209). Believing in the free hand of the market, they could only see the benefit of targeted funding for at risk children. The prime minister, personally committed to resisting targeted funding, pushed through a more universalist funding system against the odds and under considerable time pressure, as his tenure as prime minister was coming to an end.

Education historian Professor Helen May suggests a number of other important factors contributed to this era of governmental interest in childcare. Most notable was that it reflected the growing voice of women in the trade union movement, and within the ranks of the labour government and its ministerial offices. The rise of femocrats (Brennan, 1994) like Sonja Davies within the Labour Party, coupled with the elevation of women into prominent positions in the prime minister's office, were instrumental to furthering childcare as a bigger political issue. It is also noteworthy that women's rights to childcare were gaining political attention at the same time that neoliberal economic reforms were undermining some of the key sectors of employment for women (like education), and stratifying the female workforce along the lines of ethnicity and class (Larner, 1996).

In keeping with the neoliberal optic of marketization, Manning (2016) suggests that the relationship between government and the childcare sector that was envisioned at the time was ultimately viewed as contracting out service provisioning. Childcare services were understood not as state owned or organized resources, but rather as autonomous units enmeshed in new governance relationships with the MoE. This analysis would hold in the light of statements from the prime minister in parliamentary debates, noting that

> There is absolutely no prospect of the government's desiring or being able to afford to buy private premises. ... The Government does not want to become the owner of a squad of private child-care centres. What those people do well they ought to do, in contract with the Government and subject to the safeguards that are essential for children. (Lange, 1988: 8229)

The government effectively became a co-purchaser of childcare, alongside parents, but did so at a considerable distance from the market. However, as I illustrate in the next sections, to say that the state took a 'hands-off' approach to the childcare market merely reinforces the neoliberal fiction of state-market relations. While the aspiration from government was to remain as distant as possible, framing the market inevitably involved considerable work to pacify childcare and enrol actors in order for it to, hopefully, succeed. As a market of collective concern, meeting the care and education needs of some of the most vulnerable in society, its success became a considerable political issue over the coming decades. The discursive groundwork for the creation of the market assemblage was set during the late 1980s, and both the state and market, as relationally constituted entities, were intertwined in the process. Once political commitment to funding the childcare sector was secured, the complex work of state-led marketization began to gather momentum.

Framing the childcare market: the Before Five reforms

In the following sections I will document the two main attempts to frame the childcare market in New Zealand: the Before Five reforms (1988) and the Strategic Plan (2002). Drawing on SSM, I have argued that state-led marketization requires two things to be achieved: the pacification of childcare for exchange in the market, and the necessary creation of calculating agencies in order for the market to operate. One of the primary calculating agents in childcare markets are parent consumers. While much attention has been focused on how parent consumers fail to materialize in the ways imagined within neoclassical renditions of the market, in this chapter I take a step back to see how the parent consumer is constituted within two different market making moments.

Creating the childcare market from the vestiges of what already existed involved considerable social, cultural and economic work. Feminist geographer Gibson-Graham (2006) notes that in society childcare is performed within diverse economies of care, ranging from the informal to formalized spheres. Childcare in Aotearoa New Zealand had a diverse face, with a range of philosophies and approaches to practice, from largely care based to a much more educational focus under an ECE framework.[3] Differentiation existed between non-profit and for-profit providers, full day and short hour sessional services, but also between services which were based on parent volunteerism as opposed to paid carers. Deciding what became framed into the emerging market required an understanding of what kind of provisioning already existed, and knowledge of the sector which government had not yet acquired. It is within this context that long time sector advocates and ECE experts were drawn into the state-led marketization process.

Incited to build on new-found governmental interest in childcare, many of the feminist activists who pushed for its recognition as more than a 'women's issue', became enrolled in establishing the practicalities of market framing. As I will discuss, a number of high-profile childcare activists and educationalists became charged with creating the 'blueprint' for each of the two funding interventions: bulk funding and the 20 hours ECE. A key proponent in the initial blueprint for the market was early childhood education practitioner and advocate Dr Anne Meade. Appointed by Prime Minister Lange as social policy advisor for education during the reforms in 1988, she was charged with convening a working group on ECE to conceptualize what a government funded sector might look like, in keeping with the broader governmental tone of the educational reforms. The report from the working group, known as *Education to be More* (Early Childhood Care and Education Working Group, 1988) or more popularly as 'the Meade Report', offered a highly influential justification as to the economic, social and cultural benefits of investment in childcare as ECE, arguing that a significant injection of governmental funding was needed to achieve these benefits. As a tangible artefact in the market making process, this report offered considerable heft to the prime minister's political and personal desire to spend on early childhood.

While the Meade Report has received much international acclaim as a statement of the social value of ECE, looking at it through an SSM lens we can reinterpret the work of this document in framing the emerging childcare market. Amid the rationales it presented for justified spending on ECE were also costings and formula for a bulk funding model. Ultimately it offered a vision for how to actualize the process of state-led marketization going forward, recognizing the diverse and variable nature of the childcare sector which was being framed. Existing diversity in the childcare sector was both a strength and problem from a neoliberal governance perspective. While it seemed to offer the necessary level of parental 'choice', designing a means of intervening into this diverse sector was extremely challenging. Most notably, its variability made the work of funding childcare highly problematic as it was not clear what was being funded. This variability of practice and standards also undermined governmental desire to pacify childcare, as there was no clear indication of what qualified as 'good' practice. From the initial market framing, the problem of how to pacify childcare into a comparable and standardized service within the market, became a central concern of government.

Different to the commodification of an object, the pacification of services like childcare are especially challenging, as what is being 'purchased' can look very different across the market. Rather than reproducing the same object, services tend to be commodified though establishing minimum tenets of provision. In order for this to occur for childcare, it had to be made into something which could be measured and evaluated to be funded by government and purchased by parent consumers. Many have observed that childcare markets tend to be organized around structural quality measures, like adult:child ratios or health and safety regulations, as a means of ensuring a standardized quality in marketized contexts (Penn, 2011; OECD, 2012). In the terms of SSM, this standardizing work is the work of pacification. Using the financial levers afforded through bulk funding meant that some baseline conditions would have to be set and agreed upon by providers in receipt of government payment.

To set the new conditions of practice for providers, a charter system was introduced to accompany bulk funding. As a binding statement of intent, the charter outlined a commitment to a minimum standard of practice, such as child-staff ratios, levels of trained staff, staff development and cultural equity commitments as per the founding document of the state, Te Tiriti o Waitangi (the Treaty of Waitangi). A key feature of the proposed charter was to have a board of management for all services, irrespective of their original governance structure. While this was already standard practice among non-profit providers, the biggest implication was for participating for-profit services to involve parents in their governance. In essence, the charter sought to bring services in line with the demands of both communities of interest: the government and parent consumers. The participation of parents on governance boards signalled the considerable emphasis now placed on them to oversee and regulate the market.

As a means of pacifying childcare the charter discursively and materially set out the particular qualities (as different from the normative understanding of 'quality') of childcare as ECE. It established a set of criteria as to what ECE *is* in the emerging market both as a crucial aspect in helping to ensure a measure of accountability for government, and that going forward parents as consumers would have more transparency as to what they were purchasing. As an important socio-technical element in the creation of the market, the charter was distilled into a 'purple management handbook', which was dispatched to all participating services, as a reminder of the conditions of the market relationships they had entered into.

Once the terms of practice were established through the charter, the second problem to be addressed was how to fund the sector, given the diversity of services already available and others which may emerge. Through deliberations by the funding working group under the guidance of Dr Meade, a formula was devised which paid services a subsidized amount, based on whether they were full time (8 hours per day) or part time, and the number and ages of children attending each service, up to 30 hours per week.[4] Recognizing the problems created by the unique funding relationship kindergartens had with government, education academic Carmen Dalli (1990: 67) noted that 'all early childhood services will be financed in accordance with the formula, irrespective of the funding history of individual services'. Funding was to be introduced in five stages, allowing services time to meet charter requirements, aiming for funding equalization across services by 1994. Additional subsidies were offered for children under two, who are typically the most labour intensive and therefore most expensive age group to work with. Believing this would even out the variability in quality across the sector, the Secretary of the MoE described the model as 'one of those simple, elegant solutions to an incredibly difficult problem' (May 2009: 211).

As the Meade Report went through consultation with the wider sector, soliciting 1000 responses, the resulting Before Five reforms had lost many of the central accountability aspects of original 'blueprint'. Representatives for the for-profit sector pushed back against the proposed requirement for them to establish a governance board. With the non-profit sector generally working under this governance model already, not applying it to for-profit services meant that the 'equalization' effect of the charter on the emerging market was weakened. The governance role imagined for the parent consumer was also undermined, meaning that another means of arbitrating quality in the market had to be established. As a result, the newly created Education Review Office (ERO) changed from its intended 'place of last resort' (May, 2009) for regulating quality, to the primary arbitrator of standards, a role that parental involvement on governance boards was anticipated to achieve. In sum, under the political weight of the for-profit sector, the first attempt to pacify childcare by forcing services to be accountable to their communities of interest (parent consumers and the MoE) had failed to eventuate.

Enrolling actors into the market

Despite the intentions of the Before Five reforms and the considerable increase in government funding to the sector, the creation of the market was not a pre-given outcome. As Ouma (2015) reminds us, markets do not impose themselves naturally, they have to mobilize adherents. Ultimately, the strength of involvement of market intermediaries is what gives markets their seeming stability and duration over time. The more 'skin in the game' by diverse actors, the more locked-in that particular form of the market becomes. The diversity of services already in the sector meant that considerable work had to be conducted to enrol childcare providers, and to translate their interests to align with the broader aims of state-led marketization. Failure to enrol a wide range of market actors in itself threatens to stymie formation of any embryonic market assemblage. In that sense we can see how the market could have failed to eventualize or continued on a different trajectory. Given the diverse range of services, across the formal and informal sectors, it may have been more likely for parents to use cheaper, unregulated forms of care instead of the new formalized care infrastructure.

As already noted, parent consumers were envisaged as a crucial part of the market framing. More than this, empowering parents as consumers was central to the logics of bulk funding, as it meant that the state could remain distanced from the consumer side of the market as much as possible, adopting a 'philosophy that devolves to the community, and, therefore, to parents' (Shields, 1990). Establishing a market in which parents could have more choice and autonomy over their childcare needs, and at a cost level which fuelled participation rather than inhibited it, was a central aspect of the Before Fives. In order to allow for parents to exercise their calculative agency to find childcare that worked for them, government sought to stimulate the amount and type of services on offer, thus rebalancing supply to match the growing demand. Characteristic of government discourse at the time, the Deputy Minister for Education indicated that 'the emphasis has been on raising quality standards, reducing costs to families, and meeting individual needs and preferences, rather than homogenizing preschool education. ... When we talk about early childhood care and education we talk about variety' (Shields, 1989). By raising the number of available childcare places, the balance of power was anticipated to be tipped towards the parent in the market, who would manage quality across the sector through their purchasing preferences. Bulk funding, by only meeting a portion of the cost of care, allowed parents the 'freedom' to spend in accordance with their own priorities and consequently guide the kinds of services which best met changing parental needs.

One of the most contentious aspects of the funding system from the early 1980s, and into present day debates, has been the political rationale to extend government funding to private for-profit providers. At the time of the Before Five reforms, the existing childcare sector was more heavily dominated by community, non-profit providers, the inverse of the market today (May and Mitchell, 2009). The emphasis of the Meade Report was to grow a more robust sector which would allow for women's participation in the workforce, as well as meeting new expectations for children's development. However, in doing so it recognized implicitly the necessity of the private sector at that time to meet demand for full day childcare, but tempered this acknowledgement with new accountability measures for the sector. From a governmental perspective the participation of the for-profit sector was also deemed necessary, to quickly build up the capital infrastructure of the sector in a financially risk averse way. In this context, the financial incentives of bulk funding, and the associated regulatory conditions, became the governmental lever used to direct the for-profit sector. Yet the perceived necessity of the for-profit sector meant that it had a greater ability to shape the conditions of the emergent market from the outset. Pushing back against the charter requirement for governance boards continued a notable difference between the for-profit and non-profit providers in the market. The inability to realign the interests of for-profit providers with the broader governmental ambitions for the market set the beginning of a difficult relationship.

The creation of the childcare market also hinged on the recruitment of workers in the sector. Many women had worked primarily as child carers rather than teachers, meaning that the pay scales and skills levels varied considerably. Enrolling women to work in childcare, and to see it as a job worth upskilling in, was crucial to meeting the social and educational goals of state-led marketization. A central aspect of the feminist advocacy work for childcare was not only women's and children's rights, but also to have the work itself recognized and remunerated in line with other parts of the education sector, particularly as it was now under the auspices of the MoE. The groundwork for the revaluation of childcare labour was laid through increasing unionization of the sector (see Box 3.1). While unionization was underway in advance of the Before Five reforms, this advocacy work was folded into the interests of government during the late 1980s. The outcome led to the first three-year early childhood teaching degree, Diploma in Teaching (DipTch), in 1988, paving the way for qualification parity (if not pay parity) with primary teachers. For the first time, workers in the sector had a clear training pathway to follow, making their skills transparent within the education sector.

Box 3.1: ECE unionization

Today, New Zealand still has strong unionization in the ECE sector, which is a notable difference with other neoliberal childcare markets (Brown, 2009). The idea to unionize the sector came from Sonja Davies, a childcare worker, trade union advocate and member of parliament in the early 1970s. Believing that the quality of care for children would be improved by having better working conditions, she foreshadowed the importance of an industrial union for childcare workers. Along with Rosslyn Noonan and the Kindergarten Teachers Association she launched a successful bid to unionize, as they were able to articulate the benefits of unionization in line with the interests of a growing workforce of women who worked with young children across the care and education sectors. Off the back of this alliance, in 1982 the Early Childhood Workers Union (ECWU) was formed. However, its establishment was on rocky ground and reaction within the sector varied considerably. As May (2009) describes, some workers responded with a burst of activism, others did not want any trouble. Employers were uncertain of the implications of the union and began to organize their own representative groups in response to a campaign against a national wage award. During the 1990s the incumbent centre right National Party introduced Employment Contracts legislation which meant achieving any national pay award became very difficult. Staff were ultimately employed on individualized contracts which largely undermined working conditions.

In 1994 ECWU joined NZEI Te Rui Roa and formed a coalition with primary teachers, solidifying ECE interests within the education system. Although the success of unionization has waxed and waned in response to different governments in the interim years, today the ECE workforce remains part of two education unions accounting for 6000 employees. There are a diverse range of collective agreements, and the Consenting Parties Agreement is the largest, although it primarily covers workers in community, non-profit services, with minimal adherence to any agreement by for-profit providers. As I will discuss later in the chapter, this has resulted in various forms of conditionality inbuilt into the funding systems by MoE to try to ensure minimum rates of pay are reaching staff.

Overflowing the Before Fives

As Berndt and Boeckler (2011) suggest, once experimental market interventions like the Before Fives enter the world, and leave the de facto 'laboratory' in which they were conceptualized, they are susceptible to mutation and change in unpredictable ways. Although market framing is a boundary making process around what is considered within and outside the market, rarely is it possible to neatly achieve this from the messy reality of markets in motion. Market actors are not solely motivated by economic logics but are also simultaneously connected to other lifeworlds which may be shaped by competing, non-economic rationales. As a result, markets are susceptible to overflow, failing in often significant ways to achieve what they were intended to do. This is an important insight into the work of state-led marketization, as it reinforces the enormous task of putting markets to work in the service of achieving collective social goals.

When funding was implemented in 1990, almost all services[5] gained a 50 per cent increase in government income (May, 2009). However, indicative of the contested neoliberal political front which childcare represents, the Before Five reforms were amended in significant ways by an incoming, centre right, National led coalition government over the course of the next nine years. Many of the changes brought about under this term of office have been described in accounts of the sector as being out of proportion with the financial contribution of government, bringing some to the conclusion that change was driven by ideological rather than fiscal justifications (May, 2009). Working under a more austere budgetary climate, spending on social services, like childcare, was severely curtailed in the early years of the 1990s (Manning, 2016). Unlike the previous government who sought out the involvement of independent childcare advocates and experts, reviews of the sector were now conducted in private, curtailing the input of this expertise. One of the first casualties of this renewed fiscal conservatism was the removal of the staged funding equalization plan for the sector, which stalled at step one, resulting in an 11 per cent cut to total funding to the sector. This change set the scene for a much more competitive childcare market to emerge.

Under the new political lens, a very different relationship between government and the private sector was cultivated. With a desire to 'free up' business conditions and remove the apparently burdensome hand of the state with regards to compliance, further aspects of the charter were removed. This impacted some regulatory requirements, leading to raised staffing ratios and lower accountability expectations by government for how funding was used beyond basic financial reporting, with the justification that these regulations 'made it unnecessarily difficult to providers to offer ECE at a reasonable cost' (Smith, 1991: 18). Sympathetic to purported concerns from the private sector that a creeping upskilling of the workforce would make the cost of care too high for parents, the previous government's aspiration to have at least one staff member in each service qualified with the DipTch by 2000[6] was curtailed. Combined, these changes amended market conditions such that the for-profit sector could develop new business models and ways of engaging with bulk funding, largely outside of the conditions of the original market blueprint. In essence, diluting the requirement of the charter undermined state-led attempts to pacify childcare, as it loosened expectations around the 'qualities' of services, again making it a challenge for the MoE to assess the sector and parent consumers to navigate the market going forward.

While a diversity of types of provisioning was aspired to in the Before Five reforms, under these amended market conditions centre-based childcare flourished. Between 1990 and 1999 the number of childcare centres increased[7] from 2890 to 4148, but participation remained dominated by Pākehā children.[8] Continuing low participation rates for Māori and Pasifika children, who were a key part of the population envisaged to benefit from childcare spending, meant that this framing of the market was not meeting its social objectives. Much of the problem of access for more economically vulnerable groups related to the ongoing cost of care for parents. An important aspect of the bulk funding system which had been overlooked was the differential cost of operation across service types. Indeed, as early education expert Professor Linda Mitchell cautioned at the time, setting a universal rate per age of child irrespective of the differential cost of service type (urban versus rural for example) set the preconditions for a variegated landscape of care, where equity of access and cost was not guaranteed (Mitchell, 2013). This led to a rise in parental costs to offset the funding shortfall. However, I suggest that governmental desire to pacify childcare in the emergent market, to attempt to standardize the kinds of care being purchased, worked counter to acknowledgement of this cost differential. Paying childcare services a different rate would mean that the government was supporting different kinds of childcare, highlighting an inherent tension in the initial framing of the market.

By analysing the Before Five reforms and bulk funding through the lens of SSM, we can see how the childcare market was neither pre-given nor inevitable. The birth of the New Zealand childcare market involved painstaking social, political, discursive and material work to frame diverse services, enrol actors into the market and pacify childcare within it. Forged off the back of a highly variable sector, and drawing together the interests of multiple different groups, the work of market making was contentious from the outset, and as a consequence highly prone to fail.

In sum, the creation and actualization of the Before Five reforms gives critical insights into the challenges of state-led marketization. As argued thus far, the pacification of childcare, and the creation of parent consumers as a primary calculative agency were key objectives in order to realize the market. However, neither of these objectives were successfully achieved in practice. While the market had grown exponentially in response to bulk funding, low participation rates for some groups and high costs to parents overall indicated the failure of parents to be able to act calculably in the market. By the late 1990s, it was apparent that not all providers were enrolled to meet the same sets of interests or goals. As Callon and Law (1982) suggest, translation requires all parties to converge around the same purpose or activity. To become fully enrolled, actors have to adapt some aspect of their identity to align with the broader goals of the market, and the market also adapts to accommodate them. However, under the amendments made to the Before Five reforms, we can see that the market assemblage adapted to a much greater extent to accommodate the interests of for-profit actors, leaving their practice and approach to the business of care relatively unchanged. Indeed, the continued legacy of this failure to translate the work of the for-profit sector to align with the social aspirations of the emergent market can still be seen today.

Reframing the market through the Strategic Plan 2002–2012

The period from 1999 to 2008 in New Zealand captures a much more interventionist role for the state in the care of young children. For many, it marked a step change in the government's responsibility for remedying the social and economic problems created under the austerity of the preceding neoliberal period. The privatization and roll back of key domains like education and health, coupled with the impact of economic liberalism, meant that unemployment and the effects of social exclusion were widespread (Rashbrook, 2013). There was growing political acceptance that the work of the 'invisible hand' was not producing the benefits envisioned, and that more market guidance by the state was necessary to offset the worst effects of the preceding neoliberal reforms. The return to power of a Labour-led coalition government in 1999 brought forth the beginnings of a more 'reflexive' market making approach, one which still believed in the benefits of markets as a means of organizing and distributing resources, but which envisioned an increased role for the state in that process (Larner and Butler, 2005). This was especially borne out for markets of collective concern, like childcare.

The changes to the Before Five reforms had resulted in a number of unanticipated effects, provoking a necessary re-problematization of the market by the incoming government. Criticisms from sector advocates were waged at the lack of 'structural underpinnings' of the Before Fives, suggesting that the sector's development had not received sufficient guidance from government. Although participation in childcare had increased, with a notable uptake in full day care in childcare centres, by 2005 58 per cent of children were being cared for in private for-profit services (May, 2009). Concerns had been raised in the lead up to bulk funding around the possibility for profiteering among private providers. With the subsequent changes to the original 'blueprint' for state-led marketization, some of these concerns seemed to have eventuated, with media documenting breaches of the system throughout the 1990s (*Sunday Star Times*, 1990).

A crucial part of the election promise for the new government was to 'close the gap' of childcare provisioning across New Zealand, acknowledging that the market had produced uneven levels of access for families. Greater government intervention at this juncture was also justified on biopolitical grounds, on the basis that a child not in early education was potentially 'at risk', and so participation became an even more central aspect in the battle to mitigate poor child outcomes. Emerging international research, such as the OECD *Starting Strong* reports (2001, 2006), was supportive of a more interventionist approach to public spending in the years before school, moving the conversation away from a focus on childcare from a women and gender equity perspective to children in their own right (Lister, 2006). To mobilize the market to address these issues, the incoming government sought to provide more structure and to make clear its medium-term plans by introducing the first ever strategic plan for the sector: *Pathways to the Future: Nga Huaraki Arataki 2002–2012* (MoE, 2002). The genesis of the plan came from commissioned work again led by Dr Anne Meade and 31 sector representatives in 2000. Like the Before Fives, the plan laid the foundations for a new kind of relationship between government, parents and the childcare sector.

The initial stated aims of the plan were to raise the quality of childcare services by advancing the professionalization of the workforce, improving access for all children and to better support the non-profit sector, as it had clearer accountability structures to its parent community. To achieve these aims the working party argued that a new universal funding and regulatory system had to be put in place. What government and parents as key 'clients' were purchasing from childcare services had still not reached any standardized level. Questions of 'quality' differentiation between services became pertinent to the strategic plan. Feeding into these debates was a raft of new knowledge and research by academics in education during the 1990s, addressing key epistemological debates about what 'quality' childcare and ECE might actually looked like (MoE, 1998, 1999).

Reflecting on this academic body of work, I suggest that what Helen May (2009) characterizes as the 'age of quality' during the 1990s, can perhaps be seen instead as the 'age of qualities' (Callon et al, 2002), as childcare and the diverse practices within the market became revalued through a new governmental lens, with the intention to clearly identify what 'good' ECE looked like. Based on the strength of emerging education research, under the strategic plan a new important distinction manifested in government's view of the sector, moving from discussions of for-profit and non-profit providers to a distinction between parent-led and teacher-led services. This change marked a significant repositioning of market boundaries, as it began to separate early education as a distinctive sphere from other prominent childcare services in the sector which relied on parental voluntarism to operate (like Playcentre and Te Kōhanga Reo). While it was claimed to be based on a quality judgement, where quality was in part equated to the level of trained early education teachers in the service, it was also a significant step towards pacifying what childcare as ECE was. Incentivized by a new funding system which was tagged to the amount of trained teachers in a service, the plan was anticipated to encourage providers to hire more qualified staff. This was especially the case for the for-profit sector, the business model of which continued to be based on a low wage and under-professionalized workforce in the wake of bulk funding.

To enrol the childcare workforce into the reframed market, financial motivation was also offered to encourage upskilling in the sector. In this sense, government incentive was used to constitute workers as economic subjects, through encouraging them to re-evaluate childcare as a potential career. Tackling head on the issue of varying skills levels across the sector, a staged process was implemented under the strategic plan to enable *all* workers in early education services to become teacher trained by 2012, citing that 'this Government knows that the most important issue with education is the quality of the teaching that is put in place' (Duncan, 2003). Funding to support this progressive initiative rose from approximately NZ$350,000 in 2002 to almost NZ$1.2 million in 2010 and was primarily channelled into grants, scholarships and allowances to early education teachers and students (Mitchell, 2013). The number of students undertaking the DipTch degree rose from 1500 in 1999 to 4000 by 2003 (MoE, 2004), and by 2007 most childcare centres had half of their staff teacher trained.

To encourage services to meet the increased costs of having fully trained staff, bulk funding was amended in 2005. Applicable to teacher-led services, funding rates were envisioned to lift in accordance with the rate of trained teachers up to the maximum of 100 per cent trained staff. The initial market framing, which did not recognize differential costs of care, sought to allow parents to choose to pay for higher quality services if they preferred to do so. Under the Strategic Plan, the government now recognized the differential costs associated with providing a 'quality' service, and that parents' purchasing power alone should not dictate their whether their child accessed quality care. Indeed, under a social investment rationale, the quality of care and education received was directly related to the life outcomes for all young children. Consequently, the reframed market was organized around a more active attempt by government to pacify childcare. Through the levers of the new funding system, providers were now incentivized to work towards a set of common objectives for the sector, notably around workforce professionalization. In that sense, the political work of defining the 'qualities' of childcare in the market fell onto the training institutions and the teacher accreditation bodies, proliferating a new domain of market framing and contestation.[9]

While sector upskilling progressed throughout the 2000s, the other related governmental ambitions of raising children's participation rates and endorsing community non-profit providers in the market, were more challenging to achieve. Of particular concern to government and many advocates of the sector was the rapid increase of for-profit providers in line with government funding of the sector, with the Minister for Education, Trevor Mallard, stating publicly that 'I think when huge amounts of government funding is directed towards these "private businesses", then government has not only a right but a responsibility to set standards that we require for our investment' (Mallard, 2002). This concern was especially pressing because the minister had been quietly costing out different options for a universal form of childcare funding during the early 2000s. As with the Before Fives, the consultative work for this intervention was conducted by some of the feminist activists who had been working in the sector and in the trade union movement. Professor Linda Mitchell, a trade unionist and ECE expert who had been critical of the outcomes of the Before Fives, was brought in to chair a working party to explore the potential of a universal childcare payment. Coming as a surprise to many in the sector, and indicative of the growing biopolitical emphasis on the preschool years, in the 2004 budget it was announced that by 2007 all three- and four-year-old children in community non-profit services would receive 20 hours' free ECE per week. As another potentially 'elegant solution', it advanced the diminishing position of non-profit providers in the face of a growing private sector, and directly reduced the cost of care for parents at the same time.

Market contestation: the 20 hours free ECE payment

'If there is a magic bullet in public policy, this Government believes that it is education.' (Mahary, 2003)

Despite the considerable funding boost the '20 hours free ECE' payment would bring to the sector, as a market intervention its introduction proved to be highly contentious. The decision to only allow the non-profit sector to offer the payment was hotly contested in the media by some parents groups[10] who raised concern that their children in for-profit centres would miss out on the funding. The private sector lobby group, the Early Childhood Council (ECC),[11] also voiced strong opposition to the payment, arguing that they would be at a significant disadvantage in the market, even after the government offered to raise existing bulk funding rates to meet new standards of practice. The Treasury argued against the payment from a different perspective, as it envisioned that there would be insufficient supply in the non-profit sector to meet demand, thus limiting the market ideal of parental choice (Dye, 2004).

The initial problem of building capital infrastructure and the need for the private sector to provide childcare places, quickly, again stifled what government hoped to achieve in its term of office. The Minister of Education was committed to supporting non-profit providers, as they were responsible to their parent communities through their charters in a way that private services were not. This he felt accorded them a higher level of accountability for public monies received. By the mid-2000s, a large proportion of the non-profit sector had also signed up to the employment relations Consenting Parties Agreement, and were working at the 100 per cent trained teacher band and remunerating staff to a higher level than most for-profit providers. However, in an election year and coming under increasing influence from what had become a large private sector lobby under the ECC, the government was forced to reverse its decision and open the scheme to the whole sector. The significance of the timing of this decision in relation to the election is noteworthy. Within the reformulation of the market assemblage, power to shape market relations ultimately flowed to parents as voters and the private sector lobby groups, who had been very adept at cultivating media attention for their cause (Bushouse, 2008). This revised decision around the 20 hours payment thus represented another important turning point in the relationship between government and the for-profit sector.

Once applicable to the for-profit sector, public debate around the payment changed to the extent and rate of the funding. Crucially the 20 hours intervention was intended as a payment, rather than a subsidy, meaning that government set a rate above which providers were not allowed to charge for those hours. Setting that rate made highly visible the differing approaches and cost bases of providers within the market. While this was understood at the time as an economic question, the practical act of setting a rate per hour also posed a normative question for government, relating to the 'just' level at which to set the payment. Because the payment was now available to the for-profit sector, it made the task of assigning a rate even harder. Debates oscillated from too little funding and no services would take part in the scheme, to too much funding and the scheme would be 'hijacked' by private providers incentivized to make a profit (May, 2009). The monetary figure set in this sense reflects the boundary of the moral economy of childcare that remains a potent problem for state-led marketization.

After deliberation, the working party settled on the rate of payment at 100 per cent of the average cost of providing ECE to the regulated standards of the strategic plan, a figure derived from data gathered for bulk funding reporting.[12] By the time the payment was applied across the sector, the resulting system had 15 different rates of funding, with the highest for all-day, ECE centres who employed 100 per cent trained teachers. Under bulk funding, cost differences were not recognized, but three rates were set for differing ages of children which were supposed to be increased over time such that all services were equally funded. This approach was intended to have an equalizing effect across the sector in the hope that it would even out the historical variability within the market. By comparison, the Strategic Plan did account for some differences in funding between services, based on quality indicators linked to staffing. More than that, as Bushouse (2008) suggests, the 20 hours payment actually accentuated these differences, by actively rewarding services who went above the regulated standards (of having the minimum of 60 per cent teacher trained staff for example) to achieve higher quality. At the same time it took the reliance off parents to drive 'quality' in the market through their purchasing ability, by tagging funding to new structural quality objectives, which it was anticipated would both raise standards and reorientate the market towards teacher-led practice. Indeed, as I will discuss, the parent consumer as calculative agent looked significantly different under the reframed market.

The work of government to enrol actors, and gain sector buy-in to the new funding model, was a major challenge. Despite agitation to ensure the 20 hours payment was made eligible to all parts of the sector, once the level of payment was revealed it was not universally welcomed by some parents nor providers. The 20 hours rate was based on an equation which linked the two dimensions of the cost base that the government could now justify paying for under state-led marketization; the number of enrolled children, coupled with the level of trained teachers in a service. However, as an average rate it was again criticized for not taking into account other costs of operation, especially capital infrastructure costs such as land values, property rates and increasingly the cost of rent,[13] an important aspect of the for-profit sector which I address in Chapter 5. Essentially, the costs of a highly variegated economic landscape of operation were to be borne by childcare business owners. The implications of using an average cost of operation as the basis for funding levels played out in highly geographical ways, as many services in locations with higher property values felt they could not meet their operating costs.[14] In order to work within the new funding system, many argued that services with higher operating costs would ironically have to reduce quality, by increasing their ratios of children to teachers, or reducing the number of trained teachers, in order to work within the 20 hours funding rates. In contrast, centres with below average operating costs would in effect be 'rewarded' by the scheme (NZIER, 2005). Despite acknowledging the different costs associated with employing trained staff, by not accounting for other kinds of cost differentials (like rent, which was understood to be outside the purview of the MoE) many for-profit providers began to make cost savings in other ways (see Chapter 4). Although heralded as government commitment to the importance of ECE, the private sector lobby conversely labelled it as 'the biggest threat to the quality of early childhood policy in our generation' (from May, 2009: 293).

While government took a more involved role in this iteration of the market, the role of the parent consumer remained crucial. The Before Fives understood parent consumers as being necessary to both governing services such that they were accountable to their communities of interest and regulating the market through their exercise of choice. As such, bulk funding sought to constitute parents as particular kinds of calculative agents, able to read the market and make informed choices among the diversity of care on offer and in line with their own needs. While the Strategic Plan still envisioned parents as calculating agents in the market, their ability to regulate it through consumer choice was now deemed to be problematic. Evidence from research conducted in the interim indicated the multiple ways in which parents failed to enact the kind of neoliberal consumer subject imagined in the previous market iteration (Robertson et al, 2007). As part of the re-problematization of the sector, the expectation that parents would regulate the market through their purchasing ability was tempered, such that parental choice was now to be exercised in a more guided manner. This occurred through the proliferation of information from the ERO to parents, like booklets on what to look for in a childcare service, along with the publication online of all ERO reports for services. The reframed market prioritized teacher-led services over the other kinds of childcare and early education options, and through the financial levers of the 20 hours payment parents were orientated towards these services. For government then, the emphasis under the Strategic Plan became more focused on the successful pacification of childcare as ECE by prioritizing teacher-led services and setting more defined structural quality indicators for the market.

As an important point of comparison, unlike bulk funding, which was introduced relatively quickly at the end of a political term to a disparate and largely disorganized sector, the 20 hours intervention had a much longer period of consultation. By 2005 the political landscape of childcare looked very different to two decades earlier, with much more sector-wide representation and lobby groups. Indicative of this, an Early Childhood Advisory Committee was created in 2004 which allowed advocacy groups to meet directly with the MoE to raise concerns and give feedback on changes. The discursive terrain was more complex than ever. Debate among representative organizations within the sector was fierce over the funding proposal. One of the most vocal groups was the ECC, who lobbied aggressively against the funding through media releases and leaflets to services (ECC, 2007a, 2007b). Setting an hourly rate above which services could not charge was deemed to be too much involvement in the business of childcare for private providers. Other groups, like the New Zealand Childcare Association (NZCA) released counter information to quell mounting anxiety in the sector and among parents (NZCA, 2007). In the 18 months leading up to the introduction of the payment, surveys were deployed as powerful tools evidencing the low or high potential uptake of the scheme, indicating the extent to which this intervention was on a knife edge. Conscious of the potential failure of the scheme, the ministry engaged in a lengthy three phase 'Free Early Childhood Education Training Plan' consisting of roadshows, conferences, and 28 regional seminars in the lead up to the implementation of the funding.

Under pressure from the ECC, and worried that there would be low uptake of the payment among providers, government again tempered some of the initial regulatory conditions of the 20 hours funding. One important concession was that there was nothing legally stopping services introducing an 'optional' fee for the 20 hours, for extra things like food or nappies which were outside of regulated expectations. For many this optional clause directly undermined the desire to reduce the costs to parents as a key barrier for participation. By the introduction of the scheme, one in seven services had optional fees in place (May, 2009: 294). Concerns were also raised by parent groups who contested the payment on the ground of the word 'free' in its title. Because there was no obligation for services to offer the scheme, it was not possible for government to legally deliver it as an *entitlement* to all children. Thus, the allowance of optional fees so services could cover their additional costs confused parent communities, who assumed it was a universal free entitlement for their preschool age children. Opposition political parties moved to capitalize on this ambivalence by labelling the payment an 'education hoax', lying to parents and providers (Key, 2007). In 2019, I had the chance to interview the minister, Steve Mahary, who oversaw the introduction of the 20 hours payment, during which he reflected on it as a political 'damp squib', something initially heralded as a ground-breaking commitment by the government to the early years community, which in the end became a 'hard fought battle to get it across the line'. Indeed, it took many months after the introduction of the scheme before the majority of the sector took part in the scheme.[15]

Market asymmetries and the growth of the private sector

Government spending on childcare increased markedly in the wake of the 20 hours payment and, as Table 3.1 illustrates, the balance of payment tipped towards the for-profit sector over the next decade. Indeed, any analysis of the 20 hours payment needs to be set within the broader context of the concerns raised by advocates of publicly funded childcare, as to the expeditious trend towards privatization occurring as a result of this government intervention. While private providers were in the market before the 1980s, it was the scale of operation of services and the kinds of new financial entities which were now taking an interest in childcare which raised heightened concerns (Duhn, 2010), a topic I consider more closely in the next chapter. Indicative of the growing attention childcare was now receiving by diverse financial entities, on announcing the introduction of the 20 hours payment Australian owned McQuarie Bank invested in the New Zealand childcare market for the first time, buying 20 centres and bringing much media attention to the changing business of care that was emerging. Another example of the changing business models at this time was the childcare corporate Kidicorp, owned by American businessman and philanthropist Wayne Wright, who publicly listed his services on the New Zealand stock market in 2003 to generate capital for expansion (Hembry, 2007). Concerned by the potential impact of these changes, the Minister for Education cautioned private providers. Indicative of the limited agency government now had on these financial trends in the for-profit sector, he stated 'we are not telling you how to do this – this is your decision to make as the owner of your service. However, neither the ministry nor I will be expecting to see unreasonable increases in fees after free ECE begins, and the ministry will be monitoring fees' (Laugeson, 2007). Shortly after this comment he received a reprimand by the Commerce Commission for stating that he would seek to stop profiteering in the private sector, an opinion which provoked a drop in the share prices of the newly listed Kidicorp. It was becoming increasingly clear that the ability for the state to control the market assemblage, once operationalized, was limited.

Table 3.1: Political and funding changes, 1986–2020

Timeline	Majority government	Major policy changes	Key funding changes
1986–1990	Labour Government	Before Five Reforms (1988)	*Bulk funding* *Discretionary grants* to non-profit providers *Childcare Subsidy*: means-tested subsidy for low-income families
1990–1999	National Government		Cuts to Before Fives staged funding plan
1999–2008	Labour Government	*Strategic Plan-Pathways to the future: Ngā Huarahi Arataki (2002–2012)*	*Equity Funding* for services in lower socioeconomic and isolated areas *Working for Families* tax credit payments *20 hours ECE* payment for 3–5-year-olds
2008–2017	National Government	An Agenda for Amazing Children (2010) White Paper on Vulnerable Children (2012)	*Targeted Assistance for Participation*: funding to build services where participation in ECE is low Cut 100% teacher funding band
2017–present	Labour Government	Early Learning Action Plan (2019–2029)	Restored 100% teacher funding band Increase in minimum salary of certified ECE teachers, and drive to align salaries in sector with kindergarten teachers

Despite the rocky start to the introduction of the 20 hours payment, in its initial years it did tip the balance of costs away a from reliance on parental fees onto the state and costs fell by 34 per cent on average in the first year (Mitchell, 2013). However, again reflective of the politically unstable terrain on which childcare policy rests, the decade after the introduction of the 20 hours payment was shaped by a new centre right government, which although loathe to upset parents by removing the universal payment, ideologically preferred more targeted funding (National Party, 2007). As a result, it undermined the 20 hours payment by stealth, whereby the dollar value of the payment in real terms received no significant increase during their decade-long term in office, with some suggesting it did not even keep pace with inflation (Walters, 2016). This produced an effective funding freeze for much of the sector, which over the course of the 2010s tipped the balance of payment back onto the shoulders of parents (OECD, 2016b) as fee rates increased to absorb the funding shortfall. It also left the professionalization of the sector in limbo, as services struggled to meet new wage expectations in a limited funding environment. Indeed, the problem of labour in the reframed childcare market, specifically pertaining to the business models of the burgeoning for-profit sector, is a central aspect of the next chapter.

Conclusion

The primary aim of this chapter has been to document the complex and fragile process of state-led marketization in Aotearoa New Zealand since the late 1980s. Focusing on two market making moments, the Before Five reforms and the Strategic Plan, I put key insights of SSM to work to make two observations. Firstly, in order to create a market to meet social and economic objectives for children, childcare needed to be pacified. The form of childcare which was favoured by government for exchange in the market had to be identified from the diverse philosophies and practices of childcare which were already in existence. From there it had to be standardized and made measurable in some central ways in order for both the parent consumer to be assured of the kind of service they were placing their child in and for government to be secure in the knowledge that funding was going towards a similar service in the market. Pacification in this sense is a prominent aspect in the framing of markets of collective concern, as it circumscribes that which is deemed to be suitable for exchange, noting that these services are also intended to achieve important social work. Secondly, parent consumers needed to be mobilized as calculating agents so that they could act as informed economic actors in the market, such that they know how to evaluate the qualities of a service in the market.

Grounding these insights in analysis of the New Zealand childcare market, I offered an alternative reading of the dilemma between idealized renditions of childcare markets actors and how they materialize in reality. While much work has shown that the imagined parent consumer fails to eventuate, for reasons discussed in Chapter 2, this chapter has sought to approach this differently by illustrating the ways in which the parent consumer is imagined in line with each attempt at state-led marketization. Drawing on a more relational understanding of market formation, I have sought to show how the parent consumer subject is constituted in relation to the market itself. This moves the debate away from the idea of whether parent consumers have the capacity to act rationally or not in response to the market, to an understanding that such capacities are always constituted in relation to the market assemblage.

While the different phases of marketization were laid bare in this chapter, in telling this narrative I have sought to highlight market making as a highly experimental frontier for policy. The Before Five reforms initiated governmental engagement in creating the market, establishing a clear 'blueprint' to guide the framing process. However, once these plans enter the world, they are subject to change and adaptation, what Callon (2007a) refers to as market overflows. It is by examining processes of market framing and overflow that we can trace the challenges of state-led marketization, as it seeks to achieve collective social goals through the creation of the market.

4

Private Providers, Childcare Labour and the Problem of Finance

In this chapter I will consider the other set of calculative agencies in the childcare market: the providers. A major concern in recent literature has been the privatization of childcare services, particularly notable in markets with a demand side funding system. The outcome has been both a proliferation and diversification of for-profit childcare providers, ranging in scale from single owner-operators to large scale shareholder driven corporates. For critics of childcare markets, this diversification has posed a conceptual problem, as while they all in theory operate under a profit-making rationale, there is a considerable range of business models within what is referred to as the 'private sector'. Reflective of an increasing desire to produce a more nuanced understanding of for-profit provision, rather than assume it is all morally moribund a priori, there have been calls to explore what different parts of the for-profit childcare sector actually looks like (Press and Woodrow, 2005).

Speaking to this gap in knowledge, in this chapter I examine for-profit providers as calculative agents who deploy different financial strategies to operate in the emergent market. Focusing on two types of provider that have proliferated in Aotearoa New Zealand, namely the individual owner-operator and the consolidated childcare chain, I explore the strategies and economic calculations these actors have made in relation to the work of childcare since 2002. In the process I demonstrate the relational nature of this calculative work, adjusting in response to both the demands of the parent consumer and the interests of government in the sector. Building on the analysis of the previous chapter, I argue that the strategies deployed by these actors in response to state-led marketization are generative of the kinds of competitive market dynamics which have provoked significant criticism during this time.

While the aim of making a profit is important to these actors, ultimately the broader question of *finance* shapes their business strategies. As I illustrate, the problem of finance for childcare owner-operators manifests in diverse ways; financial management, cashflow, raising capital and securing loans to name but a few. In the first instance, remaining solvent is a paramount concern, but so is extracting a profit. How money moves in the market to create profit is shaped by the confluence of government funding practices and the strategies of for-profit actors in response. Maintaining stability in the market since the 20 hours payment has required a diversification of strategies for managing finance, and over time the necessary involvement of other financial actors, some existing like banks, some more bespoke like childcare finance companies, to allow money to flow.

A secondary analysis of this chapter considers the role of labour within the financial strategies of for-profit providers. Indeed, much of the public and academic criticism of the for-profit sector in childcare has hinged on the fact that in the business of care, labour is the largest cost yet the least remunerated form of work. Political economic critiques of marketized care suggest that the overwhelming outcome of the involvement of the for-profit sector is the exploitation of care labour. This argument is based on the weight of evidence of how care is devalued both socially and economically through the market (Duffy, 2011; Green and Lawson, 2011). The result has been the prevalence of financial strategies which seek to suppress rates of pay for those employed in care, in order to return greater profit (Teghtsoonian, 1997; Fraser, 2013). While I do not contradict these findings, in this chapter I suggest that the dynamics of how the for-profit childcare sector engages with the issue of labour is dependent on the nature of the market framing itself. In my examination of the financial strategies of for-profit providers in New Zealand, I found that *paying labour* in the first instance has become a central financial concern since 2008. Tracing these specific market dynamics suggests that feminist political economy critique of the exploitation of care labour may miss some of the contradictory and more nuanced outcomes of state-led marketization.

Contesting the value of childcare labour

In this section I will outline in more detail the problem that was created for the sector between the aims of the Strategic Plan, which was structurally tagged to the professionalization of the early education workforce, and the subsequent economic and social devaluation of childcare labour under an incoming centre right government in 2010. Undermining a primary ambition of the Strategic Plan, and the broader aim of pacification, the incoming government significantly reduced the incentives for workers in the sector to upskill, over time producing a childcare skills shortage. This background discussion is not incidental to the broader aim of the chapter, as it illustrates the creation of a new problematic within the financial strategies of for-profit providers: namely the challenge of hiring and maintaining qualified staff as a key structural quality indicator in order to access the maximum amount of government funding.

While the skills shortage did not solely affect the for-profit sector, as I will discuss later in the chapter, non-profit services have tended to achieve better staff retention, in large part due to their participation in the Consenting Parties Agreement, which has protected wage levels and working conditions in the market. However, the growth of for-profit childcare centres after 2008 meant that a considerable proportion of employment in the market was in these services. By 2017, the face of the childcare sector had altered significantly in response to state-led marketization. Data gathered by MoE, coupled with academic studies of the sector, indicate that there had been a significant change in the structure of the market. From my analysis of the *Education Counts* datasets, of the approximately 5000 licensed childcare services available in 2017, half were childcare centres. Indeed, the growth in childcare centres after the introduction of the 20 hours payment was notable, increasing from 1900 in 2007 to 2558 a decade later. While childcare centres are located in both the community, non-profit and for-profit sectors, it was the latter that proliferated the most in response to government funding. MoE statistics indicate that non-profit childcare centres have experienced minimal growth (increasing from 725 centres in 2002 to 807 in 2017), while the number of for-profit centres has more than doubled during the same time (from 887 in 2002 to 1751 in 2017).[1] Pertinent to this chapter, the structure of the for-profit sector also changed, leading to some increased involvement of corporatized, large scale chains,[2] as well as a more general consolidation of services into owner-operators with between three and ten services.

Governmental desire to raise the qualification levels of staff in the childcare market has been an ongoing facet of both 'blueprints' of state-led marketization. Whereas under the Before Five reforms it was anticipated that skill levels would increase as parent consumers came to value trained staff over childcare workers, the Strategic Plan for the first time made a clear statement of the importance of teacher trained staff to achieving the social goals of childcare as ECE. As Labour MP and union advocate Helen Duncan vociferously argued in parliament at the time, 'This Government knows that the most important issue with education is the quality of the teaching that is put in place. That is particularly important at the early childhood level, because those young children are so vulnerable and deserve absolutely the best' (Duncan, 2003). This view was consolidated by a government commitment to have 100 per cent trained teachers in licensed services by 2016, accompanied with a considerable increase in spending on training grants for the sector to fast-track upskilling. Apart from its perceived importance in achieving social and educational goals for children, making skills levels comparable across different services was a crucial step in making childcare measurable within the market. In that sense government expenditure was going towards a particular kind of commodified service, one which was distinguished as 'teacher-led' and newly defined through the training and accreditation body of the New Zealand Teachers Council.

As described in Chapter 3, childcare has been a frontier site for neoliberal politics in Aotearoa New Zealand, perhaps more than any other part of the education system (Press et al, 2018). This has produced contradictory political views on key issues like how to fund the sector, the extent of its regulation and its professionalization. For the Labour Party, which initiated most of the proactive market interventions over the past 30 years, the standardization of skills and the professionalization of the childcare workforce became viewed over time as a crucial aspect in ensuring the market achieved its intended policy goals. Alternatively, for the more centre right National Party, an expressed social conservatism around the nature of childcare work, coupled with a faith in the market to decide on the appropriate skills level required, left childcare workers with little financial incentive to professionalize. Characteristic of this latter view, the newly elected National Party Prime Minister John Key made his sentiment immediately known by stating 'it is a matter of personal belief as to whether a high proportion of all [childcare] centre staff should be qualified' (*New Zealand Herald*, 2010). Against an emphasis on the professionalization of childcare staff under the previous government, this rhetoric set the tone for the next ten years of government.

Taking office in the wake of the GFC, the National Party froze the education component of the ECE funding in the 2010 budget, meaning that any increase in wages to meet costs of professionalization had to come from other revenue sources (usually parent fees). Further fiscal tightening led to a large scale reduction in funding for professional development and training grants, and the removal of the 100 per cent funding band for services with fully trained staff. With the government's interests in 'finding the right balance between regulation and choice' (from May, 2009: 308), services could have a minimum of 50 per cent trained teachers in their service and still be eligible for lower rates of government funding. The top rate of funding for services was reduced to 80 per cent, meaning that many services who had a fully teacher trained staff were now 'over-qualified' and paying out more in wages than they were funded for.[3]

These labour changes had two important effects on the market. Firstly, it again undermined attempts to raise the skills level across the sector intended to make childcare more standardized and ultimately measurable, a problem which had plagued governmental attempts to pacify childcare. Secondly by widening the scope of practice, such that services could employ anywhere from 50–80 per cent of trained staff and still be eligible for funding, it laid the terrain for a new wave of economic experimentation in private sector childcare, as owner-operators developed complex financial strategies to access the most from the 20 hours 'pot of gold' payment.

Yet, contrary to the governmental intention to make the regulatory environment more 'business friendly', the political and financial withdrawal of commitment for the professionalization of the sector after 2010 had a negative impact on the for-profit sector through creating a skills shortage. MoE data on this period paints a stark picture: a 55 per cent plunge in domestic students training in ECE between 2009 and 2019 (Collins, 2019a). Relatedly, the proportion of unqualified staff in teacher-led services rose from 29 per cent of the workforce in 2014 to 37 per cent in 2019 (Education Counts, 2020).[4] By the time a Labour-led coalition party came to power again in 2017, the sector was beleaguered by a significant skills shortage. Pressured to maintain the supply of trained staff, as an interim measure the government placed ECE teachers on the immigration skills shortage list in 2019.

From the outset, most for-profit providers were nervous about the 20 hours payment, concerned that the amount set by government would not cover their costs, or that compliance would create an administrative burden. However, once it was introduced, and as more services came on board, parental demand drove the remainder of the sector to offer it. Although funding was linked to the child, the rate of payment was also tied to the level of trained teachers each service employed, hoping to incentivize providers to hire more qualified staff. Linking funding to qualified staff in the market essentially produced a new economic calculation for for-profit providers to work with in order to access government funding. Too few staff and they would lose the financial security of government funding, too many and they may not be able to cover the increased cost of wages in the context of a skills shortage. Finding a balance between labour costs and government income has become central to the diverse financial strategies of for-profit providers after the 20 hours payment, as most childcare centres rely on accessing the maximum government funding as part of their business model. Indicative of this financial reliance, the 2019 ECE Census conducted by the MoE indicated that 95 per cent of childcare centres operated to the 80 per cent+ teacher funding band (MoE, 2019).

Box 4.1: How business models impact engagement with children in services

From my experience as a parent consumer on entering a childcare service, there is increasingly a material difference in the appearance of a community non-profit service and a for-profit service as the market has become more competitive. In general, because of the tendency of non-profits to put revenue back into wages in keeping with a commitment to professionalization of the sector and the benefit of qualified ECE teaching for children's wellbeing, less money tends to be left to invest in the premises (Mitchell, 2019a).

The different financial calculations taken by owner-operators are not solely expressed at a managerial level, but can have a direct impact on the way the care environment is ordered and experienced. From visiting centres, it is evident that there are notable differences in the philosophy and practices of care depending, to some extent, on the kind of financial lens adopted. An example of this was evident from some non-profit services I visited while looking for a childcare option for my own children. A number had adopted an 'attachment based learning' (ABL) approach (Degotardi and Pearson, 2009). This model was much more labour and staff intensive than a typical 'rota' based system, where staff are delegated a set of tasks for the day (for example one staff member on bathroom duties, one on sleep duties and so on). Under the ABL model, children had a key carer and a secondary carer who were responsible for their daily needs, from putting them down for a nap to ensuring they got their food. This system only worked well when staff/child ratios were high, and staff had time to spend with children, something I will consider further in Chapter 6.

While on paper having the majority of childcare centres working to the highest funding band would suggest that a key indicator of quality in the market is being met, this statistic sits in tension with the rise of complaints in the media and within childcare discussion forums about the poor conditions many staff now work in. The on-paper calculation of for-profit providers has been to meet government expectations to be in receipt of the most amount of funding possible, hence the 80 per cent band being the most prevalent. However, in order to pay qualified staff to maintain this funding band under a skills shortage, costs and standards of practice have been significantly lowered in other ways. Although qualified childcare workers do have more mobility in the market due to the skills shortage, finding good working conditions has not been easy, especially in the growing private sector. In keeping with international research, New Zealand analyses suggest that since the 20 hours payment for-profit services are generally more likely to offer fewer professional development opportunities, minimum annual leave and sick days and have higher staff turnover (Mitchell, 2002; NZCER, 2007; Mitchell et al, 2019a). Media reports have also provided anecdotal insights of the ways owner-operators are experimenting within services to access government revenue while remaining compliant. One frequently cited example was centres having the unit manager classified on paper as a teaching staff member, so as to meet government ratios and teaching funding bands, even though they may be primarily occupied with office work (Gerritson, 2018a; Walters, 2020). Given most centres are only visited by the ERO on a three-yearly cycle, it is difficult to pick up such breaches in the system.

Although I focus on the issue of paying labour in this chapter as the key problematic for private sector actors in the current market, it is important to note that remuneration is far from the only criteria of importance to workers in deciding on a 'good' childcare employer. A survey of 4000 ECE teachers by a sector watchdog in November 2020 suggests that a quarter would not send their own children to the centres they were working at due to poor care conditions (Childforum, 2020). The adult:child ratios, size of service, number of children and management of the service are all significant to the experience of workers and to the ability of providers to maintain stable care environments. With this in mind, the remainder of the chapter will consider the strategies of two distinct types of providers which are present in the New Zealand market since the 20 hours payment, childcare corporates and small scale owner-operators, to examine how they secure revenue and address the problem of labour.

Bigger is better? Childcare market consolidation as a financial strategy

> Strong growth and a socially responsible profile have made this [childcare] market attractive for investors and with the market still being highly fragmented, there are still benefits to be gained from consolidation. It also holds the possibility of accretive earnings per share since nurseries are usually worth more in a group than as discreet entities, and there is the chance of outperforming the market by making better commercial decisions. (LaingBuisson, 2019)

The economic assumption of 'bigger is better' is one which increasingly shapes the financial analyses of and consulting interjections into neoliberal childcare markets over the past 20 years. Quotes like this one from a major UK economic consultancy serve to generate a 'regime of truth' around the idea that bigger is better in the world of childcare business. Such a discourse is both destructive and generative in equal measure: it undermines existing practices and business models and lays the terrain for new ways of envisioning and doing childcare. In that sense the discourse of consolidation has performative agency, paving the way to realize that which it describes. I suggest that it is in this light that we have witnessed significant attempts in New Zealand and internationally to consolidate childcare markets, to capitalize on the seemingly vulnerable position of a sector that is discursively understood as fragmented, and all the financial opportunity that that proposes to bring.

Within the context of markets of collective concern, like childcare, the 'bigger is better' discourse tends to be coupled with another potent discourse of being 'too big to fail'. With the rationalization of business operations comes economies of scale, making the work of childcare in an expanding market seem like financial child's play. As the owner of the influential ABC Childcare Australia was quoted as saying, 'this business is a recession proof growth industry' (Fraser, 2004), indicating much about the growing reliance of governments on large for-profit providers like ABC. As egregious as this statement may seem, there is some element of truth in the sense that large scale corporate failure in childcare markets is not an option. As a cautionary tale, the government bailout of ABC Childcare[5] after it went into receivership and the need to keep services solvent for parents while a new buyer was found, speaks to the changing balance of power which is accrued through consolidation (Moss, 2014)[6]. This is particularly the case in sectors which provide services that can (and many say should) be considered as a part of the foundational economy (Foundational Economy Collective, 2018).

Large scale childcare providers take on a diversity of forms, from publicly listed on the stock market to privately owned chains. Moreover, the business status of large childcare organizations is not static, often changing in response to market dynamics. For example, in New Zealand the childcare corporate Kidicorp began as a privately owned chain which floated on the stock market in 2003, was then reprivatized in 2007 only to be controversially registered to operate with charitable status seven years later (Nippert, 2020). This example indicates the ongoing experimental nature of the business of care in New Zealand, in response to increased government spending in the sector after 2008. The diversity of forms of large scale provision has also made the task of defining corporate childcare a challenge, as there can be a very wide set of practices to account for. Attempts to establish some definitional clarity have been context dependent, relating to the size and nature of the market being studied. Sumsion, writing from the highly privatized Australian context, suggests that childcare corporatization is a process borne from 'rapid expansion and escalating market share of childcare services owned and/ or operated for-profit by public companies listed on the [Australian] stock exchange' (Sumsion, 2006: 100). Others take a different approach, focusing instead on the business rationales of the for-profit sector and the corporate logic of profit making, whereby an owner with five or more services could qualify (Farris and Marchetti, 2017). If we take corporatization to be this broader definition then any service with over four centres or with a minimum aggregate capacity of 200 children could be included (Richardson, 2011). With that lens in mind, corporatization can be viewed as a widespread trend in neoliberal childcare markets.

Apart from the administrative benefits of rationalization, ownership of multiple childcare services in the market also increases the potential financial capital at your disposal. Being able to draw on, and leverage from, private equity to access the lending institutions or to generate finance from a stock market flotation, gives a considerable competitive advantage within what are generally understood as fragmented markets. As a New Zealand business commentator noted in national news media, 'Institutional investors such as Beststart Educare [formerly Kidicorp] and the Evolve Education Group are acquiring privately owned businesses to increase their market share, and the financial firepower at their disposal could make it increasingly difficult for smaller operators and investors to compete' (*Business Herald*, 2017). By exercising their financial power in this way, corporates can build up market share quickly, usually by acquiring profitable and well-established services and brands. Indeed, the strategy to consolidate market share through purchasing existing services is a common trend across many neoliberal childcare markets, visible in the US, Australia and the UK, where large companies listed on the stock market are able to obtain capital far beyond what is available to individual centres or even larger community providers to fund their expansion (King and Meagher, 2009; Blackburn, 2013; Lloyd, 2013; Newberry and Brennan, 2013; Moss, 2014; Woodrow and Press, 2018).

Within fragmented childcare markets, where the predominant ownership model is that of the individual owner-operator, the most likely means for consolidation to occur is through a service 'roll up': essentially a process of buying up well performing childcare businesses and merging them under one management and governance structure. Childcare roll ups tend to consist of smaller, individualized owner-operator services, rather than mergers of big companies, although in more advanced financialized contexts (like UK and Australia) there is evidence of this scale of rationalization (Moss, 2014). As an existing provider, the incentive to sell your service can be manifold, but as Press and Woodrow (2009) suggest, the increasing cost of compliance and administration in more regulated contexts pushes many to seek out the management efficiencies offered by corporate ownership. Indeed, as detailed in Chapter 3, some have suggested that the compliance expectations which accompanied the Strategic Plan and the 20 hours payment inadvertently precipitated the sale of childcare businesses, inciting market consolidation (King, 2008).

However, while this seems to make sense from an economic perspective, acquiring and consolidating childcare businesses is not a straightforward process. The financial affordances offered by greater economies of scale in childcare are not a certainty. Although shareholder reports and economic analyses of the industry may suggest that bigger is better for the reasons already discussed, large scale corporatization has actually been a relatively modest trend in advanced markets like the UK and New Zealand to date, when compared with the aged care sector, for example (Blackburn, 2005). The issue at hand is an awareness of what exactly is being purchased. In childcare it is not only the tangible aspects of the business you are buying, like the licence, equipment and related buildings, but also a host of very significant intangible aspects. These are largely based on non-economic attributes, including reputation, trust and rapport with staff and the parent community. In essence, you are also buying the relationships that make the service a success. This is especially pertinent in the case of a competitive, consumer driven market, where parents are incentivized to exercise choice. Bringing diverse services together under one ownership and management structure can also be impeded by the range of pedagogical philosophies which produce diverse ways of practising childcare in the market.[7] Through the analytical lens of SSM, we can see the significant work which is involved in the 'roll up' of services within an existing market. To apply this lens in context, in the next section I offer an analysis of the emergence of New Zealand's second largest corporate, Evolve Education.[8] As a publicly listed company which was established through a service roll up, it offers a pertinent case in which to consider the economic logic of childcare consolidation at work. In this analysis I will explore how its financial strategies developed both in response to the conditions of state-led marketization and the problem of labour in the market.

Childcare financialization: the case of Evolve Education

The New Zealand Government has a strong focus on ensuring New Zealand Children have access to high quality ECE. One of the Government's Better Public Service targets for ECE is that 98% of children starting school in 2016 will have participated in quality ECE. Government expenditure has almost trebled since 2007. ... The ECE market provides Evolve Education with further opportunities to grow its license base and capitalize on the priority ECE is accorded by Government. (Evolve Education, 2015)

Evolve Education made an aggressive entry into the New Zealand childcare market in 2014, when it launched an Initial Public Offer (IPO) for investment to purchase existing childcare services, fully underwritten by international banking giant Goldman Sachs. The IPO raised NZ$132 million, with high competition for shares. Keen to get involved in a seemingly burgeoning market, some large investors only received half of the shares they applied to buy. Indeed, like other successful childcare 'roll ups' in Australia (see Box 4.2) the highly fragmented nature of the New Zealand childcare market suggested clear scope for Evolve to rapidly establish its presence through 'selective acquisitions'.[9] Having access to private equity through the IPO offered them a competitive edge. Openly recognizing the seeming similarities between childcare and other successful care markets, Evolve's new chair told national media that 'ECE has the potential to become just as big a share market success as aged care' (*New Zealand Herald*, 2014). Drawing on the sector knowledge of specialized childcare sales and brokerage companies to seek out well-functioning centres, it undertook an aggressive purchasing strategy of high performing childcare centres across the country. By the end of its first year it had acquired over 100 centres, rapidly making it the second largest for-profit provider in New Zealand.

Box 4.2: Intermarket connections

The Evolve Education childcare roll up was most likely inspired by another similar venture in Queensland, Australia the previous year. Australian company *The Affinity Education Group* owned by the Guiffre family, raised A$81 million to purchase 57 services in Queensland and New South Wales. A promotor and lead advisor to this float was Greg Kern, of the Kern Group. Both he and the Guiffres were instrumental in advising the Evolve bid in New Zealand. They also have a link back into the successful Australian corporate G8 Education. As economist Tim Hunter notes, the day Evolve floated on the exchange was the first day of operation for the company, short-cutting the traditional private equity roll up in which the merged businesses trade for a while before an IPO is made. The upshot is that investors are taking on more risk from the outset and the creators of the roll up get paid out earlier. Evidencing this, for the Kern Group and their related associates, they received 100 per cent return on their investment once Evolve listed on the stock market (Hunter, 2014).

At the time, Evolve's purchasing strategy caused many sector advocates and even some for-profit providers to raise concerns about the inflated amount that was being paid to acquire services. Owner of the largest corporate, Kidicorp, noted the financial volatility of this approach, suggesting that 'They're buying centres at five or six times earnings and putting them on their books at ten times earnings' (Blakie, 2015). This practice served to inflate the value of the newly formed company, with some suggesting it made accessing finance from the lending institutions easier. Yet, an unanticipated outcome of this aggressive purchasing strategy was that it raised interest from other kinds of investors in childcare property, fuelling a host of speculative property practices, some of which I will address in the next chapter. Despite the growing competition from individual mum and dad investors for childcare property, Evolve's prospectus signalled that the financial fire power which the public listing offered allowed them to rapidly achieve the 'benefits of scale' necessary to compete in the market (Evolve Education, 2015). On paper it appeared to be a textbook example of the 'bigger is better' approach to childcare markets.

Indeed, the first shareholder report seemed to give weight to these benefits of scale, noting buoyant returns for shareholders which exceeded initial financial expectations. The first year saw an increase in revenue for newly acquired centres of 14 per cent (equivalent to NZ$26 million), 69 per cent of which came from government funding. Shareholders were also told of a higher-than-average occupancy level of 87 per cent, coupled with a below predicted wage to revenue ratio of 53 per cent. Putting this into context, Penn and Lloyd (2013) suggest that wage revenue for for-profit services is generally not less than 60 per cent. Combined, analysis of the first shareholder report would suggest that reducing the cost of wages within newly acquired services was a key part of the financial strategy under the consolidated structure.

Shareholder reports and accompanying media coverage of Evolve over the next five years show that the company hit choppy financial waters early on. Contrary to its initial report, its 2016 version indicated that the company would have to 'divest' some underperforming centres, as it failed to meet anticipated returns for shareholders that year. Being publicly listed meant that any financial problems were made very evident in the media, and the negative discourse around projected revenue losses directly impacted their stock market position. A change of CEO to someone with direct childcare sector experience was intended to 'restore momentum in the business, and to recover lost ground', assuaging the investor market (Boot, 2017). This did not eventuate, and in 2018 shares fell to 60 per cent of their purchase price, with another failure to meet predicted profits. Under a second change of CEO in less than 12 months, the company posted a NZ$100 million loss, sending the board into crisis mode. Chris Scott, one of the founders of successful Australian education corporate G8 Education, took over the day-to-day running of Evolve after buying a 19 per cent stake during the share price drop in 2018. One of his immediate acts was to appoint other Australian business experts from his previous education venture onto the management team.

Analysis of the financial problems of Evolve gleaned from business media and company reporting to shareholders gives important insights into their business strategy and the calculations they made to access revenue within the conditions of state-led marketization in New Zealand. The first reason the company offered shareholders for their ongoing financial difficulties was the unanticipated challenges of integrating acquired services under one management structure. Having acquired services from across 60 different brands, each with their own philosophy, management structure and manner of operation, 'rolling them up' into a coherent organization was not straight forward. In the process, some services once handed over by original management began to 'underperform' under the new structure. Taking a hard line on these services, the proposed remedy for this underachievement was to performance manage them 'either to get back to performance levels previously achieved, or if that is not able to be achieved, then for divestment to be considered so that our capital can be re-deployed elsewhere' (Evolve Education, 2017: 7). The surprisingly quick pace of action towards these services was shaped in large part by a desire to be seen by shareholders, and the stock market more generally, to be proactively addressing any shortcomings.

By 2018 it was becoming clear that more was afoot than some individual services underperforming. A raft of changes had been made to both the services and the management board, with little improvement to the company balance sheet. Roseanne Graham, CEO in 2018, offered a sober account to shareholders of the failure of the company to produce the anticipated returns.[10] A more serious problem was that parents were leaving Evolve's services in significant numbers since their acquisition. A review of centre occupancy rates showed they had dropped from an initial average rate of 87 per cent in 2015 to 78 per cent in 2018, indicative of endemic problems with the acquired services. While this drop may not sound overly problematic, centres were running on tight margins based on a very specific equation regarding occupancy rates, which meant that even a small drop off in children attending could have significant implications for meeting their profit expectations to investors. Parental dissatisfaction in services was compounded by an especially high staff turnover, recorded in the 2018 Chair's address to the AGM to be one in three staff (Evolve Education, 2018). While worker mobility in the market had increased as a result of the skills shortage, the links between staff turnover and the lower than anticipated wages to revenue ratio in the first year of operation would suggest that changes to working conditions and pay may have precipitated this effect.

According to the 'bigger is better' business model, one significant means of generating increased profits from service consolidation is through generating new efficiencies in the running of the services, such that it is cheaper to meet administration and compliance costs. Conducting in-house research, Evolve found instead that centre managers were overworked due to a lack of centralized systems and supports in an increasingly regulated environment, something which was anticipated to be one of the key benefits of scale from rationalization. The materiality of the services had also been overlooked, and maintenance had declined with services reported to be looking tired and worn. Combined, these findings would suggest that by lifting the managerial gaze off the day-to-day running of services, the company had essentially undermined many of the reasons why these services were successful in the first instance. In 2019, seeking to address these problems, the company restructured its support office, making a cost saving of NZ$3 million and citing 'a key reason for doing this was to focus resources on our centres. We believe that decision making needs to be closer to our centres and our teachers – it is after all our teachers who interact with our families on a day by day basis' (Evolve Education, 2020). One of the highlighted changes at the centre level was the ability for centre managers to establish more 'flexible and responsive' staff rostering as a means of reducing labour costs. What that actually looked like on the ground was unclear, but the tenor of this comment is suggestive of broader trends in the for-profit sector like redeploying trained staff across services in real time to maintain government compliance. As I will discuss in Chapter 6, the integration of childcare management software platforms into the operation of centre-based childcare has greatly facilitated the ability for staff to be moved between centres, ensuring that on paper the right people are in the right place, so compliance with the funding bands can be maintained.

However, while important changes like these were made at the level of centres and the day-to-day running of services, as a highly financialized entity much of the work of improving the financial position of Evolve occurred on paper. In 2018 a three-year action plan was developed to improve the financial position of the company, as a means of being able to access better credit from banks and to build up their credibility among shareholders. The plan sought to 'improve the performance of the 50 weakest centres ... and also negotiate more flexible terms from its lenders – ASB – for the next four quarters, but that is tied to a capital review aimed at getting the firm's debt-to-EBITDA ratio below three' (Sharechat, 2018). Reducing this financial ratio is an important indicator of the financial health of a business to any potential investor or lender, as it indicates the extent to which the company can pay off debts once they are due. The lower the debt-to-EBITDA ratio, the better financially positioned the company is to meet its debt obligations. To achieve this aim, Evolve was recapitalized, effectively selling more shares to generate revenue, which in turn was used to pay off existing debt. In addition, NZ$25 million was earmarked to purchase ten new centres in Australia, as a means to 'diversify and broaden' earnings for the company. As Box 4.2 indicates, links to the Australian childcare market were evident since the initial listing of the company, but the decision to leverage off another buoyant market to support business interests in the New Zealand childcare sector was a new direction within their financial strategy.

While Evolve's shareholder prospectus (Evolve Education, 2019) acknowledges the importance of skilled staff and good working conditions as part of their business model, changes over the last seven years would indicate that labour costs were viewed as a site from which savings could be generated. However, as I have suggested decisions around staffing within the business strategies of for-profit providers is more than simply a case of meeting on-paper funding calculations of rates of trained staff or the number of adults to children. Childcare as a service is heavily reliant on the people, as opposed to *staff*, it employs. As most centre managers will attest, retaining carers who have formed long-term connections to the children in their charge is of paramount importance to their business model, as high staff turnover disrupts the experience for children and their family. Employing qualified staff[11] and offering better working conditions, through lower adult:child ratios, tends to lead to better staff retention.

The case of Evolve Education represents a clear attempt to bring to the fore a childcare business model which benefits from economies of scale in the market. The purchase and consolidation of existing, successful childcare services was viewed as a means of building up market share expeditiously, as this did not require the time lag generally incurred for a new service to become established in the market. This was important in two ways: it allowed the company to enter the market while it was still growing in response to the demand for the 20 hours funding; and allowed shareholders to access a return on investment quickly, from existing services. Yet, the financial advantages of rationalization in childcare markets are not inevitable nor pre-given. In this instance the market conditions since 2010 have meant that the ability to hire and retain qualified staff has become central to the financial calculations of for-profit actors, presenting an unanticipated financial problem for Evolve on entering the market. In response, the company has sought out new means of financializing their work, initially through recapitalization to bring in more equity and recently leveraging off the more buoyant childcare market in Australia.

Borrowing from the future: the financial strategies of small scale providers

> 'I found myself in a position where I didn't want to lose Sheree as a staff member, but she had a lot of personal debt and was looking for a better paid job. All I could do was to bundle up her debts for her so she could pay them back at less interest, as a way of helping her out financially. Luckily it was enough.' (Hilary, childcare centre owner, Auckland)

Although media discourse would suggest that neoliberal childcare markets are on a track towards consolidation, much like other kinds of care markets, in this chapter I argue that this is not an inevitability nor is it the only significant business strategy that can be seen in these markets. While the 'economies of scale' analysis involves a particular configuration of financial actors under one umbrella, small scale providers have developed their own financial strategies and calculations involving a different configuration of actors from those already described. In this section I will explore what this alternative configuration looks like, noting that again the range of financial intermediaries being drawn on have little involvement in the day-to-day business of childcare itself. While the banks and lending institutions remain significant to the financial strategies of small operators, more recently specialized childcare finance companies have emerged with tailored loans to directly offset the problems created by the government funding model. As I will demonstrate, the particularities of state-led marketization, and the nature of the funding model endorsed since 2002, has actually created the space for these new financial actors to emerge.

Despite the inherent tension in for-profit provision to suppress wages as the highest operating cost, this tendency is challenged by the fact that childcare workers are not 'disposable' (Folbre and Nelson, 2000). Individuals matter greatly to the business of childcare. Operating within the 80 per cent+ funding band to access the highest amount of government revenue is one important aspect in keeping childcare centres solvent, but so are parental fees. While the funding regulations do not distinguish between centres based on staff turnover, focusing instead on the average rate of qualified workers in a service during a given time period, *who* the carer is matters to parents and their children. As was discussed through the case of Evolve, downward pressure on wages and working conditions for skilled staff ultimately results in high staff turnover and parent dissatisfaction. Thus, the other side of the business strategy for providers then pertains to the importance of staff stability in order to maintain good, long-term working relationships with parents. Within the conditions of the New Zealand childcare market, how then are services maintaining staff in the context of high labour mobility? While Hilary's account earlier is relatively unique, it is indicative of the extreme measures many owner-operators are going to in the current climate. As media releases from the ECC have noted, a more common way to retain staff has been to increase their wages relative to what could be earned in competing services. As a consequence, they claim that for many for-profit providers wages have become an uncontrollable cost (ECC, 2018). While some services have sought to raise parental fees to offset the extra cost of wages (such as childcare chain Kindercare), for others the strategy has been to financialize: to borrow from future governmental income to pay labour in the present.

The rising cost of wages relative to income has produced a cashflow problem for many small operators. The four-monthly funding payment has set in place a complex business cycle which has disciplined them as calculative agents in particular ways. Indeed, waiting for the bulk payment to arrive from MoE has become a nervous time, as discussed further in Chapter 6. With the intention to explore aspects of the financial wellbeing of the sector over the past decade, in 2019 I conducted a nationwide online survey into the extent to which providers were using short-term finance to meet operating costs.[12] The results mirrored media coverage of the financial pressure on many smaller providers, as they have less access to finance than larger corporates to offset any shortfall in funding, and as the survey indicated they often lack sufficient cash reserves to buffer against fluctuations in income. The survey findings suggested that owner-operators with one service were statistically more likely to have used short-term finance since the introduction of the 20 hours payment, with a quarter stating that they used it three or more times per year during that time. Although banks were primarily used for bridging loans, other sources had also become heavily relied upon, like family and personal savings, and more recently childcare finance companies. Within the research a much greater proportion of private providers had used short-term finance (65 per cent), irrespective of whether they were located in an urban or rural location, indicating the extent to which this was linked to structural issues within the sector. Perhaps not surprisingly, 71 per cent of those who used short-term finance also stated they had no cash reserves.

While the emergence of childcare finance companies can be interpreted as a response to for-profit providers becoming over-extended in the market, this does not account for their rapid expansion in the face of other, more traditional forms of finance, like the banks. Again, to explain why this source of finance has gained traction, it is important to view it in relation to the funding conditions of state-led marketization. By the time of writing in 2021, there were three specialized finance companies offering loans tailored specifically to childcare providers to smooth cashflow 'bumpiness' between bulk payments (see Box 4.3). The bulk funding model, and the business cycle that providers are wedded to, has not only punctuated their cashflow in particular ways but it has also generated a window of opportunity for new finance companies to meet the financial problems being created by the funding structure. The quarterly funding horizon, where payment comes through based on the enrolment rates over the last four months, leaves much room for financial miscalculation on the part of the owner-operator. This is especially pertinent given that government funding currently accounts for up to 70 per cent of the income of childcare centres. Survey responses noted heightened levels of stress and anxiety among senior staff and owners in the month leading up to the bulk funding payment, as an indicator of the increasingly tight margins to which they were working and the challenges of maintaining cashflow.

Box 4.3: Ease your finance concerns!

We know Finance and we know Childcare. We know the financial stress involved when child numbers fluctuate, or unexpected costs arise before your funding comes in. We have built our company from the ground up specifically to solve your cash flow problems. We're the largest specialist loan provider to the Childcare industry in New Zealand. We've seen it all in Childcare, the stress, the sleepless nights, the angry creditors, the frustration from bankers.

Source: advert from a childcare finance company

The need for short-term loans to meet operating costs has become relatively common place, particularly among small scale owner-operators. While findings of the Financial Wellbeing Survey suggest that most providers still turn in the first instance to their banks for such loans, the increased frequency of this practice and the amounts required mean that over time they have had to look elsewhere. A primary selling point of the childcare finance companies is that the traditional lending institutions fail to understand the nature of the childcare business model and uniqueness of the funding cycle. When asked to elaborate further, one finance company manager responded:

'There is a fundamental lack of understanding by accountants and bankers of the nature of childcare as a business. This is not helped by the inability of providers to produce a convincing report for the banks so as to evaluate their application. No indication of the risks identified and how they will mitigate them, of the projections for income etc. A good loan officer would go out to the service and try to understand better the nature of the business, and work with them to co-produce the application so that the credit advisor might approve it. Most don't. That's where we come in.'

Indeed, in a follow-up interview in 2019, four years after the first, the same company manager stated that their business was booming in the interim period, with at least a 50 per cent increase in loan requests year on year during that time. Another important difference they noted during that four-year period was an increase in the average volume of funds borrowed per client. However, as short-term cashflow loans, there is also an acceptance among lenders that their clients generally do not have good credit relationships with their banking institution, which is why they have turned to them. As was admitted by another company manager, "these loans are usually when they service cannot access the traditional lending facilities, either through not being able to put together a convincing application or because they have used up their credit at the banks and have maxed out other options", suggesting the potentially desperate point at which providers would turn to short-term lenders.

Despite acknowledging that providers using their loan services often have poor credit relationships with their lending institutions, finance company managers viewed lending to the sector as relatively low risk. In direct comparison to the banks, having a strong sense of the childcare business model and the relationship of for-profit providers to government funding allowed these finance companies to devise a lending structure that minimized their risk. Covering up to 70 per cent of the costs of centre-based care, the nature of the MoE funding system largely determines how financial risk is perceived by providers and funders, and ultimately minimized. As clearly described on the finance company webpages, the funding payment from MoE *is* the security required to make this kind of lending relatively low risk. Indeed, childcare lenders only grant loans to services in receipt of government funding. After filling in a short application form (estimated 5–10 minutes) you can be loaned up to 60 per cent of your anticipated next bulk funding payment up to a maximum of NZ$500,000, based on an average of your last three payments. Twenty-five per cent of this money is a 'wash up' from the previous quarter once the actual number of children in your care over that time is confirmed. This income is certain, even if there are major problems with the service, thus greatly minimizing chances of services defaulting on their loans. The loan period is short, and payment is taken directly from the incoming bulk funding. The repayment fee on loans varied between 7.5 per cent and 9.5 per cent depending on how early on in the funding cycle the loan was sought. To that extent, lenders acknowledged that these loans were not cheap, and were rather a 'loan of last resort' than the first port of call for any service.

New Zealand is not unique in the creation of these kinds of financial intermediaries. An online search of the UK childcare sector brings up similar finance companies, although they advertise to provide loans for buying, updating and expanding capital infrastructure, reflective of the different market conditions. By contrast, New Zealand finance companies explicitly stated they were not for this purpose, with one interviewee suggesting that

> 'we had been offering loans for 2 months, but providers were using them for reasons other than to meet cash flow issues. They were using them as deposits for new centres so they could make an application for bank funding or to extend centres by placing deposits on contractors for building work. This is not what our loans are primarily intended for as it's too risky for us.'

Returning to the key business problem of labour in the New Zealand market, where wages are seen as an 'uncontrollable cost', accessing finance to pay and top up wages is now the primary reason given for seeking short-term loans. While this is not a sustainable practice, and ultimately the ongoing cost of wages will have to be sought elsewhere, it did buffer providers against fluctuations in staffing costs between bulk payments, and as Hilary's narrative suggested, potentially retain staff in a competitive labour market. Interviewees also recounted stories of loans being used to 'poach' staff from neighbouring centres, particularly in very competitive urban contexts. Others were using the borrowed money to top up staff wages, as a disincentive to look elsewhere for work.

In essence the short-term lending process is allowing providers to make calculated financial decisions around retaining and paying staff, by allowing them to borrow into the future against expected funding from government. These lenders are now an increasingly important part of the network of financial actors that enable the calculative agency of small scale providers. Given the significance of bulk funding and the 20 hours payment to reducing the cost of care for working families, there is a certain political 'lock-in' to this funding ensuring it will continue. However, for providers to borrow into the future with any certainty they need to be relatively secure in the knowledge that their enrolment rates will not have significantly fluctuated in the time between payments. This certainty is hard to establish in childcare, as a highly volatile business in which parents can take their children out of care for a range of reasons. Indeed, as I will discuss in Chapter 8, the economic crisis arising from the COVID-19 pandemic has stymied any sense of stability for providers in the market, as families have had to dramatically rethink their childcare needs. Nevertheless, the financialization of small owner-operators, where money is accessed today based on future expected revenue, gives an indication of the fragility of the business models emerging in the current market. Some childcare lenders have recognized that their booming business over the past five years is indicative of a deepening problem in the for-profit childcare sector, with some now offering business mentorship to owner-managers who are repeat loan customers, one suggesting that "if they aren't being really smart, and running all their efficiencies, they will run into financial trouble pretty quickly".

Conclusion

Set within the context of the trend towards privatization in neoliberal childcare markets, this chapter has sought to offer two key insights. Firstly, in order to better capture the diversity of the for-profit sector which is emerging in response to government funding of childcare, we need to understand the different kinds of business strategies and financial calculations which are being adopted by these actors to access funding. How they operate does not take place in a social or moral vacuum, in the sense that their calculative agency in the market is shaped by the broader conditions of state-led marketization. This chapter has sought to explore the complex financial strategies and related fragility of the for-profit sector as a means of highlighting the new axes of instability in the market sector. Taking a relational approach to understanding the growth of the for-profit sector, which has been identified in existing literature as causing the most volatility in childcare markets (Bushouse, 2008), we can see how market dynamics are not solely attributable to the fact that these services are orientated to make a profit per se. Instead, it opens out the analysis to consider how these diverse business strategies are developed within the conditions of the market assemblage, but also in relation to the business strategies and interests of other kinds of actors (like the banks, investors or finance companies).

Building on this relational approach to the market, the second insight of this chapter pertains to the configuration of other financial actors which are central to the business strategies of both large and small scale operators. Seeking out access to high amounts of finance through private equity and lending institutions in order to achieve economies of scale is one response to state-led marketization that we can see occurring the market, but there are others. Tracing the work of small scale owner-operators, we can see different strategies being devised, approaches which also involve the use of finance, but which draw on a different configuration of financial actors. While bridging loans from lending institution remained commonplace, for many smaller operators borrowing from specialized childcare loan companies has become a crucial part in their financial strategies. Through the lending practices of these companies, services are able to leverage off future enrolments and ultimately government income. In both the cases of private equity and shareholder investment, and childcare finance companies, it is the government's financial and political commitment to maintaining the childcare market that has opened the space for these new financial actors to emerge.

Tracing the ebb and flow of the childcare market thus far, one of the most revealing aspects of market making is that what eventuates is often far removed from what was planned, as the work of the childcare finance companies documented in this chapter indicates. Overflows from the market 'blueprints' are the norm, rather than the exception. In the next two substantive chapters I take this idea further to examine how childcare markets become entangled over time with other kinds of markets and market actors, namely the property investment market and the software market, to the extent that they have become infrastructural to childcare itself. Spurred on by the privatization of the childcare sector in the wake of the 20 hours payment, and keen to find low-risk sources of investment, in the next chapter I will explore how investors have taken an interest in childcare property to derive value from the capital assets of the sector, rather than the care of children, as alternate means of accessing government revenue.

5

The Childcare Property Investment Market

It goes without saying that childcare centre investment has
become a must consider commodity of the more astute investor
in recent times.

Savills News Australia, 26 July 2016

In the previous chapters I explored what state-led marketization looks
like at its core. This work detailed the active strategies of the state in
the formation of key calculative agencies (parent consumers, workers
and providers), the related attempts to pacify childcare as a commodity
purchased in the emergent market and the financial strategies of for-profit
providers in response to state-led marketization. The significant increase of
government spending on childcare, particularly through demand side funding
mechanisms, has been argued to incite the interest of for-profit providers,
to the detriment of the quality of care in the market. However, as more
watchful commentators of neoliberal childcare markets have noted (Mitchell,
2013; Penn, 2013; Moss, 2014), private providers are not the only set of
for-profit interests now involved. At the margins of these commentaries,
it is possible to find property speculators and investors among others. The
presence of these seemingly peripheral actors is an additional signal of the
burgeoning desire to find new ways of extracting revenue from what has
become a government funded sector.

In this, and the final empirical chapter, I will consider in more detail the
engagement of what are seemingly tangential actors to the marketization
of childcare. As the first of those two chapters, the focus here will be on
the work of childcare property sales experts and investors in the wake of
the 20 hours payment. In tracing the work of these actors, I will highlight
the changing understanding of childcare property from a crucial part of the
work of care, to a lucrative investment asset for financial actors with little
knowledge, or indeed interest, in the daily practice of care. As a direct result

of state-led marketization, the property assets of care services are being viewed as having 'latent' potential which can be unlocked through assetization, changing the view of childcare property from a building to an asset in an investment portfolio. New Zealand is not unique in this trend. Childcare property investment has become a burgeoning part of the 'alternative real estate' markets of the UK (Penn, 2013; Christie and Co., 2019) and to a greater degree Australia[1] (Newell and Marzuki, 2019). To that end an Australian property report made the claim that childcare was the fastest growing commercial real estate investment class in 2017, the new 'golden child' for investors (Shield, 2017).[2] As discussed in Chapter 1, Australia and the UK have also developed a government funded childcare market over the past 20 years, which has led to a boom in parental demand for childcare services and an exponential growth in private for-profit providers during this time (Lloyd and Penn, 2013).

This chapter reinforces the conceptual claim of the book that childcare markets are not discrete, bounded entities and we should not study them as such. As socio-technical assemblages, childcare markets intersect with other markets, in this case the property market, in complex and unanticipated ways. Focusing on these market intersections shows the challenges of state-led marketization, as the childcare market becomes shaped by processes and logics rarely within the purview of the state. Building on this provocation, I argue that investor interest in childcare property was not the result of an economic problem in the childcare market, leading to the financial need for providers to sell capital assets to remain solvent. Rather in the New Zealand context it resulted from an alignment of economic rationales across the two markets: one of private providers looking to release equity to expand in the market; and the other a demand for low-risk property investment options in a burgeoning property market, to which childcare property became an attractive solution. The financialization of the New Zealand economy, a trend advanced in the wake of the global financial crisis, has led to increasing speculation in secondary circuits of capital derived from asset ownership and rentiership. Within this changing political economic context, the built infrastructure of the childcare sector has been hotly sought after by investors to derive income as passive proprietors through renting premises to childcare providers. Tracing this process, I show how the conditions of rentiership have significant implications for the way childcare is provided, and the future sustainability of the sector. Consequently, I argue that these market actors are not solely peripheral, or indeed parasitical, to the childcare market, but increasingly *infrastructural* in their involvement.

The chapter will proceed as follows. Firstly, I will consider the limitations of researching the childcare property market, as it exists outside the purview of the state and as such reflects a political blind spot for most governments. I pay specific attention to the discursive and performative work of repositioning childcare property as a potential asset, through analysis of the role of specialized childcare property specialists. The New Zealand childcare property market has grown since 2012 in line with the advanced privatization of the sector. Indicative of the specific conditions of this market, the primary investor subject in question is that of the 'mum and dad' investor. I will consider what the childcare market offers to these investors, and the impact they are having on the sector. With a particular focus on the urban childcare property market then, this chapter asks:

- Why has childcare property become a site of speculation and investment?
- What actors are involved in reframing childcare centre buildings into property assets?
- And what are the implications for the sustainability of private providers operating under rental conditions?

Researching a governmental blind spot

Capturing the extent of property investment and rentiership practices in the childcare sector was challenging, illustrating the political blind spot which exists around for-profit childcare in New Zealand. Within the initial market framing in the late 1980s, increasing the presence of the private sector was an assumed answer to the governmental problem of rising capital infrastructure demands. Yet, while the capital resources of the private sector have been necessary to meet the ambitions of state-led marketization, an acknowledged blind spot around this infrastructure has existed since the initial framing of the market, when Prime Minister Lange made it evident that 'the ownership of the land and the buildings is a matter of sublime indifference to the Government' (Lange, 1988: 8230). To that end no data has been collected by the MoE on the extent of for-profit services operating under rental conditions. However, from my research I have a working estimate of between 40 and 50 per cent by 2019.[3] This estimate is based on responses to the ECE Financial Wellbeing Survey, in which participants were asked to indicate if they rented or owned their premises, coupled with interviews with childcare property specialists, in whose interest it is to have an informed sense of this information.

Much of the potential 'data' on the property investment space is fleeting and somewhat ephemeral, housed in the domains of newspaper supplements, online advertisements and the like. As a result, the empirical material in this chapter is drawn from a range of sources. The primary source data came from analysis of 47 online childcare sales documents, property advertisements and news articles in national and the regional papers between 2012 and 2018, at the point when childcare property was gaining most attention in the print and online media. 2012 was chosen as a starting point for analysis as it was noted that childcare property sales advertisements had begun to change from being targeted towards the 'users' (the licensees) to towards property investors with an emphasis on the passive nature of childcare property investment. Box 5.1 gives an example of the headlines and the tone of the marketing material during this time. Extended articles about why childcare property was a good investment were also apparent in the property media from 2012. Approximately two-thirds of the analysed advertisements were for childcare property in urban centres, with Auckland holding prominence. In terms of my analysis, I understood this media as a having an active, performative role in creating the childcare property market.

Box 5.1: Creating a market in childcare sales

'Booming Childcare Sector Draws Investors', *New Zealand Herald*, 4 February 2017
'Childcare Centres a Growth Investment', Colliers International Online, 4 July 2017
'Why Childcare is the Next Asset Class to Watch', *Property Observer*, 4 July 2017
'Childcare Property, Investment that Adds Up', *New Zealand Herald*, 18 July 2017

Research drawn on in the following sections also derives from a set of interview questions pertaining to the nature of the childcare property sales and investment space, its framing and justification as a 'real estate asset class', and potential issues on the horizon for the childcare property market. Interviewees who had used advertising media in their work were asked to reflect on the role and importance of these media in fostering the childcare property investment space, as well as their own role in fuelling the childcare property sales market. Data from an online nationwide ECE Financial Wellbeing Survey was also drawn on to help evidence increasing points of financial tension among childcare providers over the previous three years (2016–2019), during which time participation rates in services had begun to drop.

Property investment and the problem of finance

The story of investor activity into childcare property in Aotearoa New Zealand goes hand in hand with the privatization of the sector. State-led marketization, discussed in Chapter 3, boosted business confidence and led to a significant increase in private for-profit providers with the number of new childcare centres growing by almost 30 per cent between 2007 and

Table 5.1: Government funding of childcare by sector type, 2008–2018

	Private for-profit		Community non-profit	
Year	NZ$	Enrolments	NZ$	Enrolments
2008/09	505,569,999	73,848	521,218,416	106,435
2009/10	602,379,111	82,580	566,945,873	105,756
2010/11	664,934,603	87,707	590,969,359	105,834
2011/12	712,906,622	92,218	592,907,640	103,789
2012/13	777,035,095	98,863	611,753,161	101,491
2013/14	860,191,945	103,956	648,502,374	95,546
2014/15	942,711,425	106,669	664,978,428	91,722
2015/16	1,021,793,334	110,451	677,139,403	90,810
2016/17	1,070,703,823	113,505	683,082,610	88,900
2017/18	1,123,185,318	116,909	682,494,513	83,355

Source: derived from MoE Education Counts Funding Datasets, 2008–2018

2018 (MoE, 2019). Table 5.1 illustrates this growth with regards to the level of government funding now channelled to private for-profit providers, who occupy 60 per cent of the New Zealand market at the time of writing. At present, government funding accounts for up to 70 per cent of the operating costs of childcare centres, illustrating the extent to which it has become a state backed business opportunity (MoE, 2019). The greater Auckland region holds the largest proportion of childcare providers and the greatest concentration of for-profit provision (Gallagher, 2017), in part accounting for its prominence in the analysed property advertisements.

While the sale of childcare property is not new, what is distinctive since 2012 has been the extent of the demand for childcare property, particularly within New Zealand's urban centres. As evidenced by Table 5.1, it aligns with the point at which private sector involvement also began to grow in the market. From the introduction of the 20 hours payment in 2008, until participation rates of children began to plateau in 2017, the business of childcare attracted considerable interest from the for-profit sector (Kett, 2017). Although Chapter 4 highlighted finance as a pressing issue for the for-profit sector, in light of the funding freeze and labour shortage, the full impacts of this did not manifest until well into the 2010s, by which time there had been a flurry of activity to capitalize on the 20 hours payment. While this may seem to run counter to the analysis of financial strife presented in Chapter 4, needless to say that private providers do not always approach the market in economically risk averse ways. As discussed in Chapter 4, there was a notable change in the business models of some private providers, as economic actors, who saw an opportunity to best meet the changing market conditions through service consolidation. As one property broker explained when asked about the property he typically sells, "The single operator model is a dying breed at the moment. You need to have at least two to five centres, in cities certainly, to make it financially viable". The outcome has been a desire among many existing providers to release equity from the sale of their childcare property, so that they can establish more childcare businesses to benefit from increased government funding. As I will discuss in the next chapter, this process of business extension and consolidation was aided by the large scale introduction of childcare management software to centre-based care at the same time.

The rise in property investor interest, along with a desire among providers to release equity in order to open more services, precipitated a relatively swift change in property ownership of a significant portion of the for-profit childcare sector. For many providers this occurred relatively expeditiously through a 'vendor leaseback' property arrangement where services were maintained as a going concern. As I discuss later in the chapter, much of the work of childcare sales brokerage specialists during this period involved selling childcare property under the radar to investors, so as to not alarm parents using the service. A similar trend of vendor leaseback has been noted by early years expert Helen Penn in the UK (2011). Indeed, as urban theorists Aalbers et al suggest, the story of property assetization can be one of 'opportunity rather than constraints' (2017: 574). That is to say, it has not tended to be financial constraint which has led to property being sold by providers, but rather to release equity in order to extend to meet rising demand.

While the desire to sell childcare property may have been present as a result of the specificities of state-led marketization and the increase in funding, in itself this does not account for the rise in property investor interest in the sector. Some understanding of the particularity of the property investment market is necessary to explain why childcare property has become of interest at this point in time. Unlike Australia and the UK,[4] large scale investment vehicles like Real Estate Investment Trusts (REITS) for childcare property investment have not been common in New Zealand. In the absence of REITS or other large investment vehicles, the primary route for anyone wanting to invest has been through purchasing property for rent or leaseback as part of an individualized investment portfolio. Consequently, childcare property investment has been driven by another kind of investor subject, known colloquially as 'mum and dad' investors. The term 'mum and dad' investor was favoured by Prime Minister Sir John Key, in office from 2009 to 2016, in the lead up to selling off 49 per cent ownership of four state owned energy companies in 2012. As part of the political discourse justifying that particular wave of privatization, he encouraged 'ordinary New Zealanders' to take ownership of their country's infrastructure assets by buying shares, arguing a more democratic community ownership model would be possible.[5] However, this call to invest is part of a much longer history of a middle class investor culture in New Zealand during the 1980s and 90s as a result of the neoliberalization of the economy[6] and the change in asset-based wealth during this time (Broome, 2009). Reliance on property investment over other forms of speculation was compounded by the effects of the 1987 stock market crash, which resonated particularly badly in New Zealand. A boom in house market prices from 2002 to 2007, whereby housing prices almost doubled nationally, fuelled strong conditions for property speculation (Murphy, 2011). This has been particularly pronounced for Auckland, the largest city accommodating 30 per cent of the population, where the average price for a standalone house went from NZ$900,000 in 2010 to almost NZ$1.4 million in 2016 (*New Zealand Herald*, 2016).

However, as critics have noted much of the wealth accrued during this time went to those of the 'baby boomer'[7] generation, many of whom already had access to the property ladder by the time property prices started to rise. Unlike other parts of the world, New Zealand was relatively insulated from the global financial crisis and experienced a minimal drop in house price values (Murphy, 2011). In 2014, 20 per cent of participants in a national household financial survey reported investing in real property; the largest proportion of these were mortgaged investors with two or three properties (Commission for Financial Capability, 2014). That said, it is undoubtedly not the case that these investors are ordinary New Zealanders, as the moniker of 'mum and dad' would suggest (Raschbrooke et al, 2017). Analysis of the childcare property advertisements for Auckland in particular suggest that the average price for purchasing a childcare investment property in the region by 2014 was around NZ$1 million. As the property sales agents I interviewed pointed out, the investors they were primarily targeting did not want to invest more than NZ$1.5 million in a single investment, after which it became too financially risky for their portfolios. In cities like Auckland, this price range has tended to equate to childcare property which has been created from converted residential buildings,[8] rather than new-build properties which typically command a much higher price. As was noted by a property broker during an interview, "a childcare centre is at a price point that mums and dads can afford, and therefore they value very highly because there's a lot of competition to buy them". It is here that we can see how the economic logics of the childcare market and the property investment market have intersected since 2012.

Although childcare property investment is a recent trend, it is important to note that since 2017 the investment space has already begun to diversify with the emergence of some REITS.[9] Investment practices look different under these investment vehicles, as investors derive income through being shareholders in the ownership of a portfolio of childcare buildings rather than as individualized proprietors. A change in investor subject has also become evident in media coverage of childcare sales, as illustrated in more recent advertisement:

> The PMG Direct Childcare Fund contributes to the education of young New Zealanders through the acquisition of recently built, quality childcare centres. It is an example of the diversity of choice we offer our investors. PMG Direct Childcare Fund provides a secure and stable income for investors thanks to the long-term leases of the experienced childcare operators running these centres.

As detailed in Chapter 3, by 2017 the childcare market was understood to have 'peaked' with 95 per cent of children having access to some form of childcare before school. Within this context, property investment has turned towards new-build premises, generally located in urban areas where there is an anticipated population growth (such as new suburbs). The childcare properties are built and managed by the property fund, and run by established tenanted childcare providers, adding further complexity to the financialization of the sector.

Childcare property: from building to asset

Like the childcare market itself, creating the childcare property investment market required considerable effort, involving a range of different actors and calculating agency. While growth in demand for childcare, coupled with the security of government funding for the sector, has undoubtedly been an important aspect driving the property investment market, making childcare property 'investable' has also involved a change in the social relations of childcare property ownership (Sayer, 2020). Focusing on the social relations of property enables us to consider what kinds of discursive work has taken place to change the understanding of childcare property from the building in which children are educated and cared for, to being viewed as an asset in an investor portfolio. The involvement of different forms of expertise, like property consultants, valuers, and sales agents, has been crucial to this discursive shift. Their description of childcare property for sale is not neutral: it is performative in the sense that they create that which they describe and in so doing make new (property) worlds possible (Mackenzie et al, 2007). This performative work is central to creating the necessary separation of childcare property from the practice of care, which ultimately allows for assetization to occur.

A significant part of the constitutive work of property specialists was conducted through the different forms of online and print advertising media they used as a means of aligning interests around childcare property (see for example Box 5.1). As one broker commented,

'I have been working hard to let people know just how good childcare property is from an investment point of view. I spend a lot on media, print and social, but it's paying off. I have a steady stream of potential investors and buyers on my books now, waiting for a good opportunity to come up.'

Evidencing the surge in investment interest, the labelling of childcare as a 'real estate asset class' began to appear in the New Zealand media around 2014, reflecting a similar trend which had been evident in Australia for some time (Colliers International, 2016). The characteristics of this new property asset class were advertised to be high yields relative to other commercial investments, low financial risk, with long-term tenancy agreements and in a sector backed by substantial government funding for the foreseeable future (Bell, 2017). As Ouma (2020) has illustrated through his work on assetization in the agriculture sector, categorizing something as an asset class is an important performative step in the creation of the investor market as it allows potential investors to locate new types of property within their wider investment portfolio. Indicative of this, one sales representative stated

'well, investors need to diversify, to split the risk, right. Calling it an investment class lets them understand what a childcare property could mean for their portfolios and their return on investment. They're not just investing on a fad, but in something which will be around for a while. I think of it just as a tool to help people understand their different investment interests.'

While the work of property agents has been necessary to enable childcare property investment to occur, at the same time their work is inherently relational within the property market. To that end they are embedded in a range of economic networks involving, among others, financial institutions, all of which need to be brought to view childcare property as an investment. The lending institutions were referred to at various points by all interviewees as having the power to either facilitate or stymie the embryonic property market they were trying to create. As a consequence, property specialists also saw it as part of their work to effectively persuade lenders that childcare property was legitimate in investment terms. As a specialist builder commented:

Interviewee: It's been interesting to watch how much information the banks have required to lend on a childcare property

Interviewer: over the last few years. At first it was really detailed, like information about the licensee, the size and type of the business, its income and all of that, alongside information about the building itself and its rental return. Now it's a lot less.

Interviewer: Why do you think that is?

Interviewee: Well, it's partly the softer climate for getting loans, but also I think that childcare is now more recognizable as a legitimate investment than it was even five years ago.

Attendance by sales agents and brokers at industry events, like expos, gave them the opportunity to speak with loan specialists from the various banks who were in attendance to build up their industry knowledge. This was viewed as a key space in which to persuade bank representatives of the immanent financial potential of childcare property. As such they envisioned themselves as 'educators' of future property investment trends, one commenting that

> 'the banks are getting presented with all sorts of propositions, right. They don't necessarily understand the ins and outs of every one, so they have to reach out to sector contacts to find out more. I like to keep myself involved by offering the sector information, like for childcare. It's in my interest to know that they are thinking too, don't forget.'

Childcare property specialists also shaped the investment space through their daily practices of valuing and priming childcare property for sale. This economizing work involved on-the-ground knowledge of the specific locations, clients and businesses they were trying to sell. Such local knowledge became especially important when assessing risk for prospective buyers, as I will discuss further in the next section. As was described by one property broker before an interview:

> 'I spent the weekend in [a medium sized city] looking over two potential properties for sale. It takes a long time and quite a lot of work to get to know the properties or businesses you are selling. You look from top to bottom, then over the books as such. I need to know as much as possible so I can find the right buyer.'

Their relational work was crucial for matching potential buyers and sellers, and aligning the interest of different parties in an expeditious manner. For services which are a going concern, licensees generally sell the property without parents knowing as it can cause anxiety among the parent body about changes (such as increased fees). In these instances, sales are conducted privately through brokers. Brokers and sales specialists spoke of the benefit in having a database of potential investor buyers in the hundreds to work from, which they suggested in itself was a productive artefact used in conversation to generate interest as it gave the impression to prospective investors that they may lose out if they did not act when an opportunity arose. Having a raft of specialized childcare property sales agents, who were networked to both the lending institutions and an established base of potential investors, has undoubtedly been a significant part in the relatively rapid growth of the childcare property market.

However, the structure of the childcare market, discussed in Chapter 4, also shaped how investment opportunities were viewed by property specialists and investors alike. The particularities of the childcare sector in New Zealand are such that it remains highly 'fragmented'. In effect, this meant that childcare property was more likely being sold as a single sited investment opportunity, rather than a suite of services. As a consequence, interviewees stated that these kinds of investments were most readily purchased by individualized 'mum and dad' investors or sometimes family trusts. For the most part these investors tended to be passive, with little direct involvement in the day-to-day running of services. As an Auckland based sales agent explained:

'I would say 90 per cent of our investors are passive investors ... they're thinking look I just want to buy an investment with a long-term lease in place and then all I need to do is just collect the rent and there's nothing much I need to worry about. ... The thing is, once these investors buy them, they don't come back onto the market again for a long time. They hold onto them.'

The particularities of the investor subject being imagined matters to how childcare property is being marketed and for how ownership of the capital infrastructure of the childcare sector is being reconfigured. For example, Horton (2019) suggests that there was a faster, five- to seven-year investment turnaround among institutional investors in her study of the aged care sector, as they were focused on restructuring and selling on assets to realize profits for shareholders. As a point of difference, the individualized investors in this research were attracted by the long-term investment opportunity childcare property offered. In order to gain the benefit of the investment in terms of rental return (which is around 6–10 per cent per annum) but to also benefit from capital gains, property specialists advised investors to hold onto properties for up to 15 years. Thus, to understand the particular dynamics of childcare property investment, it is important to consider the type of investor subject being imagined and the differing temporalities on which they are operating (Konings, 2018), as it has direct implications for how restructuring happens in place.

Rentiership and the cost of care

While there are financial benefits to ownership of property in New Zealand purely from the perspective of capital gains, childcare property is also anticipated to produce an ongoing return on investment from rentiership. As such, examining the legal, social and economic relations which underlie the particular form of rentiership at work in the market offers a point from which to consider the complex ways that childcare property investors intersect and shape the work of childcare. Here again we see the productive work of the socio-technical, through the use of formulae which, over time, have black boxed the rental process out of public and governmental scrutiny. The creation of a rental formula specifically for childcare property is relatively recent, brought about by a perceived 'failure' of property valuers to apprehend childcare as a business and the nature of childcare property as distinct from other types of commercial property. Interviewees referred to the traction the new formula had gained among childcare property experts, which had been designed by one of the research participants, as being more technically in tune with the differentiated business landscape of for-profit providers. While ongoing government funding makes the business of childcare appear relatively low risk and confers investor confidence, the new formula placed emphasis instead on the financial contribution of parents through fees as the basis of calculating rent. Over the past 20 years there has been a shift from deriving rental rates as a set figure per year, based on overall income of a service, to "looking at the direct relationship between parental fees, what they can afford to pay, and the actual rent to be charged" (John, childcare property sales expert). Rent in this case is calculated in relation to the financial elasticity of parent income to meet the rising costs of care. The higher the perceived socioeconomic status of the parent community that the centre serves, the higher the rental rates to be charged. In that sense the conditions of the rental system have a direct impact on the rising costs of care for parents in the market.

However, in more competitive locations, where parents have alternative care services to choose from, or if assumptions about the capacity of parents to meet rising fees is incorrect, increased rent payments become absorbed by providers in two ways. The first relates to the rate at which the rent is estimated in relation to the financial ceiling of parental fees. The rental formula is based on an estimated rate per child per week, purportedly acknowledging the socioeconomic position of the parental community using the service. This rate can range from NZ$40 in lower socioeconomic communities to an upper limit of NZ$65 per child per week in more affluent locations. However, if the rate per child is set too high, services may not be able to recoup enough through parental fees to meet it, producing a financial shortfall. As Mark, a property surveyor described it:

'So in some of the very best ritzy suburbs in Auckland, where the parents truly are paying a lot, they're paying NZ$500 plus a week. For those suburbs where the parents can afford to pay that, you could have rent easily set at NZ$55–65 a child, per week. For a centre with a 100 kids, it would be 100 x 55 x 52 weeks, that NZ$286,000 of rent per year. And so consequently that's a fair rent. Now where you come unstuck is if you have a rent which is NZ$52–53 a child and it's in an average suburb where the parent fees are only NZ$250 a week. Then rent is too high to be sustainable.'

The second problematic aspect of the formula is that it calculates rent on full occupancy. Rent is estimated based on the number of children the service is licensed for, rather than actual enrolments. In a competitive market, this heightens the challenge for providers to continue to fill vacated childcare places. For many early childhood advocates, the pressure to maintain occupancy rates is reflected in increased evidence of services offering a range of 'extras' to entice parents, like food and nappies, while cutting more expensive wage costs through having higher adult:child ratios for example.

While the way rent is calculated can pose immediate financial problems for providers, the longer schedule of rent reviews adds another layer of pressure. Guided by commercial rental law,[10] childcare lease agreements have scripted into them a schedule of rental review to ensure that rates are keeping pace with inflation and the Consumer Price Index (CPI). In theory this process offers a form of protection for renters, as well as keeping pace with investment earnings for property owners. If rent is deemed to be too high, as the result of an economic downturn for example, then it could be reduced through the review. As such, providers can call forward a review if they felt they were being overcharged. However, this is a risky strategy as there is no guarantee that their rent will not increase rather than decrease as a result. Over the duration of this research the New Zealand economy had been performing strongly, with unemployment dropping and demand for childcare relatively stable, meaning that rent reviews tended to favour the interests of investors as property owners, with rents increasing rather than decreasing. Rental increases in line with CPI in New Zealand tend to be locked into a two-year cycle, with a separate market rent review every three to five years. Being subject to this review process can have significant impacts on childcare providers, as the cumulative amount of rent paid over the course of a lease agreement builds up over time. As a childcare property consultant contextualized it:

'Well for argument's sake, if you work out NZ$60 per child and then with the CPI or rent review at 3 per cent per annum, then you know that's a 30 per cent to 40 per cent increase in 10 years on your rent. So, rents typically used to be 12 to 15 per cent of the turnover of a centre, and now with the formula and the review processes we're starting to see them above 20 per cent. It's scary where it's going and like a lot of small businesses, people just assume that tomorrow's going to be the same as it is today, and in childcare it's not.'

This section has sought to give insight into the increasing complexity of the property investment and rentiership relations now visible in the for-profit childcare sector. The discursive reframing of childcare buildings as an asset in an investment portfolio is an important part in changing the social relations around childcare property, but it is only one part in the creation of the investment market. As I have shown, the investment market has also required investors, and other notable actors like the banks, to view childcare property in financially calculable ways in order to see where they can derive a profit. We can see this evidenced most clearly through the conditions of rentiership which have emerged in the market, whereby providers in rental situations are working under unsustainable annual rates of increase. An expected market response to these challenging rental conditions would be to relocate to another premise, in the hope that rental conditions would be more favourable or that the business would be better able to sustain the rental costs. However, as I will now go on to discuss, this strategy is not available to most for-profit providers, especially in urban areas. In the next section I will explore how the materiality of the childcare property matters to the business of childcare.

Non-human matters

The intersection of the property investment market with the childcare market is not solely a financial matter for those providers operating in rental conditions. There are considerable problems associated with the disentanglement of the built care environment from the practice of care through these investment logics, which undermine the work of childcare on a day-to-day basis. One tragic illustration of this came to light in November 2016, when a tree fell into a playground of a childcare service in central Auckland. Four children were injured, two of them critically (RNZ, 2016). The centre was operated by a small for-profit childcare chain, but the land on which it operated was owned by a third-party investor. The operator had made complaints to the owner's management company about the dead tree in the preceding months, but they received no reply. Responsibility for the tree hung in a socio-legal limbo. In the wake of the event news reports focused on issues of health and safety and government regulation, but at no point did coverage dwell on the fact that the land on which the centre operated was owned by an absentee property investor. Indeed, while the story of the injured children made front page news for a brief time, a steady stream of articles about childcare property as an investment opportunity were appearing in the property supplement at the back of the same newspapers.

The previous sections have examined how government funding fuelled the privatization of childcare provisioning, at the same time inciting investor interest in childcare property. However, this chapter has sought to show that childcare property investors, and the conditions of rentiership, do more than extract revenue from the sector. Their involvement has become infrastructural to the childcare market itself. To take this argument further, in this section I explore in more detail how the conditions of state-led marketization intersect with logics of the urban property market, on the ground. This intermarket entanglement was summarized succinctly by a property agent when she stated that 'childcare ends up being a financially viable business model – supported by high demand and funding – yet a shortage of properties in cities to operate from. For this reason, properties with childcare tenants attract a lot of investor interest' (True Commercial, 2017). I suggest that the heightened regulatory requirements of state-led marketization have essentially limited the availability of suitable property, meaning that childcare cannot be conducted from any commercial building. Here again, we can see how the non-human matters to the way the childcare market is constituted.

As social geographers have long shown, care is a socio-spatial endeavour, such that space and place matter to how care is delivered (Conradson, 2003; England, 2010). Chapter 3 detailed some of the considerable amount of regulatory and compliance work required in order to pacify childcare, but also to ensure that as a government funded service it is meeting its social objectives for young children. From just a brief engagement with the regulatory and licensing conditions for childcare centres, it is clear to see that the built care environment is critical to the practice of childcare. New Zealand is considered to have high regulatory standards for childcare property, compared with the UK which has no legal obligation for childcare services to have access to outdoor play space, for example (Penn, 2011). In New Zealand regulatory criteria is specifically set around aspects like the number of available toilets, to the amount of space required per child for indoor and outdoor play. Because of the nature of the work involved, planning resource consent for a childcare facility is relatively difficult to acquire, particularly in mixed zone urban areas as there are parking and road access issues to consider for peak drop-off and pick-up times. As a result, childcare property is not the equivalent of any other commercial premises, but rather one which has been purposely designed and licensed within state guidelines for childcare work. However, as the childcare market intersects with the logics of property investment, the work of these regulations in the market changes. As read through a property investment lens, the regulations produce a scarcity of suitable property in the market, in turn limiting the mobility of providers to move out of difficult rental situations.

Beyond the immediate regulatory context, the practice of childcare is also entangled with the built care environment through its creation as a pedagogical and learning space (Kraftl and Adey, 2008). In keeping with different pedagogical approaches (like Montessori or Steiner for example), childcare spaces tend to be purposefully designed to allow children to explore, develop and be stimulated through that environment (Moss and Petrie, 2002; Gallacher, 2006). The design of this space can take years, as it often involves the landscaping and organization of the outside play areas as well as the internal space and its layout (Gallagher, 2012). From speaking with property investment specialists, in New Zealand the financial expense of this kind of design work in rental properties tends to be borne by the childcare provider rather than the property investor. Moreover, childcare as a business is dependent on high levels of parental trust. It can take a long time for a new service to establish a strong parental community and reach their full roll. While parents' decisions around care services are driven by factors such as cost, distance and time (Jarvis, 2005; Van Ham and Mulder, 2005), they are also motivated by the affective 'feel' for the environment. Feminist geographers have developed the idea of 'emotional stickiness' (Bondi and Davidson, 2005) to capture this affective sense of attachment to place. As a result of the work involved to create a childcare service and build up a community of parents, to relocate to another area and property is a potentially crippling decision for providers and not taken lightly.

In New Zealand's cities, where land values are high and rising for many, the regulatory framework, local government planning legislation[11] and commitment to their parent community discussed earlier mean that the ability for providers to physically relocate in the market is limited. At a point when parental demand for childcare has begun to plateau since 2017 (MoE, 2019), providers are more likely to try to make challenging rental conditions work for them than move. During the research period, urban childcare property rents tended to have a fixed growth of 2 per cent per annum and a market rent review every three to five years years. Moreover, tenancy leases for childcare property are unusually long, set at 12–15 years with two 10-year rights of renewal. That said, the rights of renewal and long lease are also significant to childcare licensees because of the nature of childcare as a business. As a property valuer explained:

> 'childcare businesses are generally accompanied by a high level of good-will tied to the physical property, so they very seldom move ... a large part of the value of the business is associated with the property and the resource consent for childcare use. This is why childcare leases tend to be very long term.'

He went on to add that tenants invest heavily in their properties, much more than expected from a standard commercial rental, taking responsibility for things like maintenance, property tax and insurance, leading to low levels of obsolescence and high levels of income stability for the property owner.[12] Consequently, most childcare providers in urban locations who are operating under commercial rental agreements are in a disadvantaged position within a maturing market, as a result of their relative inability to move from potentially exploitative rental conditions. Indeed, as the narrative about the fallen tree suggests, it is imperative for licensees to address any issues which arise on the property in a timely manner as it may have severe consequences for those in their charge. With such compliant tenants, it is unsurprising that the childcare sales market has blossomed in a relatively short time making childcare an ideal passive investment. As such, the materiality of how childcare is practised in the market shapes how the property investment market intersects with it.

Once a childcare property comes on sale, the work of the property specialist involves translation of risk for investors, who often become involved in childcare property investment as 'uncertain subjects' (Langley, 2007), trying interpret information about a relatively unknown sector. It is in this context that property agents as market intermediaries are poised to capitalize from identifying less risky spaces of investment. As interviewees disclosed, in the current market childcare properties in urban settings make risk averse investments for a range of reasons. Although return on investment is not as significant as other commercial sectors, the attraction for 'mum and dad' investors is in the length of lease. The relative immobility of providers, especially in the main urban centres, plays a large part in determining the level of risk involved in each potential property investment. As a point of contrast the balance of power can tip in favour of the renter in less urbanized areas, where land values are lower and the opportunity to re-establish your childcare business is greater. In these situations, risk for the property investor was deemed to be high. As one broker explained in the context of discussing risk management for investors, urban childcare property is always preferable.

'So the landlord says I want to increase the rent by 5 per cent, or whatever and the tenant says nah I'm not going to do that. I'll buy the house next door and I'll create my own childcare centre and take the parents with me. And straight away the landlord is stuck between a rock and hard place. This is why I predominantly don't encourage investment out of Auckland, because the cost of buying an alternate building is too low.'

Beyond tenant stability, urban childcare property can offer multiple angles from which to further mitigate risk for the investor even after the care service closes. Childcare services in cities are more likely to be located in mixed residential zones, intended to meet the work–life needs of parents living in proximity (McDowell et al, 2006). As a result, a significant proportion of the childcare building stock in New Zealand has been based from converted residential property in order to gain access to an existing residential zone. This adds to the attractiveness of childcare property for individualized 'mum and dad' investors, who as stated earlier primarily buy into converted childcare property as it is less expensive than a new-build premise. As one valuer explained, working from converted premises leaves the investor with options for the property beyond childcare: "Well, if the tenant leaves, or the bottom falls out of the sector, investors have some comfort in knowing that they essentially have options to revert to residential use with their building. They have some security in that." Moreover, the regulated child-space ratios in New Zealand of at least 2.5 square metres of indoor and 5 square metres of outdoor play space per child mean that childcare centres are often situated on relatively large sections of land. In instances where investors decide to change the purpose of the building to residential use, they have the potential to in-fill the section with more houses than originally existed. Indeed, some of the interviewees stipulated that they only advise buying a freehold property so that these risk-mitigating strategies were available, illustrating the complex rationalities at work in how capital switching occurs with regards to the social infrastructure of cities (Harvey, 1982; Christophers, 2011).

As this section has argued, the materiality of the built environment is of central importance to childcare providers, from the perspective of retaining their licence to practice, but also as a reflection of the pedagogical approach embraced by that service. Childcare property is not the same as any other commercial building, even though it may operate under the same lease conditions. The specificity of childcare property in this case means that it can be challenging to find an appropriate location for a service. The effect of this scarcity is especially pronounced in urban contexts, where the costs of land and the opportunity to relocate are further reduced. As a consequence, relocating in the market is not an easy option for providers in urban contexts. It is the materiality of how childcare is practised in the market which opens the possibility for these kinds of urban property investment markets to emerge.

Conclusion

This chapter has sought to outline the complex ways in which the childcare market has intersected with the property investment market since 2012. Childcare property became viewed as a relatively low-risk option for property investors within New Zealand during the 2010s, facilitated by the growth rationales of the private for-profit sector coupled with a business model which is largely backed by the state. However, studying the genesis of the childcare property market in New Zealand reveals that it was more than just the economic incentives of private providers which stimulated property investment interest. Understanding what is happening to childcare property requires us to look beyond childcare, into the spaces of financialized capital and the related drive to find new sources of revenue not from production, but from assetization and ownership of property. In New Zealand this process has manifested in the proliferation of a particular kind of investor subject, 'the mum and dad' investor. Thus, as I have shown the growth of a childcare property investment market is the product of an alignment of the rationalities of two different economic subjects: that of the private provider and that of the so-called mum and dad investor.

However, like the childcare market itself, forging the childcare property investment market has involved considerable discursive, material and technological work, involving a range of diverse actors and expertise. Tracing out this expertise led me to visit with a host of market intermediaries who I would not have imagined at the beginning of this research. Although property speculation has been noted in existing work on neoliberal childcare markets, it tends to exist on the periphery of analysis. In this chapter I have sought to give an insight into the kinds of performative work these actors achieve in actually creating the property investment market. Their work is not peripheral to childcare, but has very real, tangible effects on the daily practices of care to the extent that they are becoming infrastructural to how childcare is practised.

Yet, the impact of property investment practices remains black boxed, couched in commercial property law and lease agreements, and rendered invisible to government. One example of this can be seen in the long-term structure of the rental system, which sets in place potentially unsustainable financial relations between private childcare provider and property owner. At a point when 95 per cent of three- to five-year-olds in New Zealand are now already in some form of outsourced childcare, and centre occupancy rates have plateaued since 2017 (MoE, 2019), the discursive framing of childcare property as a low-risk investment sits in tension with the reality of the annual rate of increase written into commercial lease arrangements for childcare properties. The 'terrain of compromise' (Harvey, 1982) between investor landlord and the childcare provider as renter has started to skew towards the property investor, particularly in urban centres. This has potentially significant consequences for the sustainability of the sector when faced with rental contracts which seek to continually increase. In the next chapter I will explore another example of intermarket engagement which has led to some crucial changes in how for-profit childcare is being practised and organized. This analysis will focus on the relationship between the childcare sector and childcare software management companies, highlighting how it has also become infrastructural to the business of care.

6

Childcare Management Software and Data Infrastructures in the Market

'Back 20 years ago you really had to sell the computer as well as the software. ... We only got a few services on board who were a bit more, you know, forward thinking. There wasn't a lot of MoE compliance, unlike today. Now I would estimate 95 per cent or more of centres have our software platform or one of our competitors. It's nearly impossible to manage without it.'

Tom, childcare management company owner

The previous chapter opened out the analysis of childcare markets to the work of property investment practices as a means of illustrating the infrastructural role they now play. Continuing to develop the conceptual argument of childcare markets as shaped by the rationales and logics of other kinds of economic actors, who are relatively invisible in the existing work on childcare, this chapter turns attention to software companies. Over the duration of the research I have been afforded the opportunity to document the changing face of some key aspects of childcare technology in New Zealand (Gallagher, 2018a). One of these frontiers has been the childcare management software sector, which has experienced an expeditious uptake within childcare centres in particular. Like other topics addressed in this book, this trend is not particular to the New Zealand childcare market. Indeed, the growth of childcare management software companies is a notable development within most advanced childcare markets over the past 15 years. An industry report from the US has projected the continuous expansion of their domestic market for the software, anticipated to be worth US$293 million by 2027 (Reportlinker, 2019), in large part due to the integration of artificial intelligence into these platforms. A brief internet search for childcare management software reveals pages of international tech companies all pertaining to offer the latest, most integrated software package for providers.

Although expeditious in its uptake, the development of the childcare management software market in New Zealand is not a Silicon Valley style rise to prominence. Rather it is a story of everyday incremental and embedded developments in response to the demands of state-led marketization, where emerging companies vie for a share of a relatively small market. When I began scoping out this project in 2013, there were only two companies providing specialist childcare management software. One of these had been in operation for the best part of 20 years, although childcare software was only one aspect of what they delivered due to low demand. At the time of writing seven years later, there were seven companies almost entirely dedicated to childcare software as their focus. Despite the small, light-footed nature of these companies, their impact in the childcare market, and on how childcare is organized, is now considerable.

In this chapter I document the growth of the childcare management software market in Aotearoa New Zealand, as occurring in direct response to state-led marketization in the wake of the 20 hours payment. A cursory analysis of this trend would suggest that its growth is another example of speculative activity within the private sector, in an attempt to capture governmental revenue. However, I will take this view as just the starting point for my analysis and will go further to show the mediating and infrastructural role this technology now plays in shaping the market assemblage. Since the Strategic Plan in 2002 heightened governmental expectations as to the kind of childcare (that is to say its 'qualities') in the market, and the desire to generate evidence of the benefit of increased government spending, has led to a demand for new knowledge about how childcare is being practised. Childcare management software proliferated in the first instance as a necessary addition to the day-to-day running of centres in order to meet new regulatory and governance requirements. Yet over time this software has moved from an optional addition to the daily work of childcare for centre owner-operators to being an integral aspect in how childcare is organized and commodified in the market. In the language of SSM, it has become a market device.

The epistemological claim as to the agency of the non-human in framing market relations is a central tenet of SSM. As I outlined in Chapter 2, non-human actors like technologies, material objects and formulae can all operate as a market device: that is to say they intervene directly in the construction and consolidation of markets (Callon et al, 2007). Read in this light, technological interventions like childcare management software may not be merely inert additions to an existing system, but have the potential to exert their own form of agency. If the market conditions are right, they can become central to inducing new kinds of calculated market responses in the users (such as the MoE, the owner-operator, the care worker or the parent). In this sense, these devices become a necessary aspect of the market over time to guide action, whether this occurs through means of facilitation or even through more punitive forms of enforcement.

Governing the market through data

In February 2018 I flew to Auckland, New Zealand's largest city, to attend the 'Great ECE Expo', one of the first trade events of its kind in the country. Pulling into the regional showgrounds I was directed to join a snaking queue of cars filing into an orderly parking area in front of a large event centre. Joining the contingent walking towards the door, I was struck by the large number of women in attendance. On entering I was handed a bag filled with various kinds of advertising material, and an informational map to help navigate the venue. At first glance the room held about 50 stands, each housing a different exhibitor. The din of conversation between exhibitors and potential customers rose high in the lofty space. Not there as a consumer, I began to feel ill at ease walking up to stalls, as exhibitors were keen to sell their wares and establish sales relationships with the attending childcare services. Stepping back I took in the range of objects and services on offer: specialist architects, builders and outdoor garden suppliers, educational toys and materials, childcare recruitment and software management companies. Any uncertainty I had about attending the Expo was set aside as I looked around, replaced with a feeling that I had been afforded a unique opportunity to see the childcare market in active creation.

While childcare software companies were only one of a range of vendors I encountered at the Expo, their visible popularity among attendees was indicative of the importance they now have in the childcare sector. Understanding why management software has become so pervasive over the last decade in New Zealand involves thinking about the broader socio-political terrain into which this technology was envisaged to make a difference. In that sense, using a SSM lens invites us to consider not only what the *problem* was to which management software became the solution, but also why it was viewed as a problem at this point in time. While there are multiple potential answers to this question, some pertaining to the broader political framing of neoliberalism which has proliferated the search for new, more 'efficient' management techniques across a range of unexpected domains (Clarke and Newman, 1997; Clarke, 2004a), the question of why now also speaks back to a problem of biopolitical governance central to the recent investment in childcare and ECE. Since the early 2000s state-led marketization of childcare has had a distinctive biopolitical ambition; to mitigate the long-term effects of childhood deprivation in later life. Over time, government expenditure on childhood was anticipated to directly improve poor child outcomes, ultimately reducing welfare spending in adulthood. While this social investment ideal has now become generally accepted within policy communities (Adamson and Brennan, 2014), how to evidence the benefit of expenditure has become a pressing epistemological issue for government. Into this domain, many have documented the rise of new forms of data generation as a means of making the return on government investment more knowable, evident in an instrumentalist policy trend which is prevalent across the education and care sectors of many neoliberalized economies (Ball, 2015; Bradbury and Roberts-Holmes, 2017).

Childcare in Aotearoa New Zealand has been influenced by similar policy concerns. The emergence of a more reflexive and interventionist form of state-led marketization in the wake of the Strategic Plan in 2002 raised new questions about the comparatively hands-off approach taken within the initial framing of the market. Since the introduction of the 20 hours payment, governmental desire to know how childcare is being practised, and to evidence the benefits of increased spending on children's educational progression has heightened to a new level. As I have argued, pacifying childcare by setting out the 'qualities' of funded childcare in the market has been a central concern of state-led marketization. Much of the work of pacification has been conducted through the levers afforded by the different funding models for the sector since the 1980s. While the bulk funding system had a more arms-length governance model linked to the use of a charter of operation, which ultimately made pacification difficult to achieve, the Strategic Plan and related 20 hour payment had a clearer idea of the desired 'qualities' of government funded childcare. This was manifest in the new distinction between teacher-led and parent-led services and the focus on childcare as ECE. The capacity of the various governments to know whether these new operating criteria were being met by providers in the sector became an important aspect of the second phase of state-led marketization after 2002. Read through the lens of pacification, making childcare more measurable and standardized as a necessary part of the creation of the market was also the basis on which new forms of data could be derived about the sector.

While governmental need for more in-depth information on the operation of services became evident after 2002, for the most part MoE officials had very little engagement with the software companies during this time. Data about services, like participation, staffing and age of children, was required to be manually uploaded by providers to an online MoE platform. This was generally scheduled in line with the funding cycle, to allow for payment to be processed and any service audits to be conducted. Direct engagement between MoE and the software companies occurred during discussions around the introduction of the Early Learning Information (ELI) system in 2014, when it became evident that these companies already had a strong presence in the sector. Under a National Party government which preferred more targeted forms of funding, the inability to clearly quantify the link between ECE spending and improved child outcomes became a political problem. In response the ELI system was introduced to generate longitudinal, 'joined up' data, by linking children's access to early education with their progression across the rest of the education system. Initiated in keeping with the governmental *White Paper on Vulnerable Children* (Ministry of Social Development, 2012), the ELI system sought to address the gap in knowledge about young children by assigning a student number to each child on entering formalized childcare settings, rather than at primary level schooling as had been the case. From a governmental perspective, this number would allow children to be traceable throughout their educational journey, one which began in childcare and ECE settings. It would also provide a means of viewing how *some* children, notably those classified as being 'at risk' in light of the aforementioned White Paper, were accessing the system and if ECE spending was making a notable difference to them.

This exercise in knowledge production required a data infrastructure for the sector which the state did not yet have. Within the context of a need to generate more information about children in services, the MoE began to view childcare management software companies in a new light. By 2014, management software had been well established in the sector and most providers had integrated some version into their daily operation to meet compliance requirement for the 20 hours payment. It is at this point that we see a deepening of relations between MoE with the childcare software market, evidenced by interviewees' descriptions of invitations to visit the MoE offices to present on the capability of their platforms. The result of this engagement has been the development of the platforms to include a monthly, automatic data upload function to MoE with information pertaining to children's times and days of attendance. To facilitate the automated nature of this new form of reporting, the software platforms have all migrated from a system where information is manually input and uploaded to MoE, to a cloud-based platform in which service data is stored online and can be transferred overnight with little administrative imposition.[1] Indeed, the transition to cloud computing in childcare centres was actually precipitated by the data requirements of the ELI system, as one software designer noted: "Before ELI there wasn't any good reason for most providers to have cloud computing, other than convenience and the flexibility of being able to log in from multiple places. Most centres just ran off and stored information on their desktop, and that was it." As I will discuss later in the chapter, the use of cloud computing technologies in relation to the management of childcare centres has precipitated important changes in the organization, and ultimately the commodification, of childcare itself. Demonstrating the extent of these changes, in the following sections I will focus specifically on three key aspects of the day-to-day work in childcare centres which have been impacted: managing finance, managing staff and the relational work of childcare.

Managing finance through the software

The increasingly narrow margin of error within which childcare owner-operators now work has become evident over the past five years. On one hand, this is necessarily the case as an 'error', be it through poor judgement or deliberate negligence, has serious implications for those in their charge. Nevertheless, the heightened levels of target setting related to funding compliance and regulation has augmented the emotional and financial pressure most centre owner-operators currently experience. The conditions of state-led marketization in the wake of the strategic plan has produced a highly challenging regulatory and administrative climate, with many small services ultimately closing under the weight of new compliance costs (King, 2008). As one software company manager described:

> 'there's been two big things that have really rocked the sector if you like. The first one was the ratios of teachers to children and trying to get those right. ... So, when that kicked in, that was a very difficult thing for people to do on the back of an envelope, so we made quite a sales jump there. And the second one was the 20-hours free, which basically drove our user base diabolical that year. We went up by about 50 per cent in 12 months'.

For those services who did continue in the market, adherence to these new structural quality indicators (like the ratios for example) and the related reporting work to MoE created a much higher administrative load. The childcare management software market developed in the first instance in relation to the need for childcare centres to deal with higher administration work associated with the new funding initiatives, and ultimately over time become more efficient at it.

While the introduction of the 20 hours payment has been noted as inciting considerable interest from for-profit providers, with concerns raised that that profiteering was a driving motivation (Mitchell, 2019a), the small scale owner-operators who I interviewed reflected primarily on the complicated financial landscape that they faced in order to access the payment. Invariably, their largest challenge to acquiring funding was maintaining the levels of compliance around staffing, most notably the ratios of adults to children, and the level of trained teachers working in the centres during a funding cycle. The nature of the funding system, which remains wedded to a four-monthly payment cycle, poses a difficult timeline for providers to operate within. Any mistakes made during the four-month reporting window, such as a drop in the overall percentage of trained teachers employed over the period, or a miscalculation around children's attendance, could lead to less money coming through at the end of the funding cycle. A representative from the ECC described the management work now required to remain compliant with funding expectations as follows:

'You know, when you have a mixed aged centre (0-6 years old) with 50 kids say, and they've got flexible start and finish times, and you are trying to maintain the 80 per cent band of qualified staff over the four months for funding, because that's what you are budgeting on, its exceptionally challenging to do. In winter when there's more illness around, on a bad week you have 50 per cent of your teachers out sick with relievers in. If they get their calculations wrong, they could get slapped on the wrist [by MoE] and loose funding through, say, having a lower rate of registered teachers'.

As centres become increasingly reliant on government funding, failing to meet funding expectations could profoundly impact their financial sustainability. These issues were often only revealed through MoE audits at the end of a funding cycle. Consequently, concerns about missing out on the full extent of their funding payment was a key factor motivating the large scale uptake of management software, as the four-monthly funding cycle allowed too much potential for human error to occur.

Apart from becoming a necessary component in managing the financial relationship with MoE, the software has also to some extent reshaped the financial relationship between childcare centres and parents in the market. A key demand of the parent consumer subject has been for increased flexibility and choice in the type and availability of services to suit changing family needs. While the 20 hours payment sought to narrow the range of choice for parents by linking funding to teacher-led services, at the same time the payment heightened flexibility for parents by offering them 20 paid hours to use at their discretion.[2] Accommodating this increased flexibility within teacher-led services has produced a complex weekly web of children's attendance. What has manifested in the wake of the 20 hours payment is a highly variable landscape of participation, creating a new administrative problem for centre owners.

Managing increased parental flexibility in hours of usage has been one way the software has aided providers to remain financially solvent, but it has also intervened in the financial relations between providers and parents in more unseen ways. Despite a reduction in costs to parents as a driving rationale for the 20 hours payment, for-profit owner-operators have turned their attention towards the landscape of parental fees in the wake of its introduction, in part because of rising operating costs. As discussed in Chapter 3, under the initial framing of the 20 hours payment, which was based on the average operating costs of services, any services who had above average costs were forced to either find ways of reducing those costs or recoup this money elsewhere. Over time this tension has led to fee changes for parents under two different financial calculations. The first has been in locations where parental demand is high, such as higher socioeconomic urban areas. In these instances, any shortfall in government income has been displaced onto parents in the form of higher fees for the hours in care outside of the paid 20 hours. Indicative of this calculation, while it was noted that the 20 hours made a considerable difference to the cost of care in the first year after it was introduced (Mitchell, 2013), recent analysis suggests that childcare fees have increased by a third in the nine years until the end of 2017 (Collins, 2019b). In terms of where the extra fees have been added, owner-operators who I interviewed stated they tend to look at the fee structure of the hours outside the 20 paid hours and also for children under three who are not in receipt of the 20 hours payment, as the means to recoup income.

However, a second calculation impacting fee structures occurred in locations where competition between services was high, and centres were having to review fees to try to attract parents to use their services. In these instances, owner-operators often sought to design a fee structure which would undercut their competitors (Paull, 2013). The lack of a centrally planned system in New Zealand for the allocation of childcare services based on a local needs assessment means that services can essentially open wherever they want once they meet local planning and licensing regulations. Media reporting since 2017 has highlighted that many of New Zealand's largest cities are now experiencing the problem of an oversupply of services in some locations, most notably in new suburbs (Aldridge, 2019). The impact of competition between services was noted by software company interviewees as another key reason necessitating their technology, as one commented,

> 'So if you had a billing system where you were charging people NZ$4 an hour or something like it was, it was nice and simple. But you know very few people do that now. They come up with all kinds of cunning schemes to charge, by looking at the two centres on either side of them and trying to find a competitive rate'.

Moreover, recognizing the importance of keeping parental fees flowing into the service, most software platforms had either designed in-house, or integrated with, some type of financial software to allow for an individualized payment schedule for parents. Through these financial additions to the platform, parents could establish a customized payment schedule with an automatic direct debit facility from their accounts to the childcare service. As was highlighted on one childcare software website: 'New parents have high expectations for those caring for their children – and that includes a fast and modern payment system. Government subsidies around childcare are also changing regularly, meaning more customers and different prices. Are you ready?'[3]

Although the software allowed providers to make new kinds of economic calculations around fee structures for the children in their care, having a steady flow of children into their centres to replace any who may leave was also critically important to their business sustainability. Navigating a financial route through these demands has proven a challenge for for-profit providers. As a result, one central business calculation for providers to access funding is the number of children, increasingly referred to within the for-profit sector as the 'occupancy rate' (as different to participation rate) in their centre. As a business term more readily associated with areas like property tenancy and investment practices, its increased use over the past decade in the New Zealand childcare market is in itself indicative of a changing view of the business of childcare, and the relationship of the attending children to the financial viability of a service. Most private providers had a specific occupancy level in mind, below which their business model became unsustainable (generally around 70–80 per cent). Managing children's rates of enrolment and levels of participation are critical to maintaining childcare centres on a financial even keel. Given the business conditions which had arisen through the government funding freeze over the past decade, any fluctuation in the number of children in a centre undermines its ability to meet outgoing costs, like wages or rent. Economic downturns, demographic changes or everyday changes in family life can all lead to children being unenrolled with little warning. In an attempt to gain some certainty around occupancy rates in a highly uncertain business, providers have grown reliant on the extended functionalities of the software packages to help them plan and manage for variability in demand. As Box 6.1 details, the management software now enables providers to stagger enrolments, automatically follow up on any enquiries, and in larger centres plan the transition of children between junior rooms to more advanced 'preschool' environments, as tools to mitigate fluctuations in occupancy.

Box 6.1: Management software capabilities

Maximize occupancy by tracking, managing and converting leads and enquiries for your centre or group of centres:

- Eliminate your centre's daily attendance data entry.
- Enjoy faster and easier staff roster management.
- Avoid invoicing and payment mistakes.

- Fully automate your waitlist management, invoicing and more.
- Enjoy easier training and use than competitors' systems.
- Secure, modern technology for your sensitive data.
- Access securely from anywhere, with real time reporting.
- Multi centre management drag and drop reporting.
- Nappy charts, sleep charts, messaging and newsletters, direct debits and much more.

Source: advert from childcare management software company

While it has been acknowledged that parents are treated in the market as the de facto consumers of care rather than children, the design of the demand side funding system means that children are increasingly the basis of providers' economic calculation in the market. From the perspective of an owner-operator, as more amendments are made to the funding system, forms of governmental funding have become defined by who the child is:[4] notably shaped by their age, hours of attendance, or if their family are in receipt of a social welfare benefit. Although children have always been an important part of the financial calculation of owner-operators under both versions of state-led marketization, the integration of management software has heightened levels of financial calculation by enabling services to stratify children based on their enrolment information. Evidencing further the work of the software as a market device, some companies I spoke with had developed a formula to allow owner-operators to interpret each participating child through a more economic lens. Ultimately the software offered providers a way of weighting the potential financial contribution of each child to the service as a means of deciding which children were most financially advantageous to enrol. Indeed, as Press and Woodrow (2005) have identified in the Australian context, highly competitive childcare markets eventually produce a tendency towards stratification and residualization, such that younger children who are more labour intensive to care for become less appealing to for-profit providers as they may only financially break even for owner-operators. The desire for financial differentiation in a competitive childcare market produces a host of perverse market effects, as providers begin to act and ultimately 'see like a market' (Fourcade and Healy, 2017).

In sum, although the software has been widely adopted as a seemingly banal efficiency measure in the face of growing compliance requirements under state-led marketization, it has become crucial to the financial management of services. Over time the calculative agency of providers has been augmented by the software, rendering it as a market device which is becoming central to how the childcare market operates. Heightening the financial calculability of providers in the market depoliticizes the relational labour of childcare, extending market relations deeper into the work of care. Much of this work involves important, normative judgements, particularly around enrolling children and developing a relationship with their family, decisions which are becoming hidden within the functionalities of the platforms.

Data analytics and managing services in 'real time'

I met Heather, a centre owner-operator, at the end of 2019. Having trained and worked in various parts of the sector as an ECE teacher for more than two decades, her desire was always to own her own service. Spurred on by the increase in demand that the 20 hours payment created, she ventured out on her own, renting a premise with the backing of her partner. She started her first service in 2007 in a major New Zealand city where she worked part time as a teacher, managing the service at the same time. Today, Heather runs three services, each ranging in capacity from 48 to 100 children, accommodating ages 6 months to 6 years. Her typical day starts early, from home. She logs in to her cloud-based management system to see if there have been any issues with staffing which need to be resolved before children begin to arrive. From her home office she can access a host of information about her services: any notable illnesses within centres, issues with enrolments and payments, health and safety logs and if any injuries occurred on the grounds recently which may require further investigation. Surprised by the information she can also get about staff/child engagement through the reporting functions on the platform, she comments about how the new 'data' being produced will help evidence good practice when it comes to the ERO audit next year.[5]

Heather's description of using the software to manage her childcare services is not atypical. Childcare centres are an increasingly complex assemblage of human and non-human elements, mediated more than ever by new forms of data production and analytics on the day-to-day business of care. As childcare management software companies have become more advanced in their platform functionalities, their analytics and reporting functions have also become more sophisticated. At a glance, managers can roster staff, organize attendance records, keep pace with parental payments and overdue fees, receive alerts for health and safety compliance, teacher registration and manage teacher ratios over the bulk funding period, with the relative ease of various colour coded charts. Moving beyond the impact of management software on the financial decision making of owner-operators, this section will explore some of the ways the software also directly shapes how childcare is viewed and practised on the ground.

One of the primary rationales for consolidation of services in a competitive market has been to establish greater efficiencies around compliance costs, by centralizing administrative and other common tasks. Although the childcare software has generally made compliance work easier for providers at all scales, the move to a cloud-based operating system has made the off-site management of services an option for many. The creation of centralized, more remote management systems has been of benefit to larger chains and corporates, but as my interviews with software company owners suggests they see it as also an important contributing factor in the growth of smaller childcare chains of 3-10 services in the wake of the 20 hours payment. As noted by a software company manager,

> '10 years ago a lot of people had one centre and had a handle on the admin side for funding and regulations etc. Then they decided okay, I've got my model down, I know what I'm doing, it's easy to buy a few more with the increased funding coming in. So, from our perspective, we have seen a strong trend in our existing providers, especially for-profit ones, extending from one service to have three or four during this time'.

Like Heather's experience, having a system in place which allows a centre manager to make changes to things like rostering and scheduling staff in real time across multiple nodes, has heightened levels of calculability in the day-to-day management of centre-based care.

As a market device, the software has shaped how owner-operators view and respond to staffing problems in the wake of the 20 hours payment and the related teacher shortage. While the software produces coloured charts to help owner-operators keep track of staffing levels within services, both in terms of the number of trained teachers and the staff/child ratios, over time it has allowed for other kinds of calculative practices around staffing to emerge in the context of the teacher shortage. For owner-operators with multiple services located in relative proximity to each other, being able to look across services in real time means that they can now move qualified staff between services in order to stay within their funding band for each licensed service. As one owner-operator I interviewed who had three childcare centres in the same medium sized city described it, "if I'm down staff in one centre, I can just move others across, to make sure I don't have lots of relievers in one centre at any given time. It's not ideal, but we are left with little choice with the shortage of trained staff. That's one *major* advantage of the overview that the software gives me". While this practice may make good sense from a business perspective within the regulatory conditions of the market, it is not necessarily favourable for the children in their charge to have such worker mobility, leaving questions about the nature of the care model being endorsed. If the focus is primarily on meeting regulations by ensuring the 'correct' bodies are in the 'correct' places on a given day, then a stable care environment for children, based on strong relational bonds between them and their carer, may not eventuate (Bowlby, 2007).

Childcare software designers have come to occupy a crucial place in the New Zealand childcare market, through their ability to interpret, influence and design the digital interface providers now rely on to run their childcare services. From on-site observation with some of the software companies, it is evident that they do more than basic technology support. As one software company owner with 30 staff suggested,

'these days we are selling a support service rather than the software, both up to MoE and down to providers on the ground. It has meant that we have had to add staff for this role, and ideally, we need people who are aware of the sector. Providers ringing up want you to understand what they are working with, not just a depersonalized IT experience'.

This is a multi-directional relationship, and information derived by developers about the sector from their support work is ultimately folded back into the re-design of the technology to ensure it remains relevant. Designers I interviewed spoke lucidly about the importance of cultivating a good working relationship with providers, as ultimately their feedback is used as the basis for developing their platform and identifying new applications. The competitive nature of the childcare software sector means that having that insight allows them to maintain their competitive edge (see Box 6.2). Maintaining its position as a market device requires this ongoing relational work, so that it continues to meet the needs of MoE, owner-operators and parents alike.

Box 6.2: Competition in the childcare management software sector

We can upgrade you easily over a weekend and hundreds have trusted us to do that since our first centre more than two years ago, so we are getting pretty good at it!

Centres leaving our platform in the last 12 months: 0

Centres leaving other platforms in the next 2–3 weeks: 154

Our experienced helpdesk team have previously held roles in centre administration, centre management and centre ownership – so we are well placed to take customers through our onboarding process.

Source: advert for Discover Childcare, www.discoverchildcare.co.nz/Feedback

As the platforms have become a market device, the work the designers do in relation to the sector has changed from identifying and remedying a need in the sector (like maintaining MoE compliance) to actively conceptualizing new promissory applications which push the work of childcare providers in unforeseen directions. One newly created company I interviewed in 2017 had received a prestigious grant from a government agency in New Zealand charged with supporting business, science and technology innovation. Their award was granted to develop new, more promissory solutions to childcare sector 'problems' through mobilizing their expertise in artificial intelligence (AI) and blockchain technology. While these technologies have been around for some time, they are very much at the cutting edge of the childcare tech sector in New Zealand. Indeed, looking at the international market for childcare software, AI and blockchain technology presents the new frontier of expansion for childcare software companies, and is already under consideration by other major childcare platforms like *Procare* in the US and *Famly* in the UK.

While the uses of AI and blockchain technology will be specific to the childcare market assemblage they are introduced into, within New Zealand these innovations were anticipated to further promote the agency of the parent consumer in the market. An example of one area the company was exploring in terms of AI technology was that of overdue payments, an especially pertinent issue in light of the rising costs of care in the past decade. Conversations about overdue fees remains an unwelcome one for both parents and managers alike, as it brings to the fore key tensions around the commodification of care. As economic sociologist Viviana Zelizer has illustrated in her extensive work, the domain of care is often constructed through a 'separate spheres/hostile worlds' discourse, where the issue of money is perceived to muddy the integrity of the relational work of care. Focusing on a way of managing this tension for providers and parents, at the time of interview the company was working on a human-like AI interface which would allow a parent with overdue fees to make enquiries about how much they were in arrears, and to establish a new payment schedule going forward, without ever speaking to a real person. The expectation being that the topic of money and payment could be largely removed from the interpersonal communication between provider and parent.

The second terrain being explored by this company through their innovation grant related to the potential offered by blockchain technology to parents in an increasingly data driven sector. Emerging from the 'cryptocurrency' movement of the 2010s, blockchain technology offers a secure, decentralized and encrypted data system for childcare services. In the face of considerable amounts of data now being gathered by services and shared with the MoE, blockchain was envisioned as a means of giving parents autonomy to also generate data analytics pertaining to their child. In practice this would lead to the creation of reports or charts for parents about things like sleep times, eating times, eating behaviours or nappy changes, which they could, theoretically, use to gauge any patterns of change in behaviour over time. They could also use it to see any anomalies over time in the care of their child. The data and the reporting analytics produced would be secure, accessed only by the parent who generated the report as they would have the 'key' to access it. Questioning the company owner further about the level of parental demand they perceive for this technology in the New Zealand market, it became evident that the company was making a prediction based on the growing consumerist orientation of the childcare market in the light of the 20 hours payment. The increase in parents' desire to know as much about their child's day as possible as time spent in childcare services lengthens was also commented on as a factor that would drive demand (Furedi, 2008; Boyer et al, 2012; Fothergill, 2013). However, at the time of writing it was still not clear that there was an evident market for this technology, with the company manager stating that he could see a bigger demand for it in more privatized childcare sectors, like that of Singapore (Lim, 2017).

Of course, not all the promissory developments which were envisioned by the software companies gained traction, many stymied by the particular ideologies of care which ultimately shape and push back against how childcare *can* be practised in the market (Rosenthal, 1999). As a highly experimental domain, the childcare software sector drives the MoE, managers, parents and carers to recognize the epistemological and normative underpinnings of the care market. This was made evident at points of failure or resistance towards the technology. The use of CCTV cameras in the care setting presented one such point of resistance. One company owner described how they had begun to advertise their platform as being integrated with real time footage and recording functions, noting it as a point of difference to existing platforms. However, on testing the demand for this product, they found parents, carers and managers were dubious of the benefit of having cameras in childcare centres, raising issues of security and privacy among others. Another point of resistance arose around a seemingly more mundane change to a popular sign-in feature on another company's platform. The design change featured a barcode rather than a unique number assigned to each child on entering the centre. Perhaps unsurprisingly, parents took offence at their children being scanned much like a supermarket item, failing to see the benefit of this minor time efficiency.

While this section has sought to outline some of the primary ways in which childcare management software is being deployed to rethink how childcare is organized and managed at a day-to-day level, most of these changes would suggest a considerable depersonalization of the work of care for teachers and care givers. The introduction of applications, formula and analytics to offer a different way of viewing and in turn, acting on the business of childcare suggests that its heightened economization has the capacity to produce 'careless' spaces for children and their families. However, there has been little push back against the technology on these grounds, rather owner-operators I interviewed described significant support among their staff for the involvement of the technology in the daily work of care. Although I have not had the opportunity to speak in-depth with teachers and carers directly in this research, in the next section I will offer some initial insights into how the software, as a market device, has articulated with the broader, non-economic logics of carers and owner-managers. Here I will suggest that as a market device it has gained traction as it allows them to 'make time for care'.

Non-economic rationales: using the software to make time for care

It's not about having enough time, it's about making enough time.
(Astute Education, 2019)

While this far I have examined the work of childcare management software as a market device, which is formative of new kinds of economic relationships between MoE, childcare managers, parents and children within the market, in this final section I want to return to the question of care. Although the primary impact of the software has been to allow for new forms of economic calculability within the market, producing a range of effects, as Deville (2015) suggests, market devices also have the capacity to foster other kinds of non-economic logics at the same time. The impact of new management regimes has been of interest to many studying the negative effects of neoliberal forms of governance on the work of care. As care is commodified for exchange in the market, the relational work itself becomes subject to processes of regularization and standardization (Green and Lawson, 2011; Hoppania and Vaittinen, 2015). In making care measurable, documented and scripted, in accordance with increased workloads for example, time for the relational and corporeal demands of care becomes eroded (England et al, 2007; England, 2010). Consequently, a clear theme within the literature on care commodification under neoliberalism has been a concern around the *loss of time* to care in the face of increased management regimes and relatedly its datafication.

Childcare work has not been immune to these criticisms (Moss, 2014; Moloney and Pettersen, 2017). Indeed, as I have argued in this book the desire to pacify childcare as a central aspect of state-led marketization has placed increasing emphasis on making childcare as ECE more standardized. The trend towards regularization of childcare practices affects both workers and managers in the sector. As described by Moss in the UK context (2014: 23) the policy emphasis on 'high quality' in early education, as a means of achieving the desired governmental outcomes from childcare markets, has proliferated the use of technologies in the practice of childcare to ensure these qualities are being met. These can be seen not only in the regulatory and compliance regimes, but also in aspects like the achievement of curriculum goals that ECE teachers are expected to adhere to. In essence, setting these goals of practice over time forms the basis on which the sector, and its purported social and economic benefits, can be measured.

Exploring the expeditious uptake of childcare management software has afforded a different set of insights into the neoliberal governance of the sector. As the owner-operators I interviewed frequently described, the 20 hours payment has significantly increased regulatory oversight on a daily level, proliferating the amount of administrative work required to meet government funding expectations. These expectations filter down to teachers and carers, who are required to log heightened amounts of paperwork during their working day.[6] Encountering growing concerns about the impact of regulatory paperwork undermining the time spent with children, the software companies have sought to advertise their platforms as 'making time for care'. Reinforcing this claim at the managerial level, owner-operators stated in interviews that they were able to save considerable amounts of time on administrative tasks by integrating and ultimately ceding increasing amounts of the day-to-day running of the centre to the software platform. As one interviewee described her working day before she had integrated the software across her two childcare centres:

'I was starting to lose sight of why I created the centres in the first place. ... Over time as more children enrolled and the variation in their hours and days in the service grew, I was in an office job basically. I was just trying to keep on top of everything and working as a reliever when someone was out sick. That's not what I imagined owning a childcare centre would be like'.

The need for teachers and carers to document increasing amounts of their daily work in the face of heightened compliance requirements from MoE, but also expectations from parents, has impacted on their time spent with the children in their care. As discussed in Chapter 4, the business of childcare relies on a host of non-economic logics to be successful, like trust and compassion, sentiments established between carers, parents and children in the daily work of care. Being available to reassure parents at pick-up and drop-off times, and ensuring children can get the individual attention they need in large childcare settings to feel emotionally supported, require unburdened amounts of time for carers. Sharing details of the child's day is an important part of building good relationships with parents and assuaging parental anxiety. Yet, time is a factor here too, as although parents are keen to hear of their child's day, they are often in a hurry home to start the 'second shift' (Hochschild, 1989). As one owner-operator described the pick-up experience:

'well, it's often a bit fraught at pick-up. Kids are looking for their parent's attention, having been apart all day. So the parent is distracted, but still trying to talk to you about how things went. Did they sleep? Eat their food? Have a good day? Any incidents? And all of that. It can be very hard to have any meaningful conversation with them, other than a fleeting chat before they whisk out the door again'.

It is precisely the problematic of needing to make time for these interactions that the software companies are directing their recent attention. To make time for interaction between parent, child and carer, most of the companies I interviewed were working on new software applications which could be used by carers to digitally record as much detail as possible of the child's day, in the hope that it would create space for more meaningful engagements to take place at those crucial interaction times with parents. As one company who had recently launched their application advertised it: 'The newest app for educators in rooms! GoMobile! let's staff instantly update worked hours, roll calls, nappy/toilet charts, sleep charts and many more from your phone or device.'[7] Justified as part of the discourse of making time for care, these developments may have the unwanted potential to proliferate new forms of 'micro-work' for carers, pushed to log ever more detailed digital records over the course of their working day and beyond (Gallagher, 2018a). However, as the childcare market assemblage continues to proliferate to draw in new actors and forms of knowledge in an increasingly experimental frontier of care, keeping pace with the impact of these kinds of changes in response to state-led marketization becomes extremely difficult to achieve.

Conclusion

This chapter has given insight into the expeditious uptake of childcare management software in the New Zealand childcare market. At first glance, much like the property investors in Chapter 5, the software companies appear to be financially 'parasitic' in their motivation, seeking a means of accessing and syphoning off money from increased government spending in the sector. To access a share of the spending being made into a buoyant childcare market, they have in the first instance offered management solutions for owner-operators to the problem of increased compliance and administration work in the wake of the 20 hours payment. However, while this may have been the initial reason for the uptake of the technology in the sector, I have argued that this analysis overlooks the profound work childcare management software now does in the market as a market device. As a non-human agent, over time the software has engaged with the diverse needs of the MoE, providers, carers and parents, bringing them into new kinds of economic and extra-economic relationships with each other, and enabling a range of new calculable agency in the market. In that sense, childcare management software has become infrastructural to the market as a market device.

The increase in demand for new forms of data about the running of childcare services under the conditions of state-led marketization has ultimately led to childcare centres becoming increasingly digitized and data driven. This data, whether it is tracking children's attendance or managing teacher/child ratios, has become the basis of new calculative financial practices in the market. To that extent, through the lens afforded by the platform owner-operators can better interpret and respond to the complex financial landscape produced by the funding system, parents can negotiate fee structures with managers, and the MoE can audit services for reporting irregularities with greater ease. While I have documented how and why these changes have occurred at this point in the development of the market, I have also sought to indicate some of the wider effects these changes have had on centre-based childcare. Some of these changes have led to unanticipated negative outcomes, like heightened mobility of staff in real time between services, while others have more positive effects, like making more time for the relational work of care in the face of increased regulatory compliance.

However, it is important to highlight that by smoothing out processes and relations of exchange in the market, as the management platforms seek to do, market devices also have a depoliticizing effect. As we become more reliant on the functionalities of these platforms, and as services come to rely on the data analytics which are produced, this kind of technology has the capacity to occlude important aspects of the daily work of care. In the process, questions with highly normative underpinnings around equal access to care become rendered technical and formulaic. One example I identified in this research was the tendency towards 'weighting' individual children's potential financial contribution during their time in care to the centre at the point of enrolment. As more of the running of services is integrated onto these platforms, and as diverse market actors come to see the childcare market through the lens of the data and analytics now on offer, the work of these platforms takes on a new prevalence in shaping how children are cared for. The promissory work of software platforms in centre-based care presents a difficult terrain to regulate under state-led marketization, as it continues to exist largely outside government purview of the sector.

7

Conclusion

In March 2018, the incoming Minister for Education sent ripples through the New Zealand childcare sector by announcing that the forthcoming Strategic Plan (2019–2029) would 'turn the tide' away from the growing presence of private providers, to favour the community-based non-profit sector (Gerritson, 2018b). History tells us he was not the first Minister for Education to state this intention. Similar comments were made two decades earlier in response to the first Strategic Plan and the 20 hours payment, which sought from the outset to buoy the non-profit sector in the face of an increasingly competitive childcare market. Yet by the time of writing in 2021, relatively little has been done to meet this ambition, indicating the extent of the political lock-in to the current market.

This book has sought to address some of the perplexing tensions inherent in neoliberal childcare markets: that they are tasked with achieving considerable social and economic outcomes, yet are organized through highly inequitable market-based systems; they receive considerable public funding, yet are privately delivered. Media coverage and academic literature drawn on in earlier chapters home in on the problems that manifest from these tensions for those who use and work in childcare. As the proportion of for-profit services grows, these markets have been highlighted as having low(er) quality care and education for young children, suppressing pay and working conditions for staff in the sector, and resulting in the transferral of considerable amounts of public funding to an increasing variety of private entities.

One of the key questions that has shaped the focus of this book is how neoliberal childcare markets are assembled and held together over time, in the face of considerable criticisms and problems. In an interview with the Minister for Education who was in office for the introduction of the 20 hours payment, he queried my assumption that childcare markets were markets at all. In his opinion they were not, as he stated, "government has had a considerable hand in regulating and managing them". In many ways his comment speaks to the crux of the argument of this book: if they do not resemble a typical neoclassical rendition of a market, then what do childcare markets actually look like? To answer this question I have suggested that the literature on markets of collective concern can offer some important clarity in distinguishing what childcare markets, and other markets which are charged with achieving significant social goals, actually look like on the ground.

There are two reasons why I have claimed childcare markets can be studied as markets of collective concern. The adoption of more 'third way' or social investment approaches to remedying complex social issues has been a marked feature of the post-neoliberal era from the late 1990s. Under this lens, childcare has become a crucial part of the social infrastructure of neoliberal welfare economies, tasked with meeting new political ambitions for working families and children. Yet, despite the growing importance of childcare, especially as ECE, to achieving social and educational goals, the use of markets and market mechanisms to develop the childcare sector has been commonplace. As a market of collective concern, childcare represents a highly experimental frontier of policy making in which markets are continually problematized and repaired. Over time these markets have become constructed as policy instruments in themselves, because policymakers expect them to offer the best possible solutions to the childcare problem. Throughout this book I have sought to demonstrate how policy interventions within neoliberal childcare markets have occurred under the political rationale of 'fixing' existing versions of the childcare market, despite the weight of evidence pointing to the ways in which they continually fail to do so (Lloyd and Penn 2013; Moss, 2014).

The second reason I have drawn on the concept of markets of collective concern is that it offers a potent means of understanding how neoliberal policy communities over time have become reliant on markets to achieve social aims. As Peter Moss (2014) has convincingly argued, the use of markets to meet childcare needs has become discursively and politically 'locked-in' within anglophone neoliberal policy communities, producing what he terms an effective 'dictatorship of no alternative' (DINA). Recognizing the hegemony of the market model, he illustrates how this reliance is neither necessary nor inevitable. The importance of this work as a discursive counterpoint to the dominant neoliberal rendition of childcare markets is unquestionable. Reading across this varied literature, increasing the role of the state in direct provisioning is understood as a potential antidote to the current problems of marketization. However, as I have argued, calls for the state to intervene in this context fail to recognize the changes that have occurred in the nature of the post-neoliberal state itself in order for childcare markets to be sustained. To explore the nature of the deepening relationship between state and market in the provisioning of childcare, I have developed the concept of state-led marketization.

As the case study for this book, the childcare market in Aotearoa New Zealand offers a pertinent example of state-led marketization at work. In the New Zealand context childcare has had a turbulent journey, situated at the forefront of competing forms of neoliberal politics since the 1980s. Although both major political parties (Labour and National) believed in the use of markets to meet childcare needs during this time, there has not been any significant cross-party agreement on what the market 'blueprint' should be, especially regarding how much the sector should be regulated and funded, and the role of the private for-profit sector. Lack of political agreement as to how to provide childcare, even within a market model, has undermined the social aspirations of state-led marketization. This has been evident in the way the two market 'blueprints' introduced under a Labour government were subsequently altered, resulting in significant market overflows like the skills shortage or the rising cost of childcare for parents. As a result, it is fair to say that childcare and early education have been affected by the whims of neoliberal politics more than any other part of the education portfolio in New Zealand.

When examining the emergence of the New Zealand childcare market, it is evident that the inability to realize the market blueprint as imagined in the initial Before Five reforms of the 1980s and the subsequent Strategic Plan in 2002 meant that the work of state-led marketization in the sector became one of continuous repair and maintenance for government. Although there has been some political desire to 'turn the tide' towards non-profit providers and a public system over the last 20 years, successive governments have largely resorted to making ongoing amendments to the existing market system in response to emerging market problems. Reliant on demand side funding levers like the 20 hours payment to try to direct the market towards achieving desired governmental outcomes has conversely led to a downturn in the non-profit sector and a proliferation of for-profit providers. As explored in earlier chapters the decision to extend funding to the for-profit sector has precipitated a wave of economic experimentation to find new ways of making childcare economically profitable. In the New Zealand market, the outcome of this heightened economic calculability can be linked to perverse trends evident in the for-profit sector, like the movement of qualified staff between services in order to maintain regulatory compliance for funding, or the effective 'weighting' of children according to their financial contribution to the service.

Ultimately, this book has sought to open up analysis of childcare markets to show the complex ways in which the state actively supports and directs their creation as markets of collective concern. In the process I have suggested that we need to develop a different approach to analysing childcare markets, one which is attentive the complex everyday work of market making. The Social Studies of Markets literature, housed in the disciplines of economic sociology, anthropology and economic geography, offers a new direction in this regard.

State-led marketization and the fragility of childcare markets

In this book I drew on SSM to make the analytical shift from a discussion of markets as a handmaiden of neoliberalism, to studying markets in their own right as tenuous, practical accomplishments. Changing analytical registers in Chapter 2 allowed me to develop the conceptual language of SSM, based on a more-than-human reading of market relations, to offer insights into how state-led marketization actually works on the ground. Privileging neither the actor nor the system, this approach gave weight to the complex interplay of both human and non-human actors which inform the construction of markets as distinctive socio-technical arrangements.

Taking on board the role of the non-human in the creation and sustenance of care markets involves a more active research engagement with the plethora of *things* now entangled in the practice and organization of formalized childcare. As documented throughout earlier chapters, childcare centres and the care and education they provide are now replete with regulations, materials, technologies, formula, discourses, forms of knowledge and rationalities, which are drawn together in particular ways to shape how care is commodified and experienced as a service for sale. Focusing attention on the constitutive role of the non-human offers new possibilities for how we examine marketized childcare, noting how things like charters serve to align the interests of diverse market actors, or how software management technology shapes the calculative agency of parents and providers. In that sense I have sought to demonstrate that taking a market assemblage approach is not just useful on a theoretical level, it has significant practical implications for how we view and act on childcare markets, and for recognizing what kinds of non-human elements might actually fuel marketization.

Putting the SSM approach to work in the analysis of the New Zealand context has allowed me to trace out the broader contours of the market, and the work involved in its creation, more than a typical historicized account could do. Drawing on the insights of SSM to consider how state-led marketization works on the ground, I made two key points in the process. Firstly, state-led marketization requires the creation of calculative agency in the market in order for childcare to be successfully commodified and exchanged as a service for sale. In the context of neoliberal childcare markets, the primary calculative agencies are the figures of the parent consumer and the childcare provider, both encouraged to act in economically rational ways to enter into relations of exchange around childcare as a purchased service. Secondly, to allow these actors to behave in economically calculative ways, childcare itself needs to be pacified in the market. In the process the diverse range of childcare practices which exist across paid and unpaid care economies need to be 'tamed' (Callon, 1998), whereby the kind of childcare that is aspired to under state-led marketization is consistently offered by providers and purchased by parents. In a market associated with the achievement of considerable social goals for children and families, much hinges on the government's ability to identify and standardize a particular form of childcare that is deemed to meet these goals, while at the same time marginalizing those that do not. We can clearly see this framing effect gaining heightened traction in the New Zealand market over the past 20 years, with the preference for childcare as early education and the emphasis on teacher-led services to the detriment of other kinds of parent and volunteer-led provisioning (Gallagher, 2021). Pacification in essence seeks to reduce practices of childcare, by making standardizable and measurable key aspects of its practice. This in turn allows for market actors to come together around the commodification of a service with a common set of qualities. Within the context of state-led marketization, achieving pacification of childcare is crucial, as it means that parent consumers can feel assured they were purchasing well for their children and governments can be confident in the knowledge that they are funding a particular quality of care across the market.

Yet, as I have demonstrated, in practice these objectives around pacification and calculability are very hard to achieve. While calculative agency is aspired to, not every actor achieves this to the same extent. Taking this insight on board we can trace how calculative agency is not derived from something innate to the individual, but is an effect of the relationships they have in the market assemblage. It is also the result of their propensity to draw on a range of market devices to aid action. For example, it is well noted that parents fail to ever realize the aspired agency of the imagined parent consumer in neoliberal childcare markets. Even for actors who are empowered to engage in more economically calculable ways, like for-profit providers, the outcome of their calculability may work counter to the social aspirations of the market framing itself. We can see this becoming apparent in the New Zealand market by tracing out the ways different kinds of for-profit providers have responded to the changes in funding structure, as endorsed through both phases of state-led marketization. Indeed, approaching the dynamics of the childcare market through the lens of calculative agency re-politicizes much of what is being rendered invisible through the increasing normalization of the 'business case for childcare' (Prentice, 2007), which shapes not only how government funding to the market is justified but reaches all the way down to the daily practice of childcare.

As a contestable field, Callon and Muniesa remind us that 'open discussions and even public debates on the way of organizing calculations (or on the way of excluding certain modes of calculation) are possible. In short, it restores to markets the political dimension that belongs to them and constitutes their organization as an object of debate and questioning' (2005: 1245). SSM offers a more agnostic starting point for analysing childcare market relations by drawing attention to how action in the market is a relational rather than individualistic endeavour, the result of a configuration of human and non-human elements as much as a desire on the part of the individual market agent themselves. Throughout the book I have suggested that this perspective offers a different vantage point from which to analyse the predominant trends identified in neoliberal childcare markets, such as the rise of the private for-profit sector in its diverse forms. Examining market relations through the lens of calculative agency shows how the behaviour of market actors occurs in direct response to the particularities of state-led marketization.

The analytical contribution of market making as a contested process of framing and overflow highlights that childcare markets are never discrete entities. Through market overflows, childcare intersects with a host of other markets and market actors in complex and largely unforeseen ways. Ultimately, making this point has both analytical and political import, as for the most part the governmental gaze of state-led marketization assumes that childcare markets can be managed through the levers of the funding and regulatory system as a relatively discrete entity. Taking the example of the childcare property investment market discussed in Chapter 5, we can see over time that state-led marketization has precipitated the involvement of investors in for-profit childcare centres, who are drawn to childcare as a relatively low-risk, government backed business. Yet, rather than merely trace this as an example of money being syphoned out of the sector through rentiership, I have sought to show how these intermarket relationships shape the sector in fundamental ways. In the case of the childcare property market, by exploring the conditions of the rental system in place, a process which is largely hidden within the for-profit part of the market, I illustrated how property rentiership practices are directly linked to the rising costs of care for parents in the New Zealand context. In this book I have argued that to better understand neoliberal childcare markets today, and to advocate for change, we need to also be attentive to these sites of intermarket engagement.

While the primary aim of using SSM was to advance how academics studying care markets may approach this endeavour differently, in the process this book also advances the SSM literature in new directions. To date there are few studies in the SSM literature which consider care markets, favouring instead studies of commodity and financial markets in the main. As such this book makes a novel contribution to this literature by exploring the diverse economic and non-economic logics around care through the lens of market making. In the process it also opens new ground in the use of this analytical framework by documenting a sustained example of intermarket engagement. While existing work in the field of SSM has given many examples of market overflows, few have traced what this looks like once the economic logics of different markets intersect, as in the case of the property investment or software markets with childcare. In doing so I have considered how these markets actually fold back onto the work of care, changing the care practices and disciplining childcare market actors in new ways. To that end, I have argued that they have become infrastructural to the childcare market.

In sum, an SSM approach sets out a research framework through which to capture the fragility of childcare markets and the considerable work involved in creating and sustaining them. Despite the continuing prevalence of the neoliberal discourse of markets to solve social problems, the practical challenges of framing and creating markets to do this work means that this endeavour is inherently prone to fail. Set in this light, it becomes evident that deploying markets to meet significant collective social outcomes will never involve a reduced role for the state, such that it merely steers the market in the way imagined by proponents of neoliberal forms of governance. As this book has demonstrated, through these new entanglements of state and market we are seeing a fundamental transformation in how social provisioning occurs through the proliferation of markets of collective concern. The question then becomes how to address the complex task of regulating these markets.

Childcare markets: going forward

The research informing this book sought to take a step back from the immediate daily work of childcare to consider the broader economic logics, practices and actors which are shaping the terrain in which centre-based childcare now operates. While the research did not directly engage with children and parents, throughout the chapters I have indicated where the analysis inevitably has implications for how childcare is being practised 'on the ground'. For-profit childcare centres are providing the care and education of the largest proportion of children in neoliberal childcare markets today, and how this part of the sector adapts to the conditions of state-led marketization has a direct impact for children in their care. One of the major questions to ask at this juncture is how best to regulate or oversee childcare markets, given the growth of the for-profit sector and its propensity for overflow which continually undermines governmental attempts to manage the market. As White and Friendly (2012) presciently noted of the New Zealand context, 'even when a government attempts to develop standards regarding planning, delivery of services, staffing and training, the choice of delivery agents can undermine those efforts'.

Childcare markets today are shaped by a much wider constellation of actors than what has been accounted for in existing studies. Extending knowledge of the diverse actors now involved, the research informing this book engaged with property specialists, finance companies, and software developers, most of whom only appear on the margins of existing studies. The book also drew on a much wider array of 'data' to evidence the work of these actors, involving media and advertisements, websites, shareholder prospectus and more, pushing my individual capacity to follow the market and its actors into terrains which were largely unfamiliar to me. Yet as the childcare market proliferates to involve these actors, they remain largely outside the capacity of governments to either regulate or hold accountable to the broader aspirations of state-led marketization. Returning to the story recounted in Chapter 6 of a fallen tree in the playground of a childcare centre in Auckland, three years later an official health and safety investigation laid culpability for the first time at the feet of both licensee *and* property owner. Fines were imposed on both parties, although the licensee carried the bulk of the financial penalty. Importantly, the investigating officer at the official hearing found that 'both parties had a duty of care that they failed to meet'.[1] This outcome is significant, as it illustrates the changing nature of the terrain of responsibility now required to monitor these new forms of financialized, intermarket entanglements.

In many ways greater accountability over childcare property practices can be achieved within the existing structures of the state, once the political will is there to do so. For other changes in the childcare market, like those at the frontier of software development, this will be much harder to achieve. Through the examples given in Chapter 6, we can begin to envision the impact of ongoing childcare software integration into childcare settings as part of the broader trend towards what Amoore and Piotukh call 'algorithmic life' (2016). The generation of greater amounts of data about childcare settings, from attendance details through to more specific data on sleep times and food habits of children, presents a new horizon in the codification of the everyday work of care. With this development fuelled by increased government regulation, I have given some insight into the kinds of economic calculability which has unexpectedly been made possible through these platforms. As more of the decision making around the daily running of childcare services is driven by the analytics derived from these kinds of platforms, it becomes possible to see the potential this technology will have in mediating the crucial relational work of care. Reflecting on this broader trend towards datafication in society, Amoore and Piotukh (2016) pertinently ask 'how do new digital calculative devices, logics and techniques affect our capacity to decide and act and what are the implications?' While state-led marketization has proliferated the demand for these kinds of software platforms at the level of childcare services, it also needs to set in place some way of accounting for the effects this intermarket involvement now has in the domain of care (Mayer-Schönberger and Cukier, 2014).

To conclude, stepping back from the specifics of childcare markets, in this book I have sought to contribute to the growing critical literature on the use of markets to achieve important social and collective goals. While I have offered an insight into the complexities of marketized childcare in neoliberal contexts, as one example of this political work in action, the analysis and findings also have relevance to other kinds of care markets, like that of the aged care sector (Schwiter et al, 2018; Horton, 2019, 2021; Dowling, 2021). Here too research has shown how state-led marketization has proliferated the involvement of a range of new economic actors, with little direct knowledge or involvement in the work of care (Bayliss and Gideon, 2020). Processes of privatization and financialization are opening new avenues for economic calculability in how the care of the young, and indeed the old, is being provided. Laying bare the role of the state in actively paving the way for new forms of economic experimentation in social care is the first step in rethinking how we engage with this highly contested domain.

8

Epilogue: Market Responses to COVID-19

At the time of writing in early 2021, New Zealand had remained relatively unscathed, both social and economically, from the COVID-19 pandemic. Swift action to close the borders to non-residents, mandatory isolation coupled with an early lockdown of ten weeks from 25 March 2020 positioned the country as having instigated one of the best public health responses to the virus in the world (Robert, 2020).

However, like other parts of the world the childcare industry in New Zealand has been significantly affected during this time. Childcare services across the country closed from 25 March until 14 May 2020, with full health restrictions only lifted by 8 June. Although childcare is a relatively volatile business in normal conditions, the rapidly changing levels of parental demand for childcare in response to the pandemic has turned any sense of certainty on its head. The significant drop in both the length of hours and the number of children participating in the system has heightened increased reliance on the state to uphold the childcare infrastructure in the face of a crisis. While the uniqueness of the COVID-19 situation cannot be overstated, in the New Zealand context the severity of some of the problems beleaguering the sector can be linked back to state-led marketization of the sector.

Although attendance in childcare services stopped during periods of lockdown, concern was raised by sector advocates that fewer children would return to services after restrictions were lifted. A report into the impact of COVID-19 on the ECE sector in New Zealand noted that 55 per cent of managers who responded rated a prolonged drop in attendance as the most significant long-term problem for their sustainability. Cognisant of this issue, the MoE maintained a detailed weekly account of attendance rates across the country, noting the regional variability. From this data it was found that children in formalized ECE services attended 111 hours less on average than for the same period in 2019 (MoE, 2020). While the strong public health response meant that the social and economic effects of the pandemic have been minimized, and attendance has strengthened again to almost the same levels as pre-COVID, there remain notable differences in the amount of hours children have returned for and a reduction in the number of children actually starting ECE services.

When the pandemic hit New Zealand's shores, and childcare services had to close to reduce the transmission of COVID-19, it became apparent that a relatively unusual clause was present in the insurance policies of over 1500 childcare centres, more than half of childcare centres in the country. After the financial impact of the SARS outbreak to insurers in 2002, most had written pandemic cover out of their newly issued policies. However, insurance company Crombie Lockwood, with whom most of the for-profit providers were insured through an arrangement with their main advisory group, the ECC, had unexpectedly retained a pandemic clause. When news of the pandemic cover broke, the Chief Executive of the Insurance Council of New Zealand was quoted as saying:

> This arrangement is very unusual. By far almost all business interruption policies these days, and for a number of years, have had an exclusion in them for pandemics, and they have exclusion for war and other things that are just too catastrophic and astronomical in their costs to be able to insure. (Insurance Business, 2020)

The terms of the pandemic insurance from Crombie Lockwood covered up to 25 per cent of the centre's annual earnings, and for many in the early days of the pandemic it was seen as a financial lifeline for the sector.

However, recognizing the heavy reliance the sector had on government funding, bulk funding payments were also continued for services based on the number of children enrolled in the service pre-COVID. As broader government plans for economic support were formalized, an alternative source of income to sustain the sector also emerged. This was part of a wider support package for businesses during lockdown to enable them to retain staff and pay wages. The COVID-19 Wage Support Scheme[1] was eligible to any business that could demonstrate that it had incurred at least a 30 per cent drop in earnings compared to the same time the previous year. As the pandemic rolled on over the course of 2020, and a second, more localized lockdown for Auckland was initiated, it became apparent that those who had been in receipt of the insurance payment had taken a financial hit as it made them ineligible for the government wage subsidy, which was ultimately more financially beneficial. The uptake of the government wage subsidy by some of the major corporates in the sector caused consternation in the media. Notably, the largest childcare provider in the country, Beststart Educare, was criticized for taking NZ$26.9 million in subsidies despite having accrued large cash reserves through returning a profit of over NZ$46 million in the previous two years (Edmunds, 2020).

While the wage subsidy was intended to cover the costs of retaining staff in employment, many noted that the for-profit sector did not adhere to the ethos of the subsidy, instead taking the opportunity to make labour cost savings and changes during the pandemic. Evolve Education gained negative media attention in 2020 when it responded to a NZ$13 million loss by asking staff to move from full time to flexible hours contracts, with a minimum of 20 guaranteed hours of work per week. The proposal was met with vehement rejection by the education unions and the MoE, as at that time the company was also in receipt of the COVID wage subsidy. Under public pressure it offered an 'alternative employment agreement' to staff in order to allow centres to downsize in the face of the economic challenges presented by the fallout from the pandemic. However, financial reporting for Evolve in the latter half of 2020 noted that the company had made a considerable financial uptick on its books. In the six months up to 30 September 2020 it recorded a NZ$6 million profit, the first in a long time for the company. The continuance of bulk funding payment and the COVID wage subsidy resulted in a 25 per cent raise in government funding revenue to the company to NZ$39.5 million. It is notable to situate this figure alongside the company's employee costs, which in the first half of 2020 fell by 30 per cent (Morrison, 2020).

Although data on the impact of COVID-19 remains limited, it does appear that uncertainty created by COVID-19 in many cases has been used as justification for some childcare centres to downsize, change work contracts, or to push against the current wave of pressure for pay equity claims in the sector. Mitchell et al's (2020) COVID-19 survey strongly indicates that there was a notable difference in the wages paid by non-profits over for-profits during the pandemic, with 95 per cent of non-profit services offering staff full wages,[2] while only 63 per cent of for-profit services did the same. Other ongoing cost considerations, like rent, have also manifested in problematic ways for private providers. The growing prevalence of rentiership, as investors look to childcare property as a low-risk investment, has set new conditions of capital value extraction from the sector. During lockdown when services were not in use, concern was raised by for-profit providers about continuing rent payments. The government set a nationwide freeze on all rent increases between March and September, which meant that services could be protected during that time. However, for many this was not sufficient. Despite having considerable cash reserves, and being in receipt of the wage subsidy, Beststart Educare requested a 'rent holiday' for its services. The for-profit advocacy group the ECC (2020a) strongly encouraged its members to follow suit, stating that

> We're asking landlords to think of the long term. Many ECE centres are struggling to meet teacher wage costs, even with the government's wage subsidy. We fear that without rent support, centres will be forced to fold under the financial pressure so that children, parents, teachers, centre owners and landlords all lose out.

Mitchell et al's (2020) survey indicated that 16 per cent of their respondents had applied for a rent reduction in lieu of the economic downturn.

As New Zealand began to return to its new normal, with closed borders and a strong public health approach to stamping out any incidence of COVID-19, life for childcare owner-operators picked up where it had left off. However, the continued slowdown in attendance and participation rates has fuelled a much more competitive childcare market than before the pandemic (ECC, 2020b). Media coverage has begun to document a price war in many parts of the country, where the market is 'thick' and new services are vying to capture the attention of parent consumers (Collins, 2020). New centres opening in recently developed suburbs around Auckland and some of the other major cities have been caught in a bind by these heightened competitive pressures post COVID-19. As a result, considerable discounting in price is occurring, where services are seeking to undercut neighbouring centres by offering parents incentives to enrol their child,[3] knowing that once enrolled it is highly unlikely that child will leave. However, as I have documented in this book, reducing the cost of care for parents tends to be based on a change in the economic calculations of for-profit providers, meaning that cost saving is occurring in other ways to make up the financial shortfall. What these new financial pressures mean for the kinds of care and working conditions in the sector, and the ongoing sustainability of the New Zealand childcare market more generally, is yet to be revealed.

Notes

Chapter 1

[1] Sumsion (2006) states for example that for-profit provision in Australia increased by 400 per cent between 1991 and 2001.

[2] I invoke the term financialization here to mean the heightened involvement of the financial sector and related market intermediaries into all aspect of our lives, from the role of institutional investors as shareholders to the financialization of everyday life through pension funds and secondary mortgages. As many have documented, while these processes are not new, they have become especially pervasive since the Global Financial Crisis of the mid-2000s.

[3] In New Zealand, only home-based care has experienced a higher rate of growth during this time, but this is relative to a small starting figure.

[4] Drawing on Foucault here, I understand the state not as an unchanging force overarching society, but instead to be a 'composite reality' (Foucault, 1997). It therefore can be seen as a dynamic amalgamation of relations that come together to produce the institutional structure of the state.

[5] I use the term childcare consciously to refer to all extra-familial care of young children, knowing that much of what I am referring to in New Zealand and elsewhere is more recently recognized as early childhood education (ECE). The discursive battleground over the naming of this field is not one which should be taken lightly. The distinguishing of childcare as ECE is reflective of a political battle over the right to have the work of childcare recognized beyond the private domain, and the related trend towards professionalization of childcare workers. I will use the terms somewhat interchangeably at different points in the book, but I acknowledge the way the language is being mobilized in important performative ways to shape market relations.

[6] Although I have not engaged with social investment as a paradigm in considerable detail here, Adamson and Brennan (2014) note that there are two different social investment paradigms with regards to early childhood education.

[7] Compiled of the disciplines of child development psychology and neuroscience in particular.

[8] HighScope is an early childhood educational programme originally started in the US in the 1960s. The programme has a 'plan-do-review' theme as central, which seeks to reinforce processes of planning and evaluation of actions in the child and has been argued to be particularly effective with 'at risk' communities. The HighScope Foundation now has branches in many countries.

[9] However, its over extension in the market, coupled with questionable business and valuation strategies, led to the collapse of the company in 2008 at a cost of a A$22million bailout by the Australian government to keep services viable while a new owner was

found. It was eventually bought out by a consortium of community sector organizations, known as Goodstart Early Learning in 2009.

10 Maintained nursery schools offer state funded childcare in local authorities up to the age of five. They have often provided care for children with disabilities and special needs, which are not well catered for in the for-profit childcare sector.

11 As Penn (2011) notes, other than maintained nursery care, the main differences in the regulatory framework for the EYFSF is between 'domestic settings' and non-domestic settings, irrespective of the auspice of the service.

12 For example, the Transformation Fund was abolished, and the role of local authorities in arbitrating quality and regulation was reduced in 2014. In its place a centralized role for Ofsted was consolidated as the sole arbitrator of quality (see Penn, 2013).

13 Indeed, an important point of comparison to note is that in New Zealand around 60 per cent of income for childcare centres comes from government funding, compared to the UK where up to 60 per cent of income is derived from parent fees (Penn, 2013).

14 However, corporatization in neoliberal childcare markets is still relatively modest, compared to aged care for example.

Chapter 2

1 To that extent, childcare choice plays a significant part in the constitution of class-based differences through the perpetuation of parenting cultures (Vincent et al, 2008). For example, for many Chinese and Indian migrants home-based care is often a preferable choice over centre-based care in neoliberal childcare markets, in large part as it is deemed more culturally acceptable.

2 In NZ single mothers who are in receipt of governmental support have to be either in study or 20 hours employment by the time their first child is three years old, and their second is one year old. Failure to do so invokes penalties to their welfare payments.

3 The terms framing and overflow are derived from the work of sociologist, Erving Goffman (1974).

4 However, Deville (2015) poses the question as to whether devices are necessarily things, as has been the case in studies to date. Moving beyond a strong object focussed approach, we may be able to see how individuals can be encouraged to act according to very specific criteria, like in a scripted call centre role for example.

5 I am grateful to Professor Helen May for her conscientious archiving of this material.

6 Although as a commercial business childcare property can be sold by any property sales representative, there were a limited number of sales professionals across the country who openly advertise as having specialization in childcare sales and brokerage. These individuals were deemed to be the most appropriate participants for this aspect of the study.

Chapter 3

1 The Kindergarten movement has had a strong presence as a philanthropic endeavour in New Zealand since the late 1880s in response to public concerns about working class parenting practices. Over time it extended from focusing primarily on poor children to offering sessional forms of educational care for all children (as opposed to long day care). It has received direct funding from government for many years, and today all Kindergarten teachers have their salaries paid by government and benchmarked against the salaries of primary school teachers. This funding differentiation between services in the market has caused considerable backlash over the past 30 years (May and Bethell, 2017). While this service meets the needs of a significant number of families and children requiring short

care hours, in general centre based care has been used to meet the needs of working families requiring full day care.

2   The report Te Ara Hou: The New Way (1989) was named after the presiding chair of the enquiry, Sir Clinton Roper. The impact of this report was considerable, as New Zealand has very high incarceration and recidivism rate per capita.

3   New Zealand has seven types of childcare service funded by government. Today these are divided into services which are community or parent-led, such as Playcentre or the Māori cultural immersion service, Kōhanga Reo, and those which are considered to be teacher-led, like early childhood education centres, Kindergartens and hospital-based childcare. Home-based care also receives funding at two different levels (standard and quality), but home-based carers are understood as 'educators' rather than teachers and require much lower qualification levels than centre-based carers.

4   At the time of its introduction, the suggestions of the working group had been reduced to three set rates – one for children over two years, one for children under two years where a parent was not present (therefore Playcentre was only eligible for funding for the older children), and one rate for kindergartens (to ensure that they did not get less funding than they currently recieved). See Manning (2016) for more details.

5   With the exception of kindergartens, which already received higher funding.

6   Statistics showed that by 1999 35 per cent of staff had the DipTch, 20 per cent had no qualification and 50 percent had a part time qualification (May, 2009: 251).

7   Growth at this time was mainly in childcare over sessional preschool services.

8   Pākehā is a term used to refer to the descendants of the colonial settlers of Aotearoa New Zealand, largely from Europe during the 1800s. Between 1990 and 1999 Pākehā children's rates of participation rose from 50 per cent to 65 per cent, while participation rates among Māori and Pasifika children only rose from 35 per cent to 42 per cent during the same period.

9   Groups like Kōhanga Reo were controversially excluded from being recognized as teacher trained by the New Zealand Teachers Council for a large part of the 2000s, as their training process was not deemed to be in keeping with expectations around early education (Gallagher, 2021).

10   Notably the '20 hours free please' campaign by some parents who were already using private childcare services.

11   This group was formed in 1990 in the wake of bulk funding.

12   In the first month of the scheme costs fell to parents by 34 per cent nationwide (Statistics NZ, 2007).

13   Property rental costs for non-profit services is generally much less, as they are often based on the grounds of schools or universities, and only pay only a nominal fee.

14   For example, the wealthy suburb of Epsom in Auckland only had a 26 per cent uptake of the scheme among childcare centres on the day it was launched.

15   Take up of the scheme at 26 June 2007 was 62 per cent, with less than half of for-profit providers registered as participating at this stage. Kidicorp, New Zealand's largest corporate service with over 250 centres, only came on board after government allowed for optional fees to be charged.

Chapter 4

1   Data was derived from the MoE website at www.educationcounts.govt.nz/statistics/services

2   The four main chains in New Zealand at the time of writing, in order of size, are Beststart Educare (260 centres), Evolve Education (110 centres), Provincial Education (66 centres) and Kindercare (45 centres).

3   Many community non-profit services still commit to this higher quality objective, even though it was not technically funded to that rate by government (May and Mitchell, 2009).
4   A survey by National Party ECE spokesperson Nicola Willis in 2017 found that 71 per cent of ECE centres had to hire an unqualified teacher as a result of the lack of qualified teachers. See www.nzherald.co.nz/nz/childcare-fees-rise-as-ece-teacher-shortage-deepens/EXW23QFGYE6243AMNRT5I3FOCY/
5   The Australian Government had to commit A$22million to keep the company solvent before a new buyer could be found.
6   In June 2019 a new advocacy groups called Advocates for Early Childhood Excellence was created, comprised of 20 per cent of the private sector providers, notably made up of three of the four major childcare chains. This group has sought to exercise a clear and united voice in response to government changes being proposed under the new strategic plan (2019–2029).
7   Differences can be noted in the New Zealand context between Montessori based childcare and other forms of play-based learning for example.
8   Evolve is one of four major childcare corporates. I have chosen to focus on this company as it is a publicly listed company, and as such has much more available information on its operation than other kinds of corporates in the New Zealand market.
9   The acquisition process was aided by some of the childcare property and sales brokers, discussed in more detail in the next chapter.
10 The findings of internal company research were given to shareholders through a CEO address in 2018: www.evolveeducation.co.nz/media/3499/evo-ceo-asm-speech-2018.pdf
11 Although the for-profit sector may hire qualified staff, the pay rate may still be low. Most services are not signed up to the Consenting Parties Agreement, which is the collective labour agreement. Government funding stipulates that services must pay the minimum as per the agreement to be eligible for funding, yet this has produced a highly variable rate of pay across the sector.
12 The survey was conducted in conjunction with one of the two Education Unions, NZEI Te Rui Roa. From manipulation of the online registry of providers, I determined there were 2506 childcare centre licensees in the country and distributed the survey to them through their email contact on the ECE directory. I received a 22 per cent response rate (507 responses). Apart from the suite of questions I had about financial management, Union colleagues also wanted to gauge the extent to which financial concerns were having an emotional impact on providers, staff and the wider parental body. Within this context, it was concerning to find that for-profit providers overwhelmingly had financial worries most or all of the time, with just over half indicating that this had a knock-on impact on their personal family lives.

Chapter 5

1   A report by Colliers International (2016) suggested that childcare property sales in Australia had increased by 800 per cent between 2008 and 2016.
2   While this trend has only been documented in some Anglophone contexts, consideration of the prospectus of major global early education corporates, like G8 Education, suggests that interest in childcare property investment is mounting in other expanding childcare markets, such as Singapore.
3   Community based providers (such as Kindergartens) largely operate on rental premises, but for historic reasons they tend to be located on government 'Crown Land' and have rent waved or pay a nominal amount.
4   See, for example, ARENA and Folkstone childcare REITS.

5 This was largely a political fiction as subsequent reports showed that of the 113,000 individuals who bought shares, 400 investors owned a third of those shares (*New Zealand Herald*, 2013).

6 Notably this period witnessed a significant opening of New Zealand's economy under the guidance of Finance Minister Roger Douglas. Pertinent to the creation of an investor culture was the deregulation of the banking industry which gave the financial institutions significantly more freedom to lend.

7 The baby boomer period peaked in New Zealand in 1968. Statistics show that gross wealth of over 55s had risen to 47 per cent of total wealth in 2012 (Statistics NZ, 2018).

8 New builds tend to be larger and on newly developed sites close to growth areas in cities particularly. For this reason they tend to be more expensive as an investment.

9 The main investment funds in this space are the REIT Property Management Group Fund, the Erskine and Owen Childcare Property Syndicate and the Provincial Pension Fund Group.

10 Childcare freehold properties are a commercial proposition dictated by a commercial Lease prepared on a standard Auckland District Law Society Lease Agreement.

11 However, there is no state planning system, via a needs assessment for example, managing the number of services being created.

12 Under Commercial Leases the Tenant pays for the vast majority of all costs involved with the property. The following are summaries of responsibilities between the parties: https://childcaresales.co.nz/getting-lease-right-critical-childcare-business-sale and www.abcbusiness.co.nz/abc/childcare-tenants-obligations-greater-expected.

Chapter 6

1 It is possible to send monthly attendance information to the MoE without having the software in place. For those who use the 'backdoor' upload function, they still are required to confirm this information each month. Failure to upload information to ELI or in a timely fashion can result in funding being withheld.

2 The only stipulation being that they cannot use more than six hours of the 20 paid hours in one day. When I asked the minister in charge of introducing the payment why this was, he stated that it was felt to be a sufficiently long length of time for a child to be in childcare, within the context of it being intended as 'early education' hours rather than childcare hours.

3 https://www.ezidebit.com/en-nz/industry/childcare

4 The ability for stratification within enrolment processes appears to be amplified by more targeted funding approaches, which seek to tag higher levels of support to specific children.

5 The diversification of the software packages has been a recent feature of the market. Many now specialize in aspects like Health and Safety compliance or building regulation compliance. Indeed, what has become apparent in the last few years is that many of these new companies are started with the aim to be either bought out by or integrated into the larger childcare management platforms over time.

6 In my observations I noted teachers keeping logs on attendance, accidents and injuries, and children's learning stories for their portfolios. I also saw a proliferation of other kinds of records for parents relating to food consumption, toileting and sleep times.

7 https://infocaresolutions.co.nz/add-ons/

Chapter 7

1 Access to the findings of the WorkSafe investigation can be found at: www.worksafe.govt.nz/about-us/news-and-media/companies-sentenced-after-tree-falls-on-children/

Chapter 8

1   The wage support scheme was operational from 30 March until 30 September 2020.
2   This figure also includes the Kindergarten Association, which has its staffing costs covered by government.
3   Marketing strategies such as having the first four weeks of care free, which stipulate weeks one, two and five and six are free, mean that children are already well attached to their carers and environs and make it harder for parents to remove their child after the free period ends.

References

Aalbers, M.B., Loon, J.V. and Fernandez, R. (2017) The financialization of a social housing provider. *International Journal of Urban and Regional Research*, 41(4), 572–587.

Adams, R. (2021) England's nursery schools nearing extinction, *The Guardian*, 4 May. Available from: www.theguardian.com/education/2021/may/04/englands-nursery-schools-driven-towards-extinction-says-survey

Adamson, E. (2017) *Nannies, Migration and Early Childhood Education and Care: An International Comparison of In-Home Childcare Policy and Practice.* Bristol: Policy Press.

Adamson, E. and Brennan, D. (2014) Social investment or private profit? Diverging notions of 'investment' in early childhood education and care. *International Journal of Early Childhood*, 46(1), 47–61.

Akgunduz, Y.E. and Plantenga, J. (2014) Childcare in the Netherlands: Lessons in privatisation. *European Early Childhood Education Research Journal*, 22(3), 379–385.

Aldridge, J. (2019) Childcare competition heats up, *Bay of Plenty Times*, 12 September. Available from: www.nzherald.co.nz/bay-of-plenty-times/news/childcare-competition-heats-up/HB7KQV5JDB2BRNOGWPQCUGKCDM/

Amoore, L. and Piotukh, V. (eds) (2016) *Algorithmic Life: Calculative Devices in the Age of Big Data.* London: Routledge.

Astute Education (2019) It's not about having enough time, its about making enough time. Available from: https://astuteeducation.com/its-not-about-having-enough-time-its-about-making-enough-time/

Baker, T. and Cooper, S. (2018) New Zealand's social investment experiment. *Critical Social Policy*, 38(2), 428–438.

Bakker, I. (2007) Social reproduction and the constitution of a gendered political economy. *New Political Economy*, 12(4), 541–556.

Ball, S.J. (2012) *Global Education Inc; New Policy Networks and the Neo-Liberal Imaginary.* London: Routledge.

Ball, S.J. (2015) Education, governance and the tyranny of numbers. *Journal of Education Policy*, 30(3), 299–301.

Ball, S.J. and Vincent, C. (2005) The 'childcare champion'? New Labour, social justice and the childcare market. *British Educational Research Journal*, 31, 557–570.

Bauernschuster, S., Hener, T. and Rainer, H. (2016) Children of a (policy) revolution: The introduction of universal child care and its effect on fertility. *Journal of the European Economic Association*, 14(4), 975–1005.

Bayliss, K. and Gideon, J. (2020) *The Privatisation and Financialisation of Social Care in the UK*. SOAS Department of Economics Working Paper No. 238, London: SOAS University of London.

Beck, U. (1992) *Risk Society: Towards a New Modernity*. Translated by Mark Ritter. London: Sage Publications.

Bell, M. (2017) Opportunities in the childcare sector, Landlords, 11 July. Available from: https://www.goodreturns.co.nz/article/976513328/opportunities-in-childcare-sector.html

Bennett, J. (2010) *Vibrant Matter: A Political Ecology of Things*. Durham, NC: Duke University Press.

Berndt, C. and Boeckler, M. (2009) Geographies of circulation and exchange: Constructions of markets. *Progress in Human Geography*, 33(4), 535–551.

Berndt, C. and Boeckler, M. (2011) Geographies of markets: Materials, morals and monsters in motion. *Progress in Human Geography*, 35(4), 559–567.

Berndt, C. and Boeckler, M. (2012) Geographies of marketisation. In T. Barnes, J. Peck, and E. Sheppard (eds), *The Wiley-Blackwell Companion to Economic Geography*. Chichester: Wiley Blackwell.

Bevir, M. (2005). *New Labour: A Critique*. New York: Routledge

Bezanson, K. and Luxon, M. (2006) *Social Reproduction: Feminist Political Economy Challenges Neoliberalism*. Montreal: McGill-Queens University Press.

Birch, K. (2017) *A Research Agenda for Neoliberalism*. Cheltenham: Edward Elgar.

Birch, K. and Siemiatycki, M. (2015) Neoliberalism and the geographies of marketization: The entangling of state and markets. *Progress in Human Geography*, 40(2), 177–198.

Blackburn, P. (2005) *Childcare Services in the EU: What Future?* Dublin: European Foundation for the Improvement of Living and Working Conditions.

Blackburn, P. (2013) What future for the mature UK childcare market? In E. Lloyd and H. Penn (eds), *Childcare Markets: Can They Deliver an Equitable Service?* Bristol: Policy Press.

Blakie, J. (2015) Someone needs to learn their ABCs, *Education Aotearoa*, 20 January. Available from: https://ea.org.nz/someone-needs-learn-abcs/

Blanden, J., Crawford C., Drayton, E., Farquharson, C., Jarvie, M. and Paull, G. (2020) *Challenges for the Childcare Market: The Implications of Covid-19 for Childcare Providers in England*. London: The Institute for Fiscal Studies.

Bondi, L. (1997) In whose words? On gender identities, knowledge and writing practices. *Transactions of the Institute of British Geographers*, 22(2), 245–258.

Bonoli, G. and Reber, F. (2010) The political economy of childcare in OECD countries: Explaining cross-national variation in spending and coverage rates. *European Journal of Political Research*, 49, 97–118.

Boot, S. (2017) Evolve Education appoints Mark Findlay as Chief Executive, *New Business Review*, 1 November. Available from: www.nbr.co.nz/article/evolve-education-appoints-mark-finlay-chief-executive-b-209448

Bowlby, R. (2007) Babies and toddlers in non-parental daycare can avoid stress and anxiety if they develop a lasting secondary attachment bond with one carer who is consistently accessible to them. *Attachment & Human Development*, 9(4), 307–319.

Boyer, K., Reimer, S., and Irvine, L. (2012) The nursery workspace, emotional labour, and contested understandings of commoditised childcare in the contemporary UK. *Social and Cultural Geography*, 14(5), 517–540.

Bradbury, A. and Roberts-Holmes, G. (2017) *The Datafication of Primary and Early Years Education: Playing with Numbers*. London: Routledge.

Brennan, D. (1994) *The Politics of Australian Childcare: Philanthropy, to Feminism and Beyond*. Cambridge: Cambridge University Press.

Brennan, D. (2002) Australia: Child care and state-centred feminism in a liberal welfare regime. In S. Michel and R. Mahon (eds), *Australia: Child Care and State-Centred Feminism in a Liberal Welfare Regime*. London: Routledge.

Brennan, D. (2007) The ABC of childcare politics. *Australian Journal of Social Issues*, 42(2), 213–224.

Brennan, D. (2014) The Business of Care: Australia's experiment with the marketisation of childcare. In C. Miller and L. Orchard (eds), *Australian Public Policy: Progressive ideas in the neoliberal ascendency*, pp 151–168. Bristol: Policy Press

Brennan, D., Cass, B., Himmelweit, S. and Szebehely, M. (2012) The marketisation of care: Rationales and consequences in Nordic and liberal care regimes. *Journal of European Social Policy*, 22(4), 377–391.

Brodie, J. (2003) Globalization, in/security, and the paradoxes of the social. In I. Bakker and S. Gill (eds), *Power, Production and Social Reproduction*. London: Palgrave Macmillan.

Broome, A. (2009) Neoliberalism and financial change: The evolution of residential capitalism in New Zealand. *Comparative European Politics*, 6(3), 346–364.

Brown, T. (2009) As easy as ABC?: Learning to organize private child care workers. *Labor Studies Journal*, 34(2), 235–251.

Bushouse, B. (2008) *Early Childhood Education Policy in Aotearoa / New Zealand: The Creation of the 20 Hours Free Programme*. Ian Axeford Fellowship in Public Policy, Report, Wellington, NZ.

Business Herald (2017) Booming childcare sector draws investors, *New Zealand Herald*, 4 February. Available from: www.nzherald.co.nz/business/booming-childcare-sector-draws-investors/7WR6CS5PQD6W3M75H4E56LUIEA/

Çalişkan, K. and Callon, M. (2009) Economization, part 1: Shifting attention from the economy towards processes of economization. *Economy and Society*, 38(3), 369–398.

Callon, M. (1998) An essay on framing and overflowing: Economic externalities revisited by sociology. *The Sociological Review*, 46(1_suppl), 244–269.

Callon, M. (2007a) An essay on the growing contribution of economic markets to the proliferation of the social. *Theory, Culture & Society*, 24(7–8), 139–163.

Callon, M. (2007b) What does it mean to say that economics is performative? In D. Mackenzie, F. Muniesa, and L. Siu (eds), *Do Economists Make Markets? On the Performativity of Economics*, pp 311–357. Princeton, NJ: Princeton University Press.

Callon, M. and Law, J. (1982) On interests and their transformation: Enrolment and counter-enrolment. *Social Studies of Science*, 12(4), 615–625.

Callon, M. and Muniesa, F. (2005) Peripheral vision: Economic markets as calculative collective devices. *Organization Studies*, 26(8), 1229–1250.

Callon, M., Méadel, C. and Rabeharisoa, V. (2002) The economy of qualities. *Economy and Society*, 31(2), 194–217.

Childforum (2020) *Is Our Publicly-Funded Early Childhood Education Good Enough for Children?* Available from: www.childforum.com/reports/1901-quality.html

Christie and Co. (2019) *UK Alternatives Investment Index*. London: Christie and Co.

Christophers, B. (2011) Revisiting the urbanization of capital. *Annals of the Association of American Geographers*, 101(6), 1347–1364.

Christophers, B. (2014) From Marx to market and back again: Performing the economy. *Geoforum*, 57, 12–20.

Clarke, J. (2004a) *Changing Welfare, Changing States: New Directions in Social Policy*. London: Sage Publications.

Clarke, J. (2004b) Dissolving the public realm? The logics and limits of neo-liberalism. *Journal of Social Policy*, 33(1), 27–48.

Clarke, J. and Newman, J. (1997) *The Managerial State*. London: Sage Publications.

Clarke, K. (2006) Childhood, parenting and early intervention: A critical examination of the Sure Start national programme. *Critical Social Policy*, 26(4), 699–721.

Cleveland, G. and Krashinsky, M. (2009) The nonprofit advantage: Producing quality in thick and thin child care markets. *Journal of Policy Analysis and Management*, 28, 440–462.

Cleveland, G., Forer, B., Hyatt, D., Japel, C. and Krashinsky, M. (2007) *Final Report: An Economic Perspective on the Current and Future Role of Nonprofit Early Learning and Childcare Services in Canada*. Available from: www.childcarepolicy.net/wp-content/uploads/2013/04/final-report.pdf

Cochoy, F. (2009) Driving a shopping cart from STS to business, and the other way round: On the introduction of shopping carts in American grocery stores (1936–1959). *Organization*, 16(1), 31–55.

Cohen, D. (2017) Between perfection and damnation: The emerging geography of markets. *Progress in Human Geography*, 42(6), 898–915.

Coleman, L. and Cottell, J. (2019) *Childcare Survey 2019*. Coram Family and Childcare Institute, UK.

Colliers International (2016) *Childcare: Australias Burgeoning Real Estate Asset Class*. Childcare Whitepaper.

Collins, S. (2019a) Childcare fees rise and ECE teacher shortage deepens, *New Zealand Herald*, 27 August. Available from: www.nzherald.co.nz/nz/childcare-fees-rise-as-ece-teacher-shortage-deepens/EXW23QFGYE6243AMNRT5I3FOCY/

Collins, S. (2019b) Childcare costs jump to equal private school fees, *New Zealand Herald*, 25 February. Available from: www.nzherald.co.nz/nz/childcare-costs-jump-to-equal-private-school-fees/6HJRG4TFSXPFPPPCLKG2TSSUWI/

Collins, S. (2020) Choosing childcare: Price war for children as early childhood education attendance struggles to recover from lockdown, *New Zealand Herald*, 29 June. Available from: www.nzherald.co.nz/nz/choosing-childcare-price-war-for-children-as-early-childhood-education-attendance-struggles-to-recover-from-lockdown/YUVR3UWPDEUJLS6NMQIT3OA5AU/

Commission for Financial Capability (2014) *Financial Behaviour Index Data*, Wave 7.

Conradson, D. (2003) Geographies of care: spaces, practices, experiences. *Social & Cultural Geography*, 4(4), 451–454.

Dalli, C. (1990) Early childhood education in New Zealand: Current issues and policy developments. *Early Child Development and Care*, 64(1), 61–70.

Daly, M. and Lewis, J. (2000) The concept of social care and the analysis of contemporary welfare states. *British Journal of Sociology*, 51(2), 281–298.

David, M. (1999) Home, work, families and children: New labour, new directions and new dilemmas. *International Studies in Sociology of Education*, 9(2), 111–132.

Davis, M. (2005) Child care as a human right: A new perspective on an old debate. *Journal of Women, Politics & Policy*, 27(1–2), 173–179.

Degotardi, S. and Pearson, E. (2009) Relationship theory in the nursery: Attachment and beyond. *Contemporary Issues in Early Childhood*, 10(2), 144–145.

Department of Education (1988) *Before Five: Early Childhood Care and Education in New Zealand.* Wellington, NZ: Government Printer.

Department of Education and Skills UK (DFES) (1998) *Meeting the Childcare Challenge.* London.

Deville, J. (2015) *Lived Economies of Default: Consumer Credit, Debt Collection and the Capture of Affect.* London: Routledge

Dobrowolsky, A. (2002) Rhetoric versus reality: The figure of the child in New Labour's strategic 'social investment state'. *Studies in Political Economy,* 69, 43–73.

Dowling, E. (2020) *The Care Crisis: What Caused It and How Can We End It?* London: Verso Books.

Duffy, M. (2011) *Making Care Count: A Century of Gender, Race and Paid Care Work.* New Brunswick: Rutgers University Press.

Duhn, I. (2010) 'This centre is my business': Neo-liberal politics, privatisation and discourses of professionalism in New Zealand. *Contemporary Issues in Early Childhood,* 11(1), 49–60.

Duncan, H. (2003) Hansard PD, Volume 610, 23 July, p 7247.

Dye, S. (2004) Treasury opposes preschool plan. *New Zealand Herald,* 4 October.

Early Childhood Care and Education Working Group (1988) *Education to be More: Report of the Early Childhood Care and Education Working Group.* Wellington, NZ: Department of Education.

Early Childhood Council (ECC) (2007a) Early Childhood Council recommends 20 hours free be resisted by both early childhood services and preschoolers, 26 April. Available from: www.ecc.org.NZ/mediareleases/index.hph?rt=20&rid=999

ECC (2007b) *Free Early Childhood Education: Why Your Child Might Miss Out.* Information for Parents, leaflet published by the Early Childhood Council, Wellington, NZ.

ECC (2018) Govt teacher drive ignores teacher shortages in early education, Media Release, 15 October. Available from: www.ecc.org.nz/Folder?Action=View%20File&Folder_id=428&File=20181015_MEDIA_RELEASE_ECE_Teacher_Shortage_ignored.pdf

ECC (2020a) ECC urges centre landlords to consider rent holiday, 28 March. Available from: www.ecc.org.nz/Category?Action=View&Category_id=590

ECC (2020b) Early Learning centres fight for survival, 15 October. Available from: www.ecc.org.nz/news&media/BlogPost?Action=View&BlogPost_id=598

Early Learning: Everyone Benefits (2019) *State of Early Learning in Australia 2019.* Canberra, ACT: Early Childhood Australia.

Edmunds, S. (2020) Coronavirus: Multimillion dollar subsidy for childcare centres slammed, Stuff Newsmedia, 6 May. Available from: www.stuff.co.nz/business/121421548/coronavirus-multimilliondollar-subsidy-for-childcare-centres-slammed

Education Counts (2020) *Time Series Data: Number of Teaching Staff by Qualification Status, (2011–2020)*. Available from: www.educationcounts.govt.nz/statistics/staffing

Ehrenreich, B. and Hochschild, A.R. (2004) *Global Woman: Nannies, Maids and Sex Workers in the New Economy*. New York: Holt.

England, K. (2010) Home, work and the shifting geographies of care. *Ethics, Place & Environment*, 13(2), 131–150.

England, K. and Ward, K. (2007) Introduction: reading neoliberalism. In K. England and K. Ward (eds), *Neoliberalisation: States, Network, Peoples*. Oxford: Blackwell Publishing.

England, K., Eakin, J., Gastaldo, D. and McKeever, P. (2007) Neoliberalising home care: Managed competition and restructuring home care in Ontario. In K. England and K. Ward (eds), *Neoliberalisation: States, Networks, People*, pp 169–194. Oxford: Blackwell Publishing.

Evolve Education (2015) *Annual Report*. Available from: www.evolveeducation.co.nz/media/1108/evolveannualreport2015fornzx.pdf

Evolve Education (2017) Chair's Address, Annual Shareholders Meeting, 17 August 2017.

Evolve Education (2020) Chair's Address, Annual Shareholders Meeting, 23 September 2020.

Farris, S.R. and Marchetti, S. (2017) From the commodification to the corporatization of care: European perspectives and debates. *Social Politics: International Studies in Gender, State & Society*, 24(2), 109–131.

Federici, S. (2012) *Revolution at Point Zero: Housework, Reproduction and the Feminist Struggle*. Oakland, CA: PM Press.

Fielding, M. and Moss, P. (2012, 5 January). *Radical Democratic Education*. The American Sociological Association Conference, Denver, USA.

Fine, B. (2003) Callonistics: A disentanglement. *Economy and Society*, 32(3), 478–484.

Folbre, N. (2008) *Valuing Children: Rethinking the Economics of the Family*, Cambridge, MA: Harvard University Press

Folbre, N. and Nelson, J. (2000) For love or money – or both? *The Journal of Economic Perspectives*, 14(4), 123–140.

Fothergill, A. (2013) Managing childcare: The experiences of mothers and childcare workers. *Sociological Inquiry*, 83(3), 421–447.

Foucault, M. (1997) Governmentality. In G. Burchell, C. Gordon and P. Miller (eds), *The Foucault Effect: Studies in Governmentality*. Chicago: Chicago University Press.

Foucault, M. (2001) *Power (The Essential Works of Foucault, 1954–1984),* Volume 3. New York: The New Press.

Foucault, M. (2008) *The Birth of Biopolitics: Lectures at the College de France, 1978–79.* New York: Palgrave Macmillan.

Foundational Economy Collective (2018) *Foundational Economy: The Infrastructure of Everyday Life.* Manchester: Manchester University Press.

Fourcade, M. and Healy, K. (2017) Seeing like a market. *Socio-Economic Review,* 15(1), 9–29.

Frankel, C., Ossandón, J. and Pallesen, T. (2019) The organization of markets for collective concerns and their failures. *Economy and Society,* 48(2), 153–174.

Fraser, A. (2004) Child's play. *Weekend Australian,* 11–12 September.

Fraser, N. (2013) *Fortunes of Feminism: From State Managed Capitalism to Neoliberal Crisis.* London: Verso.

Fraser, N. (2014) Can society be commodities all the way down? Post-Polanyian reflections on capitalist crisis. *Economy and Society,* 43(4), 541–558.

Friedman, M. (1962) *Capitalism and Freedom.* Chicago: University of Chicago Press.

Furedi, F. (2008) *Paranoid Parenting: Why Ignoring the Experts May Be Best for Your Child.* London: Continuum International Publishing.

Gallacher, L. (2006) Making space for excess in the nursery? Or superheros in the doll corner. Paper presented at the Annual Conference of the Royal Geographical Society, London.

Gallagher, A. (2012) Neoliberal governmentality and the respatialisation of childcare in Ireland. *Geoforum,* 43(3), 464–471.

Gallagher, A. (2017) Growing pains? Change in the New Zealand childcare market 2006–2016. *New Zealand Geographer,* 73(1), 15–24.

Gallagher, A. (2018a) E-portfolios and relational space in the early education environment. *Journal of Pedagogy,* 9(1), 23–44

Gallagher, A. (2018b) The business of care: Marketization and the new geographies of childcare. *Progress in Human Geography,* 42(5), 706–722.

Gallagher, A. (2020) "A 'golden child' for investors": The assetization of urban childcare property in NZ. *Urban Geography,* 1–19. DOI 10.1080/02723638.2020.1785257

Gallagher, A. (2021) Making markets for collective concern: Childcare in a bicultural context In R. Prince, M. Henry, C. Morris, A. Gallagher and S. Fitz-Herbert (eds), *Markets in their Place: Context, Culture, Finance.* London: Routledge.

Gambaro, L. (2017) Who is minding the kids? New developments and lost opportunities in reforming the British early education workforce. *Journal of European Social Policy,* 27(4), 320–331.

Gambaro, L., Stewart, K. and Waldfogel, J. (2014) *An Equal Start? Providing Quality Early Education and Care for Disadvantaged Children*. Bristol: Policy Press, Bristol.

Gerritson, J. (2018a) Early childhood centres unsafe – teachers. Radio New Zealand News, 16 March. Available from: www.rnz.co.nz/news/national/352659/early-childhood-centres-unsafe-teachers

Gerritson, J. (2018b) Government looks to turn tide away from privatised education. Radio New Zealand News, 6 April. Available from: www.rnz.co.nz/news/national/354282/govt-looks-to-turn-tide-away-from-privatised-education

Gibson-Graham, J.K. (2006) *A Post-Capitalist Politics*. Minneapolis, MN: University of Minnesota Press.

Giddens, A. (1998) *The Third Way: The Renewal of Social Democracy*. Cambridge: Polity Press.

Gingrich, J.R. (2011). *Making Markets in the Welfare State: The Politics of Varying Market Reforms*. Cambridge: Cambridge University Press.

Glennerster, H. and Le Grand, J. (1995) The development of quasi-markets in welfare provision in the United Kingdom. *International Journal of Health Services*, 25(2), 203–218.

Goffman, E. (1974) *Frame Analysis: An Essay on the Organization of Experience*. New York: Harper Colophon Books.

Gordon, L. (1992) The New Zealand state and educational reforms: 'competing' interests. *Comparative Education*, 28(3), 281–291.

Gordon, L. and Whitty, J. (1997) Giving the 'hidden hand' a helping hand? The rhetoric and reality of neoliberal education reform in England and New Zealand. Comparative Education, 33(3), 453–467.

Green, M. and Lawson, V. (2011) Recentring care: Interrogating the commodification of care. *Social & Cultural Geography*, 12(6), 639–654.

Hamilton, M., Hill, E. and Adamson, E. (2021) A 'career shift'? Bounded agency in migrant employment pathways in the aged care and early childhood education and care sectors in Australia. *Journal of Ethnic and Migration Studies*, 47(13), 3059–3079.

Harvey, D. (1982) *The Limits to Capital*. Baltimore: Johns Hopkins University Press.

Harvey, D. (2007) *A Brief History of Neoliberalism*. Oxford: Oxford University Press.

Hembry, O. (2007) Kidicorp chief keen to shed shareholders. *New Zealand Herald*, 6 July. Available from: www.nzherald.co.nz/business/kidicorp-chief-keen-to-shed-shareholders/LZ4IVGZYDOIH4B4T7TUPFJYK74/

Hochschild, A.R. (2012) *The Outsourced Self: Intimate Life in Market Times*. New York: Metropolitan Books.

Hochschild, A. and Machung, A. (1989) *The Second Shift: Working Families and the Revolution at Home*. New York: Penguin Books.

Holloway, S.L. (1998) Local childcare cultures: Moral geographies of mothering and the social organisation of pre-school education. *Gender, Place and Culture – A Journal of Feminist Geography*, 5, 29–53.

Holmer Nadesan, M. (2008) *Governmentality, Biopower and Everyday Life*. New York: Routledge.

Hoppania, H.-K., and Vaittinen, T. (2015) A household full of bodies: Neoliberalism, care and 'the political'. *Global Society*, 29(1), 70–88.

Horton, A. (2019) Financialization and non-disposable women: Real estate, debt and labour in UK care homes. *Environment and Planning A: Economy and Space*, 0308518X19862580. 10.1177/0308518X19862580

Horton, A. (2021) Liquid home? Financialisation of the built environment in the UK's 'hotel-style' care homes. *Transactions of the Institute of British Geographers*, 46, 179–192.

Hunter, T. (2014) Weighing up roll-up risk, *Sunday Star Times*, 30 November. Available from: www.pressreader.com/new-zealand/sunday-star-times/20141130/282342563159139

Insurance Business (2020) Coronavirus: Crombie Lockwood to pay out to childcare centres, 28 March. Available from: https://www.insurancebusinessmag.com/nz/news/breaking-news/coronavirus-crombie-lockwood-to-pay-out-to-childcare-centres-218241.aspx

Jarvis, H. (2005) Moving to London time: Household co-ordination and the infrastructure of everyday life. *Time & Society*, 14(1), 133–154.

Jenson, J. and Saint-Martin, D. (2003) New routes to social cohesion? Citizenship and the social investment state. *Canadian Journal of Sociology-Cahiers Canadiens De Sociologie*, 28(1), 77–99.

Jenson, J. and Sineau, M. (2001). *Who cares? Women's Work, Childcare and Welfare State Redesign*. Toronto: University of Toronto Press.

Jessop, B. (2000) The changing governance of welfare: recent trends in its primary functions, scale and modes of coordination. In N.P. Manning and I. Shaw (eds), *New Risks, New Welfare: Signposts for Social Policy*, pp 12–23. Oxford: Blackwell Publishing.

Jovanovic, J. (2013) Retaining Early Childcare Educators. *Gender, Work & Organization*, 20, 528–544.

Kamenarac, O. (2019) Discursive constructions of teachers' professional identities in early childhood policies and practice in Aotearoa New Zealand: Complexities and contradictions. Unpublished PhD thesis, The University of Waikato, Hamilton, New Zealand.

Kamenarac, O. (2021) Business managers in children's playground: Exploring a problematic (or not!) identity construction of early childhood teachers in New Zealand. *Contemporary Issues in Early Childhood*, DOI 1463949121989362.

Kelsey, J. (1997) *The New Zealand Experiment: A World Model for Structural Adjustment?* Wellington, NZ: Bridget Williams Books.

Kett, G. (2017) ECE has become a playground for profiteers, *Education Central*, 19 December. Available from: https://educationcentral.co.nz/opinion-garrett-kett-ece-has-become-a-playground-for-profiteers/

Key, J. (2007) '20 hours free' ECE Hoax, 26 March, NZ National Party. Available from: www.youtube.com/watch?v=p0yRz3ir9_8

King, D. and Meagher, G. (2009) (eds) *Paid care in Australia: Politics, Profits and Practices*. Sydney, Australia: Sydney University Press.

King, J. (2008) *Evaluation of the Sustainability of ECE Services During the Implementation of Pathways of the Future – Ngā Huarahi Arataki*. Final Report to the Ministry of Education.

Kingfisher, C.P. (2013) *A Policy Travelogue: Tracing Welfare Reform in Aotearoa/New Zealand and Canada*. New York: Berghahn Books.

Kirchgässner, G. (2008) *Homo Oeconomicus: The Economic Model of Behaviour and its Applications in Economics and Other Social Sciences*. New York: Springer.

Konings, M. (2018) *Capital and Time: For a New Critique of Neoliberal Reason*. Stanford, CA: Stanford University Press.

Kraftl, P. and Adey, P. (2008) Architecture/affect/inhabitation: Geographies of being-in buildings. *Annals of the Association of American Geographers*, 98(1), 213–231.

Kuger, S., Marcus, J. and Spiess, K. (2019) Day care quality and changes in the home learning environment of children. *Education Economics*, 27(3), 265–286.

LaingBuisson (2019) *Childcare UK Market Report*. 15th edition, London.

Lange, D. (1988) Hansard PD, volume 494, 23 November.

Langley, P. (2007) Uncertain Subjects of Anglo-American Financialization. *Cultural Critique*, 65, 67–91.

Larner, W. (1996) The 'New Boys': Restructuring in New Zealand, 1984–94. *Social Politics: International Studies in Gender, State & Society*, 3(1), 32–56.

Larner, W. (2000) Neo-liberalism: Policy, ideology, governmentality. *Studies in Political Economy*, 68, 5–21.

Larner, W. (2003) Neoliberalism? *Environment and Planning D: Society and Space*, 21(5), 509–512.

Larner, W. and Butler, M. (2005) Governmentalities of local partnerships: The rise of a 'partnering state' in New Zealand. *Studies in Political Economy*, 75(1), 79–101.

Latour, B. (2005) *Reassembling the Social: An Introduction to Actor Network Theory*. Oxford: Clarendon.

Laugeson, R. (2007) Childcare centres warned not to profit from subsidy, *Sunday Star Times*, 6 May.

Lawson, V. (2007) Geographies of care and responsibility. *Annals of the Association of American Geographers*, 97(1), 1–11.

Lemke, T. (2001) 'The birth of bio-politics': Michel Foucault's lecture at the College de France on neo-liberal governmentality. *Economy and Society*, 30(2), 190–207.

Lewis, J. and West, A. (2017) Early childhood education and care in England under austerity: Continuity or change in political ideas, policy goals, availability, affordability and quality in a childcare market? *Journal of Social Policy*, 46(2), 331–348.

Lim, S. (2017) Marketization and corporation of early childhood care and education in Singapore. In M. Li, J. Fox and S. Grieshaber (eds), *Contemporary Issues and Challenge in Early Childhood Education in the Asia-Pacific Region*, pp 17–32. Singapore: Springer Singapore.

Lister, R. (2003) Investing in the citizen-workers of the future: Transformations in citizenship and the state under new labour. *Social Policy & Administration*, 37(5), 427–443.

Lister, R. (2006) Children (but not women) first: New Labour, child welfare and gender. *Critical Social Policy*, 26(2), 315–335.

Lloyd, E. (2013) Childcare markets: An introduction. In E. Lloyd and H. Penn (eds), *Childcare Markets: Can They Deliver Equitable Service?* pp 3–18. Bristol: Policy Press.

Lloyd, E. and Penn, H. (2010) Why do childcare markets fail? Comparing England and the Netherlands. *Public Policy Research*, 17, 42–48.

Lloyd, E. and Penn, H. (eds) (2013) *Childcare Markets: Can They Deliver an Equitable Service?* Bristol: Policy Press.

Logan, H., Press, F. and Sumsion, J. (2012) The quality imperative: Tracing the rise of 'quality' in Australian early childhood education and care policy. *Australasian Journal of Early Childhood*, 37(3), 4–13.

Mackenzie, D., Muniesa, F. and Siu, L. (eds) (2007) *Do Economists Make Markets? On the Performativity of Economics*. Princeton, NJ: Princeton University Press.

MacLeavy, J. (2007) Engendering New Labour's workfarist regime: Exploring the intersection of welfare state restructuring and labour market policies in the UK. *Gender, Place and Culture - A Journal of Feminist Geography*, 14, 721–743.

MacLeavy, J. (2011) Reconfiguring work and welfare in the UK's 'New Economy': regulatory geographies of welfare-to-work at the local level. *Gender, Place & Culture*, 18(5), 611–633.

Mahary, S. (2003) Hansard PD, Volume 610, 23 July.

Mahon, R. and Michel, S. (2002) *Childcare Policy at the Crossroads: Gender and Welfare State Restructuring*. London: Routledge.

Mahon, R., Anttonen, A., Bergqvist, C., Brennan, D., and Hobson, B. (2012) Convergent care regimes? Childcare arrangements in Australia, Canada, Finland and Sweden. *Journal of European Social Policy*, 22(4), 419–431.

Mallard, T. (2002) The politics of early childhood. Conference address, Early Childhood Symposium, 7 August, Dunedin.

Manning, S. (2016) Meade Report/'Before Five', *Dictionary of Educational History in Australia and New Zealand* (DEHANZ).

May, H. (2009) *Politics in the Playground: The World of Early Childhood in New Zealand.* Dunedin: Otago University Press.

May, H. and Bethell, K (2017) *Growing a Kindergarten Movement in Aotearoa New Zealand: Its people, Purposes and Politics.* Wellington, NZ: NZCER Press.

May, H. and Mitchell, L. (2009) *Report on the Quality Public Early Childhood Education (QPECE) Project 2009.* Wellington: NZEI: Te Rui Roa.

Mayer-Schönberger, V. and Cukier, K. (2014) *Big Data: A Revolution That Will Transform How We Live, Work and Think.* New York: Eamon Dolan/ Mariner Books.

McDowell, L. (2004) Work, workfare, work/life balance and an ethic of care. *Progress in Human Geography*, 28(2), 145–163.

McDowell, L. (2008) The new economy, class condescension and caring labour: Changing formations of class and gender. *NORA – Nordic Journal of Feminist and Gender Research*, 16(3), 150–165.

McDowell, L., Ray, K., Perrons, D., Fagan, C. and Ward, K. (2005) Women's paid work and moral economies of care. *Social & Cultural Geography*, 6(2), 219–235.

McDowell, L., Ward, K., Fagan, C., Perrons, D. and Ray, K. (2006) Connecting time and space: The significance of transformations in women's work in the city. *International Journal of Urban and Regional Research*, 30(1), 141–158.

Meyers, M.K. and Jordan, L.P. (2006) Choice and accommodation in parental child care decisions. *Community Development*, 37(2), 53–70.

Midgley, J. and Tang, K.L. (2001) Social policy, economic growth and developmental welfare. *International Journal of Social Welfare*, 10(4), 244–252.

Millei, Z. and Joronen, M. (2016) The (bio)politicization of neuroscience in Australian early years policies: fostering brain-resources as human capital. *Journal of Education Policy*, 31(4), 389–404.

Miller, D. (2002) Turning Callon the right way up. *Economy and Society*, 31(2), 218–233.

Milligan, C. and Power, A. (2010) The changing geography of care. In T. Brown, S. McLafferty and G. Moon (eds), *A Companion to Health and Medical Geography*, pp 567–586. London: Wiley-Blackwell.

Ministry of Social Development (2012) *White Paper for Vulnerable Children.* Wellington, NZ.

MoE (Ministry of Education) (1998) *Quality in Action – Te Mahi Whai Hua.* Wellington, NZ.

MoE (1999) *The Quality Journey: He Haerenga Whai Hua.* Wellington, NZ.

MoE (2002) *Pathways to the Future: Ngā Huarahi Arataki. A 10 year Strategic Plan for Early Childhood Education.* Wellington, NZ.

MoE (2004) Landmark budget for educating young kiwis. Press release, 27 May.

MoE (2019) *ECE Census 2019.* Available from: www.educationcounts.govt. nz/publications/series/annual-early-childhood-education-census

MoE (2020) *How Participation in early learning is affected by Covid-19, He Whakaaro/Education Insights.* Available from: www.educationcounts.govt.nz/__data/assets/pdf_file/0015/204603/How-participation-in-early-learning-is-affected-by-COVID-19.pdf

Mirowski, P. (2013) *Never Let a Serious Crisis go to Waste: How Neoliberalism Survived the Financial Meltdown.* London: Verso.

Mitchell, L. (2002) Differences between community owned and privately owned early childhood education and care centres: A review of evidence. NZCER occasional papers, New Zealand.

Mitchell, L. (2013) Markets and childcare in New Zealand: Towards a fairer alternative. In E. Lloyd and H. Penn (eds), *Childcare Markets: Can They Deliver an Equitable Service?* pp 97–114. Bristol: Policy Press.

Mitchell, L. (2015) Shifting directions in ECEC policy in New Zealand: From a child rights to an interventionist approach. *International Journal of Early Years Education,* 23(3), 1–15.

Mitchell, L. (2019a) Turning the tide on private profit-focused provision in early childhood education. *New Zealand Annual Review of Education,* 24, 75–98.

Mitchell, L. (2019b) *Democratic Policies and Practices in Early Childhood Education: An Aotearoa New Zealand Case Study.* Singapore: Springer.

Mitchell, L., Hodgen, E., Meacher-Lundberg, P. and Wells, C. (2020) Impact of Covid-19 on early childhood education sector in Aotearoa New Zealand: Challenges and opportunities. Initial findings from a survey of Managers, Wilf Malcolm Institute of Educational Research, New Zealand.

Moloney, M. and Pettersen, J. (2017) *Early Childhood Education Management: Insights into Business Practice and Leadership.* London: Routledge.

Morel, N., Pallier, B. and Palme, J. (2012) *Towards a Social Investment State? Ideas, Policies and Challenges.* Bristol: Policy Press.

Morris, J.R. and Helburn, S.W. (2000) Child care center quality differences: The role of profit status, client preferences, and trust. *Nonprofit and Voluntary Sector Quarterly,* 29(3), 377–399.

Morrison, T. (2020) Evolve Education turns to a profit from a loss, eyes more acquisitions, Stuff Newsmedia, 27 November. Available from: www.stuff.co.nz/business/123527508/evolve-education-turns-to-a-profit-from-a-loss-eyes-more-acquisitions

Moss, P. (2014) *Transformative Change and Real Utopias in Early Childhood Education.* London: Routledge.

Moss, P. and Petrie, P. (2002) *From Children's Services to Children's Spaces*. London: Routledge.

Müller, M. (2015) A half-hearted romance? A diagnosis and agenda for the relationship between economic geography and actor-network theory (ANT). *Progress in Human Geography*, 39(1), 65–86.

Muniesa, F., Millo, Y. and Callon, M. (2007) An introduction to market devices. *The Sociological Review*, 55, 1–12.

Murphy, L. (2011) The global financial crisis and the Australian and New Zealand housing markets. *Journal of Housing and the Built Environment*, 26(3), 335.

National Party (2007) *Early Childhood Education and Care*. Policy 2008: Education.

Neuwelt-Kearns, C. and Richie, J. (2020) *Investing in Children? Privatisation and Early Childhood in Aotearoa New Zealand*. Auckland, NZ: Child Poverty Action Group.

New Zealand Herald (2010) Budget 2010: Early childhood educators 'devastated', 20 May. Available from: www.nzherald.co.nz/nz/budget-2010-early-childhood-educators-devastated/HSRQBIJZV5MR OA3ML6GVDSA6XQ/

New Zealand Herald (2013) Wealthy grabbed big MRP share, 24 May. Available from: www.stuff.co.nz/business/8712155/Wealthy-grabbed-big-MRP-share

New Zealand Herald (2014) Barlow backs childcare growth, 27 November. Available from: www.nzherald.co.nz/business/barlow-backs-childcare-growth/VRJ522SGR7TVT7GBETOHUES6FM/

Newberry, S. and Brennan, D. (2013) The marketisation of early childhood education and care (ECEC) in Australia: A structured response. *Financial Accountability and Management*, 29(3), 227–245.

Newell, G. and Marzuki, J. (2019) *The Significance of Childcare Centres as an Alternate Property Sector*. European Real Estate Society, Vol. 78.

Nippert, M. (2020) Kidicorp's metamorphosis to Beststart Educare raises tax questions. *New Zealand Herald*, 11 July. Available from: www.nzherald.co.nz/business/kidicorps-metamorphosis-to-best-start-educare-raises-tax-questions/BB7ASNZMMJU46KRTO2EFQ43WQE/

NZCA (New Zealand Childcare Association) (2007) Free ECE – Get the Facts Right. Media release, 24 April.

NZCER (New Zealand Council for Education Research) (2007) Early Childhood Education Services in 2007: Key findings from the NZCER survey. NZCER, Wellington, New Zealand.

NZIER (New Zealand Institute for Economic Research) (2005) *Early Childhood Participation: Is '20 Free Hours' the Answer?* Report prepared for the Early Childhood Council, Wellington.

OECD (Organisation for Economic Co-operation and Development) (2001) *Starting Strong: Early Childhood Education and Care*. OECD, Directorate for Education.

OECD (2006) *Starting Strong II: Early Childhood Education and Care*. OECD, Directorate for Education.

OECD (2012) *Starting Strong III, A Quality Toolbox for Early Childhood Education and Care*. OECD, Directorate for Education.

OECD (2016a) *Starting Strong IV: Early Childhood Education and Care Data Country Note, New Zealand*. Available from: www.oecd.org/education/school/ECECDCN-NewZealand.pdf

OECD (2016b) *Who Uses Childcare? Background Brief in the Use of Formal Early Childhood Education And Care (ECEC) Among Very Young Children*. Social Policy Research Division, Directorate for Employment, Labour, Social Affairs.

OECD (2020) 'Is Childcare Affordable?' Policy Brief on Employment, Labour and Social Affairs, OECD, Paris, oe.cd/childcare-brief-2020

OECD (2021) *Net childcare costs (indicator)*. Available from: www.oecd-ilibrary.org/employment/net-childcare-costs/indicator/english_e328a9ee-en

Ongley, P. (2013) Work and inequality in neoliberal New Zealand. *Sociological Association of Aotearoa New Zealand*, 28(3), 136–163.

Osgood, J. (2005) Who cares? The classed nature of childcare. *Gender and Education*, 17(3), 289–303.

Ouma, S. (2015) *Assembling Export Markets: The Making and Unmaking of Global Food Connections in West Africa*. Sussex: Wiley Blackwell.

Ouma, S. (2020) This can('t) be an asset class: The world of money management, 'society', and the contested morality of farmland investments. *Environment and Planning A: Economy and Space*, 52(1), 66–87.

Palmer, G. (1989) Hansard PD, Vol. 500, 8 August.

Paull, G. (2013) Childcare markets and government intervention. In E. Lloyd and H. Penn (eds), *Childcare Markets: Can They Deliver an Equitable Service?* pp 227–238. Bristol: Policy Press.

Peck, J. and Tickell, A. (2002) Neoliberalizing Space. *Antipode*, 34(3), 380–404.

Penn, H. (2007) Childcare market management: How the United Kingdom government has reshaped its role in developing early childhood education and care. *Contemporary Issues in Early Childhood*, 8(3), 192–207.

Penn, H. (2011) Gambling on the market: The role of for-profit provision in early childhood education and care. *Journal of Early Childhood Research*, 9(2), 150–161.

Penn, H. (2013) Childcare markets: Do they work? In E. Lloyd and H. Penn (eds), *Childcare Markets: Can They Deliver an Equitable Service?* pp 19–42. Bristol: Policy Press.

Plantenga, J. (2012) Local providers and loyal parents: Competition and consumer choice in the Dutch childcare market. In E. Lloyd and H. Penn (eds), *Childcare Markets: Can They Deliver an Equitable Service?* pp 63–78. Bristol: Policy Press.

Polanyi, K. (1944) *The Great Transformation: The Political and Economic Origins of our Time*. New York: Farrar & Reinhart.

Pollock, K. (2021) Early childhood education and care: Government support, 1940s to 1970s. In *Te Ara – the Encyclopedia of New Zealand* (accessed 15 February 2021). Research & Publishing Group, Manatū Taonga Ministry for Culture and Heritage, Wellington, New Zealand.

Power, M. (1997) *The Audit Society: Rituals of Verification*. Oxford: Oxford University Press.

Pratt, G. (2003) Valuing childcare: Troubles in suburbia. *Antipode*, 35(3), 581–602.

Prentice, S. (2007) Childcare, the 'business case' and economic development: Canadian evidence, opportunities and challenges. *International Journal of Economic Development*, 9(4), 269.

Prentice, S. (2009) High stakes: The 'investable' child and the economic reframing of childcare. *Signs*, 34(3), 687–710.

Prentice, S. and White, L.A. (2019) Childcare deserts and distributional disadvantages: the legacies of split childcare policies and programmes in Canada. *Journal of International and Comparative Social Policy*, 35(1), 59–74.

Press, F. (2015) The Australian ECEC workforce: Feminism, feminisation and fragmentation. In V. Campbell-Barr and J. Georgeson (eds), *International Perspectives on Early Years Workforce Development*, pp 69–81. Northwich: Critical Publishing.

Press, F. and Woodrow, C. (2005) Commodification, corporatisation and children's spaces. *Australian Journal of Education*, 49(3), 278–291.

Press, F. and Woodrow, C. (2009) The giant in the playground: Investigating the reach and implications of the corporatisation of childcare provision. In *Paid Care in Australia: Politcs, Profits, Practices*. Sydney: Sydney University Press.

Press, F., Woodrow, C., Logan, H. and Mitchell, L. (2018) Can we belong in a neo-liberal world? Neo-liberalism in early childhood education and care policy in Australia and New Zealand. *Contemporary Issues in Early Childhood*, 19(4), 328–339.

Prince, R., Kearns, R. and Craig, D. (2006) Governmentality, discourse and space in the New Zealand health care system, 1991–2003. *Health & Place*, 12(3), 253–266.

Productivity Commission (2019) Chapter 3: Early childhood education and care. In *Report on Government Services 2019*. Available from: www.pc.gov.au/research/ongoing/report-on-government-services/2019/child-care-education-and-training/early-childhood-education-and-care

Raco, M. (2016) *State-led Privatisation and the Demise of the Democratic State: Welfare Reform and Localism in an Era of Regulatory Capitalism.* London: Routledge.

Radin, M. (1996) *Contested Commodities: The Trouble with Trade in Sex, Children, Body Parts and Other Things.* Cambridge, MA: Harvard University Press.

Raschbrooke, G., Raschbrooke, M. and Molano, W. (2017) *Wealth Disparities in New Zealand: Final Report.* Institute for Governance and Policy Studies Working Paper 17/02, Victoria University, Wellington.

Rashbrook, M. (ed.) (2013) *Inequality: A New Zealand Crisis.* Wellington, NZ: Bridget Williams Books.

Reportlinker (2019) *Childcare Management Software market to 2027: Global Analysis and Forecasts by Deployment Solution.* Available from: www.reportlinker.com/p05862089/Childcare-Management-Software-Market-to-Global-Analysis-and-Forecasts-By-Deployment-Solution.html?utm_source=GNW

Rhodes, R.A.W. (2005) The hollowing out of the state: The changing nature of the public service in Britain. In R. Hodges (ed), *Governance and the Public Sector*, pp 3–16. Cheltenham: Edward Elgar Publishing.

Richardson, B. (2011) Taking stock of corporate childcare in Alberta: Licensing inspection data in not-for-profit and corporate childcare centres. In R. Langford, S. Prentice and P. Alanese (eds), *Caring for Children: Social Movements and Public Policy in Canada*, pp 119–140. Vancouver: UBC Press.

Risse, L. (2010) '...And one for the country': The effect of the baby bonus on Australian women's childbearing intentions. *Journal of Population Research*, 27(3), 213–240.

RNZ (2016) Children injured by fallen tree at Auckland Daycare, 8 November. Available from: www.rnz.co.nz/news/national/317594/children-injured-by-fallen-tree-at-auckland-daycare

Robert, A. (2020) Lessons from New Zealand's Covid-19 outbreak response. *The Lancet*, 5(11).

Roberts, J. (2011) Trust and early years childcare: Parents' relationships with private, state and third sector providers in England. *Journal of Social Policy*, 40(4), 695–715.

Roberts-Holmes, G. and Moss, P. (2021) *Neoliberalism and Early Childhood Education: Markets, Imaginaries, and Governance.* London: Routledge.

Robertson, J., Gunn, T., Lanumata, T. and Prior, J. (2007) *Parental Decision Making in Relation to the use of Early Childhood Education Services.* Report to the Ministry of Education.

Rose, N. (1990) *Governing the Soul: The Shaping of the Private Self.* London: Routledge.

Rose, N. (1996) The death of the social? Re-figuring the territory of government. *Economy and Society*, 25(3), 327–356.

Rose, N. (1999) *Powers of Freedom: Reframing Political Thought.* Cambridge: Cambridge University Press.

Rosenthal, M.K. (1999) Out-of-home child care research: A cultural perspective. *International Journal of Behavioral Development*, 23(2), 477–518.

Rutter, J. (2016) Childcare Survey, Report for the Family and Childcare Trust, UK.

Rutter, J. and Evans, B. (2012) *Childcare for Parents with Atypical Work Patterns: The Need for Flexibility.* London.

Sayer, A. (2020) Rentiership, impropriety and moral economy. *Environment and Planning A: Economy and Space*, 0308518X20908287. 10.1177/ 0308518X20908287

Schweinhart, L.J., Montie, J., Xiang, Z., Barnett, W.S., Belfield, C.R. and Nores, M. (2005) *Lifetime Effects: The HighScope Perry Preschool study Through Age 40.* Volume 14. Ypsilanti, MI: HighScope Press.

Schwiter, K., Berndt, C. and Truong, J. (2018) Neoliberal austerity and the marketisation of elderly care. *Social & Cultural Geography*, 19(3), 379–399.

Sharechat (2018) Evolve shares fall on $32m write-down, 28 November. Available from: www.sharechat.co.nz/article/0c92314b/evolve-shares-fall-on-32-mln-write-down-lower-earnings-guidance.html

Shield, H. (2017) No kidding: Childcare centres the new 'golden child' of property investment. *The West Australia*, 25 November. Available from: https://thewest.com.au/business/commercial-property/no-kidding-childcare-centres-the-new-golden-child-of-property-investment-ng-b88665164z

Shields, M. (1989) Hansard PD, Volume 502, 11 October.

Shields, M. (1990) Hansard PD, Volume 506, 29 March.

Smith, L. (1991) *Education Policy: Investing in People, Our Greatest Asset.* Wellington, NZ: Ministry of Education.

Smith, G., Sykva, K., Smith T., Sammons, P. and Omonigho, A. (2018) *Stop Start: Survival, Decline or Closure? Children's Centres in England, 2018.* London: The Sutton Trust.

Sosinsky, L.S. (2013) Childcare markets in the US: Supply and demand, quality and cost, and public policy. In E. Lloyd and H. Penn (eds), *Childcare Markets: Can They Deliver Equitable Services*, pp 131–149. Bristol: Policy Press.

Sosinsky, L.S., Lord, H. and Zigler, E. (2007) For-profit/nonprofit differences in center-based child care quality: Results from the National Institute of Child Health and Human Development Study of Early Child Care and Youth Development. *Journal of Applied Developmental Psychology*, 28(5), 390–410.

Spanswick, E. (2016) Childcare providers fear 30-hour offer could result in closure. Daycare Nurseries UK, 20 April. Available from: www.daynurseries.co.uk/news/article.cfm/id/1575240/childcare-providers-fear-30-hour-offer-could-result-in-closure

Statistics NZ (2007) Consumer Price Index: September 2007 quarter, Wellington, New Zealand Statistics, New Zealand.

Statistics NZ (2018) Wealth of top 20% rises by $394,000. Available from: www.stats.govt.nz/news/wealth-of-top-20-percent-rises-by-394000

Sumsion, J. (2006) The corporatization of Australian childcare: Towards an ethical audit and research agenda. *Journal of Early Childhood Research*, 4(2), 99–120.

Sunday Star Times (1990) Misuse feared of childcare funding bonus, 19 August.

Te Ara Hou: The New Way (1989) Committee of Inquiry into the Prison Systems, New Zealand Government

Teghtsoonian, K. (1997) Who pays for caring for children? Public policy and the devaluation of women's work. In S.B. Boyd (ed.), *Challenging the Public/Private Divide; Feminism, Law and Public Policy*. Toronto: University of Toronto Press.

Tronto, J. (1994) *Moral Boundaries: A Political Argument for an Ethic of Care*. New York: Routledge.

Tronto, J. (2013) *Caring Democracy: Markets, Equality and Justice*. New York: New York University Press.

True Commercial (2017) Dominion Road childcare investment. *New Zealand Herald*, 21 July. Available from: www.nzherald.co.nz/property/news/article.cfm?c_id=8&objectid=11893670

Van Ham, M. and Mulder, C. (2005) Geographical access to childcare and mothers' labour-force participation. *Tijdschrift voor Economische en Sociale Geografie*, 96(1), 63–74.

Viitanen, T.K. (2005) Cost of childcare and female employment in the UK. *Labour*, 19, 149–170.

Vincent, C. and Ball, S.J. (2001) A market in love? Choosing pre-school childcare. *British Educational Research Journal*, 27(5), 633–651.

Vincent, C., Ball, S.J. and Kemp, S. (2004) The social geography of childcare: Making up a middle-class child. *British Journal of Sociology of Education*, 25(2), 229–244.

Vincent, C., Braun, A. and Ball, S.J. (2008) Childcare, choice and social class: Caring for young children in the UK. *Critical Social Policy*, 28(1), 5–26.

Walters, L. (2016) Here's what you need to know about childcare. *Stuff*, 15 October. Available from: www.stuff.co.nz/national/education/85336252/heres-what-you-need-to-know-about-childcare

Walters, L. (2020) Early childhood education adult-to-child ratios not fit for purpose, *Newsroom*, 10 July. Available from: www.newsroom.co.nz/ece-adult-to-child-ratios-not-fit-for-purpose

Warner, M.E. and Gradus, R.H.J.M. (2011) The consequences of implementing a child care voucher scheme: Evidence from Australia, the Netherlands and the USA. *Social Policy & Administration*, 45(5), 569–592.

Weaven, S. and Grace, D. (2010) Examining parental and staff perceptions of childcare service quality across competing business structures. *Australasian Journal of Early Childhood*, 35(2), 54–62.

White, L.A. and Friendly, M. (2012) Public funding, private delivery: States, markets, and early childhood education and care in liberal welfare states – a comparison of Australia, the UK, Quebec, and New Zealand. *Journal of Comparative Policy Analysis: Research and Practice, 14*(4), 292–310.

Wilkinson, R. and Pickett, K. (2010) *The Sprit Level: Why Great Equality Makes Societies Stronger*. London: Bloomsbury.

Williamson, B. (2020) Making markets through digital platforms: Pearson, edu-business, and the (e)valuation of higher education. *Critical Studies in Education*, 1–17.

Woodrow, C. and Press, F. (2018) The privatisation/marketisation of ECEC debate: Social versus neoliberal models. In *The Sage Handbook of Early Childhood Policy*. London: Sage.

Zelizer, V. (2013) *Economic Lives: How Culture Shapes the Economy*. Princeton, NJ: Princeton University Press.

Index

References to boxes and tables appear in *italic* type.
References to endnotes show both the page number and note number (146n6).

www.ingramcontent.com/pod-product-compliance
Lightning Source LLC
Chambersburg PA
CBHW070626030426
42337CB00020B/3925